# THE EIGHTIETH ANNUAL MEETING OF THE AMERICAN ACADEMY OF POLITICAL AND SOCIAL SCIENCE

## APRIL 9 AND 10, 1976
## THE BENJAMIN FRANKLIN HOTEL
## PHILADELPHIA, PENNSYLVANIA

For several days prior to the Annual Meeting the Academy will have held a Bicentennial Conference on the United States Constitution. Principal participants from that Conference will address each session of the Annual Meeting on the topic

## BICENTENNIAL CONFERENCE ON THE CONSTITUTION: A REPORT TO THE ACADEMY

Approximately 1,000 persons will be in attendence sometime during the two days of sessions, representing a wide variety of cultural, civic and scientific organizations.

Members are cordially invited to attend and will automatically receive full information.

- Proceedings of the 80th Annual Meeting will be published as the July issue of THE ANNALS.

- FOR DETAILS WRITE TO: THE AMERICAN ACADEMY OF POLITICAL AND SOCIAL SCIENCE • BUSINESS OFFICE • 3937 CHESTNUT STREET, PHILADELPHIA, PENNSYLVANIA 19104

VOLUME 424                                                    MARCH 1976

# THE ANNALS

*of* The American Academy *of* Political
*and* Social Science

Richard D. Lambert, *Editor*
Alan W. Heston, *Assistant Editor*

# INTERNATIONAL EXCHANGE OF PERSONS: A REASSESSMENT

*Special Editor of This Volume*

KENNETH HOLLAND
*President Emeritus*
*Institute of International Education*
*United Nations Plaza*
*New York, New York*

PHILADELPHIA

The articles appearing in THE ANNALS are indexed in the *Reader's Guide to Periodical Literature,* the *Book Review Index,* the *Public Affairs Information Service Bulletin,* and *Current Contents: Behavioral, Social, and Management Sciences.* They are also abstracted and indexed in *ABC Pol Sci, Historical Abstracts, International Political Science Abstracts* and/or *America: History and Life.*

International Standard Book Numbers (ISBN)

ISBN 0-87761-199-8, vol. 424, 1976; paper—$4.00

ISBN 0-87761-198-x, vol. 424, 1976; cloth—$5.00

*Issued bimonthly by The American Academy of Political and Social Science at 3937 Chestnut St., Philadelphia, Pennsylvania 19104. Cost per year: $15.00 paperbound; $20.00 clothbound. Add $1.50 to above rates for membership outside U.S.A. Second-class postage paid at Philadelphia and at additional mailing offices.*

*Claims for undelivered copies must be made within the month following the regular month of publication. The publisher will supply missing copies when losses have been sustained in transit and when the reserve stock will permit.*

*Editorial and Business Offices, 3937 Chestnut Street, Philadelphia, Pennsylvania 19104.*

# CONTENTS

iii

BOOK DEPARTMENT

## INTERNATIONAL RELATIONS AND POLITICAL THOUGHT

## AFRICA, ASIA AND LATIN AMERICA

# CONTENTS

## EUROPE

## UNITED STATES

## SOCIOLOGY

## ECONOMICS

# PREFACE

The May 1961 issue of THE ANNALS was devoted to "The Rising Demand for International Education." A number of authors prepared articles on various phases of the exchange of persons. Though as the special editor of that issue said, "Appropriations for this program are only a pittance as compared with those for military and economic aid," that was a time of hope and expectations for the acceptance and support of these activities. There were many encouraging and ambitious plans for programs in the field of international education, and there were even exchange programs developing with the U.S.S.R. and Eastern Europe.

But during the intervening years these hopes have not been realized. It is true that the number of students and leaders coming to this country and Americans in similar categories going abroad has increased greatly, as the article by Wallace B. Edgerton states, but the programs are still pitifully underfinanced when their potential for academic advancement, economic development, and better understanding are recognized. As Senator Fulbright states in his contribution to this issue: "We simply can no longer afford to consider this basic human dimension as a low priority add-on to the serious content of our international relations. The Department of State's well-administered programs in this field are currently grossly underfunded at levels approximately only equivalent to that of 1967. Whereas we readily spend billions for the military and hundreds of millions for propaganda abroad, it is incredibly difficult to get the administration and the Congress to invest the few score millions necessary to sustain this activity most important to the future of this country and to the peace of the world. When one reflects on the accomplishments, it is indeed disturbing that lack of funding remains such an impediment to the future potential of these programs."

In spite of the lack of adequate support there have been encouraging developments. Experience has made it possible to improve the planning, the administration, and the evaluation of these international activities as several of the articles indicate.

## The UN and the Specialized Agencies

One important development during the last 15 years has taken place in the United Nations and its specialized agencies. The numbers of individuals participating in these programs has increased dramatically until they play a major role in the work of the United Nations system. As William D. Carter indicates in his article, recent notable developments in these activities have been the establishment of regional and national training institutes, the research that has gone into determining program content and methodology, the greater emphasis on evaluation, and the coordination of the various programs within individual countries.

While the United Nations, as in the case of UNESCO with its Zionist resolution, may become bogged down in political wrangling and power blocks, the basic work of the specialized agencies for the most part goes on. As one who studied in Paris and Geneva and attended sessions of the League of Nations as it became weaker and finally collapsed, I certainly hope the UN is not following the same path. But as with the League-sponsored International Labor Office, the International Bureau of Education and the International Committee on Intellectual Cooperation, the specialized agencies of the UN, may be building foundations for long-term international cooperation.

## THE ARTS

One area not covered by an article in 1961 was the field of the arts. It has been said for many years that music is an international language, which indeed it is, and so is dance, painting, and theatre, especially mime. The exchanges in the arts between the U.S.S.R. and the U.S.A. have been, in my opinion, the most successful in bringing the people of these two potential enemy countries into limited contact and understanding.

In 1970, the Institute of International Education (IIE) held a conference called "The Arts: An International Force," which brought together artists and administrators from many parts of the world. Robert Motherwell, in the opening session of the conference, stressed the universality of art. He had observed

that all the small children of the world have a universal language, painting, a language that is taught to them by no one . . . . a child reared in solitude uses the same painting vocabulary as his more socialized contemporaries . . . a vocabulary even more universal than sexuality . . . a language of rudimentary but beautiful signs—a circular scribble, an oval, a circle, a square, a triangle, a cross . . . who would believe . . . that a universal language, the painting of small children, not only exists, but has existed unchanged or touched since the dim beginnings of mankind, of our human world. . . . One might suggest that small children need international exchange least of all and by the same token, perhaps the older one grows, the more one needs it.

In my introduction to the arts conference report, I said:

We have a strong conviction that the Arts are of special importance to mankind in these deeply troubled times. Not only do the Arts know no barriers, and speak a universal language, they contribute to the enrichment and enjoyment of mankind.

Our purpose in convening the conference was to focus attention on the need for action to restore and expand opportunities for an international experience for talented artists. Such opportunities have been drastically curtailed by reduced public and private support.[1]

The funds for the international arts programs have not been restored, as Joan Joshi indicates. This powerful instrument for unifying mankind is barely being used.

## EXCHANGES WITH CHINA

One relatively new program in the field of international exchange of persons is that with the People's Republic of China. Tens of thousands

1. Conference on International Exchanges in the Arts: The Arts an International Force, Institute of International Education, 1970.

of Chinese from Taiwan, Hong Kong, Macao, and other areas with concentrations of Chinese people have been coming to the United States following the tradition of exchanges between our two countries over the years. The Boxer Indemnity program, begun in 1907, made it possible for Chinese to come to the United States to study and is probably the best-known early program. But many other exchanges have taken place in the intervening years. The IIE's largest overseas office to interview students desiring to come to the United States has been in Hong Kong, where more than 40,000 Chinese each year came for advice on how to study in the United States. But it was not until 1971 that any exchanges with the People's Republic of China took place. As Douglas P. Murray says, these programs have sometimes been referred to as Ping-Pong diplomacy because the first exchange was of Ping-Pong players. Like the exchanges with the U.S.S.R., the numbers of Communist individuals coming from this Asian country have been limited—only 700, while some 12,000 Americans have gone to the People's Republic in almost all fields of interest. Again, like the exchanges with the U.S.S.R., the Chinese leaders coming here have been largely in the scientific and technical fields. The cultural exchanges have been in the performing arts and sports, in accordance with the wishes of the Chinese.

As with the visits to the U.S.S.R., the Americans going to the People's Republic are shown what the Chinese want them to see and so come back to the United States to describe the very best aspects of life that the Chinese can show them. We frequently hear glowing descriptions of the bright, clean school children, attentive, disciplined, memorizing docilely the teachings of Mao. No Solzhenitsyn has yet escaped from China or risked his life while within to inform the world about the conditions in those areas of China not visited by Americans.

Undoubtedly, there have been constructive changes in the People's Republic of China in the fields of agriculture, family planning, education, industrialization, and many other areas, but have they been made at the expense of millions of people, as happened in the U.S.S.R.? Fortunately, Mr. Douglas P. Murray, the writer of the article for this issue of THE ANNALS, gives a professional analysis of the present exchange program.

## INTERNATIONAL COMPANIES

Another very important development in the movement of peoples across national boundaries has come about because of the multinational or, as Susan S. Holland prefers to call them, international companies. While the international company with branches in many countries is not a new phenomenon, it has developed tremendously during the last five to 10 years. As the article in this issue indicates, some 150,000 persons are now living in a foreign country because of their connection with international companies. Companies operating overseas began a number of years ago—even before legislation required it—filling their positions abroad with nationals of the country where the operations took place. This was dictated by cost factors—a national could be hired for much less, he would know the local mores and behavioral patterns better than a foreigner, and could communicate better with the local people.

But today the overwhelming majority of the international companies should favor peace because of enlightened self-interest. Big companies need freedom of access to raw materials, markets for their products, the right of individuals, ideas, and money to cross frontiers readily, and war stops or at least handicaps these functions. An atomic war could, of course, incinerate their plants as one of the first targets of intercontinental ballistic missiles. The recognition of these facts by companies all over the world just might be a new powerful motive for peace.

International companies have, over the years, increased their appreciation and support of exchanges. Over 400 have made general contributions on an annual basis to the IIE. Some 36 of them financed fellowship programs through the IIE. The last corporate program negotiated before I retired from the IIE in 1973 was with the ITT and provided annually funds for some 60 grants to foreign students for study here or to Americans to go abroad.

## PROGRAMS OF THE DEPARTMENT OF DEFENSE

Another field that should be under continuous scrutiny is the training program of the military. Several years ago the IIE issued a pamphlet[2] on this subject which attempted to pull together such information as was available on the programs provided by our military services to foreigners. With the increasingly important role of the military in governing countries in the world, the training given to some 8,000 brought to this country each year assumes an importance well beyond the technical training they receive. The article in this issue makes new information available on this important aspect of our foreign relations.

## EAST-WEST EXCHANGES

I think it can be said that exchanges with most countries have contributed to the education and understanding of peoples the world over and have helped each participating country to solve its own problems with its own trained leaders.

But we are concerned with East-West relations and what cultural and educational exchanges might do to develop more friendly relations with the U.S.S.R. and to help us avoid those confrontations which all too frequently threaten armed conflict.

I should emphasize particularly the importance of exchanges with the U.S.S.R., our most dangerous adversary. I am convinced that the limited exchanges with the U.S.S.R. of scientists, agriculturists, teachers, lawyers, political leaders, dancers, singers, pianists, violinists, and the few students have all helped build greater realism and understanding between our two countries and, if multiplied a thousand-fold, would

2. Military Assistance Training Programs of the United States Government, Institute of International Education, July 1964.

contribute greatly to détente. It is tragic that we have had for the last 15 years only about 40 students from the U.S.S.R. in the United States each year and a similarly small number of American students in the U.S.S.R. We have 10,000 Canadians in our country and 3,000 of our students in Canada; 3,000 Mexicans are studying in the United States, 4,000 Americans there; 10,000 Indians in the United States; 2,000 French, German, and English in the United States; 400 from Switzerland and 800 Americans there. We have fewer students from our potential enemy, the U.S.S.R., than from Nicaragua, Iceland, Melawi, Hong Kong, or Bermuda.

It is folly for the U.S.A. and the U.S.S.R. to spend so much on armaments and so little on trying to bring our peoples together.

It is clear that we should be doing everything in our power to establish relations with Russian scientists and with Russian men and women in every other field.

## AREAS OF COOPERATION

A stable peace is our greatest need, and internationally educated people are required to achieve it. But there are also many other problems in the world that require cooperation.

In the field of health, for decades we have cooperated across national boundaries, especially to eradicate small pox, yellow fever, cholera, and other such diseases. Recently, there has also been international cooperation on cancer. But there are new problems whose solution requires international cooperation: the pollution of our oceans and seas, the air we breathe, the water we drink, the population explosion, and the food these new millions and billions of people will require just to stay alive. Cooperation is required in exploring space, in developing the resources of the sea, in the preservation of wildlife, especially whales.

We live in an interdependent world, but we still act as if we are living in the eighteenth century before recent development made this, indeed, one world.

It is through international educational exchanges that we might achieve a more friendly, intelligent, cooperative spirit, and this is, in my opinion, the neglected strategy. If these programs had their desired effect, and I an convinced that they would, we might then reduce the risks of war and also the tremendously high expenditures for arms and devote these funds to the development of the abundant life for all men everywhere.

KENNETH HOLLAND

ANNALS, AAPSS, 424, March 1976

# The Most Significant and Important Activity I Have Been Privileged to Engage in during My Years in the Senate

By J. WILLIAM FULBRIGHT

ABSTRACT: After World War II, it was obvious that a new approach to international relations was essential to avoid indiscriminate destruction of life and property. It was hoped that man could be diverted from military to cultural pursuits. The Fulbright Act was introduced in 1945 to enable Americans to study abroad at the graduate level and teach in an elementary or secondary school, lecture in a university, or conduct post-doctoral research. Similar opportunities are offered to citizens of other countries to attend American-sponsored schools abroad or in the United States. The program's success depends largely on the support and cooperation of private organizations and individuals. After 30 years in the U. S. Senate, I remain convinced that educational and cultural exchange offers one of the best means available for improving international understanding. The inadequacy and peril of traditional methods of solving differences among nations and the hydrogen bomb put us on notice to find a better way to deal with international human relations. Whereas we readily spend billions for the military and hundreds of millions for propaganda abroad, it is incredibly difficult to get the administration and Congress to invest the few score millions necessary to sustain this activity most important to this country's future and world peace.

---

*William Fulbright is a former Rhodes Scholar who received his Masters Degree at Oxford. He then earned a law degree at George Washington University in Washington, D.C. He lectured at that institution before joining the faculty at the University of Arkansas. In 1939, at the age of 34, he became President of the University of Arkansas. In 1942 he was elected to the House of Representatives and two years later to the Senate, where he served continuously until his retirement in 1974. It was in 1945 that he introduced the legislation sponsoring exchange programs that made him world famous.*

THE tragic horror of World War II ended 30 years ago with the unprecedented total destruction by nuclear bombs of two great cities in Japan. Such indiscriminate destruction of life and property by new and sophisticated methods suggested that some new approach to international relations was essential. In introducing the basic legislation in 1945 for the educational exchange program, it was my thought that if large numbers of people know and understand the people from nations other than their own, they might develop a capacity for empathy, a distaste for killing other men, and an inclination to peace. If the competitive urge of men could be diverted from military to cultural pursuits, the world could be a different and better place to live.

## THE FULBRIGHT ACT

The bill introduced shortly after the end of the war in August of 1945 was signed into law by President Truman on August 1, 1946, and a great program of cultural exchange began.

It is, therefore, fair to say that the Exchange Program is an instrument of foreign policy, not just of the United States, but of all participating nations—as well as a memorable educational experience for the individual participants.

These exchanges enable Americans to study abroad at the graduate level, to teach in an elementary or secondary school, to lecture in a college or university, or to conduct postdoctoral research. Similar opportunities are offered to citizens of other countries who come to the United States. The legislation also authorizes grants to foreign nationals to attend American-sponsored schools abroad.

The encouragement of the teaching of English overseas and the development of the study of American subjects in foreign universities are facets of the program which have been reciprocated to some extent in our own universities.

The success of the exchange program depends heavily on the participation of private groups and individuals, since local patrons are in the best position to facilitate the acceptance of foreign students in the American academic community. Sponsorship on the local level—both financial and personal—is invaluable to the program.

The Fulbright Act was designed to encourage cooperation between private groups and the government, the resources of the one expanding to supplement the activities of the other. Representatives of American universities have emphasized that the government's program both stimulates and supplements private investments in the exchange field and that much of this private contribution would diminish if such a program did not exist.

Private and governmental efforts also combine in the administration of the program. The Board of Foreign Scholarships, a public body whose members include outstanding representatives of cultural, educational, student, and veterans groups, is charged with the supervision of the program. The board approves the policies and projects to be undertaken, selects the institutions abroad approved for participation, and makes the final choice among candidates for awards, both American and foreign. There appears to be a steadily growing recognition of the board's success in these efforts. Furthermore, because the board is private rather than governmental, many observers feel that it has facilitated freer acceptance of Fulbright Scholars overseas.

Other agencies, governmental and private, such as the Institute of International Education, the United States Office of Education, and the Conference Board of Associated Research Councils, assist the Board of Foreign Scholarships in screening American candidates and in placement and supervision of the foreign grantees. At a local level, over 3,000 Fulbright and foreign student advisers assist applicants and grantees on over 1,000 campuses throughout the United States.

## SIGNIFICANT ACTIVITIES

After 30 years in the United States Senate, 15 years as chairman of the Foreign Relations Committee, and a fair opportunity to move around at home and abroad, I remain convinced that educational and cultural exchange offers one of the best means available for improving international understanding, and I believe that my association with endeavors to promote this mutual understanding among the peoples of the world is the most significant and important activity I have been privileged to engage in during my years in the Senate. I believe that more and improved programs for exchange of persons and intellectual interchange around the world offer the best prospect for creating the understanding and rationality necessary to avoid annihilating ourselves in a burst of nuclear missilery. I am persuaded of the inadequacy and peril of the traditional methods of solving differences among nations; in my opinion, the hydrogen bomb puts us on notice to find a new and better way to deal with human relations in the international field.

The question, of course, is if we can or will, as Secretary Kissinger has said, "muster the vision and resolution which the conduct of foreign policy requires." I believe we can; I am less sanguine that we will, for we have yet to accept and act upon the reality of interdependence for what it is: the challenge and opportunity of our time. One exception, a most significant exception, is the sustained effort of the United States to promote mutual understanding internationally. This objective motivated the legislation introduced in 1946 for the government-supported exchange of persons. Operating largely under this legislation, the Department of State's exchange programs have produced some 150,000 alumni, including over 20 who are now chiefs of state, currently more than 250 cabinet ministers and thousands of legislators, educators, journalists, and other key individuals in America and abroad.

## FULBRIGHT ALUMNI INFLUENCE

I think of these alumni scattered throughout the world, acting as knowledgeable interpreters of their own and other societies; as persons equipped and willing to deal with conflict or conflict-producing situations on the basis of an informed determination to solve them peacefully; and as opinion leaders communicating their appreciation of the societies which they visited to others in their own society. In my view, such exchange-of-person programs are among the most significant activities now going on in the world, and I am pleased that other countries are beginning to establish similar programs suited to their conditions. That is a very hopeful development. If and as these efforts succeed in establishing an international base of mutually comprehending leadership groups capable of facilitating international cooperation, then we can hope to supplant the traditional methods of solving differences of opinion according to the standards of feuding and dueling. Therein lies my principal long-term hope for the human race. But there is not much time left, and we and others still are not doing nearly enough, not giving this hopeful endeavor nearly the attention it deserves.

We simply can no longer afford to consider this basic human dimension as a low priority add-on to the serious content of our international relations. The Department of State's well-administered programs in this field are currently grossly underfunded at levels approximately only equivalent to that of 1967. Whereas we readily spend billions for the military and hundreds of millions for propaganda abroad, it is incredibly difficult to get the administration and the Congress to invest the few score millions necessary to sustain this activity most important to the future of this country and to the peace of the world. When one reflects on the accomplishments, it is indeed disturbing that lack of funding remains such an impediment to the future potential of these programs.

## INTEREST OF SECRETARY KISSINGER

Fortunately, we have a secretary of state who fully understands and also feels strongly about the importance of personal and institutional intellectual relations among nations. As he said at a meeting of the Board of Foreign Scholarships last December, "We must deal with what Walter Lippmann called the pictures in people's heads: the manmade environment in which ideas become realities." The secretary referred to our "age when the technologies of communication are improving faster than man's ability to assimilate their consequences, and when the multiplication of differing perspectives and predispositions complicate the achievement of global consensus." He recognized that "the dramatically accelerating pace of interaction among peoples and institutions would not necessarily lead to increased understanding or cooperation." He noted that "interaction, unguided by intelligent and humane direction and concern, had the potential to bring increased tension and hostility rather than less." Speaking of the exchange-of-persons program with which I am honored to have been associated, the secretary observed that "it has grown to meet new realities, promoted the solidarity of the West and now sustains exchanges between the United States and 122 countries around the globe. It expressed—it helps us to master—the growing interdependency of the world."

More than any secretary of state I have known. the present holder of that office appreciates that this type of activity is a real alternative to the traditional methods and that it is imperative to support these new ways of dealing with international human relations. I am, of course, pleased that people in the State Department, the Board of Foreign Scholarships, the Institute of International Education, the Associated Research Councils, and the Office of Education have made the exchange program so successful. Their dedication and efficiency have been so obvious throughout that, while people occasionally have questioned the program, never has anyone, including the late Senator McCarthy in the 1950s, succeeded in discovering anything discreditable in it.

## CAN WE HUMANIZE INTERNATIONAL RELATIONS BEFORE WE INCINERATE THEM?

The question remains whether we can sufficiently civilize and humanize international relations, not merely by improving our traditional way of doing things, but also by devising new techniques and inculcating new attitudes within our capacity and adequate to our needs. What we can do, through the power of creative human interaction in scholarly and other fields, is to expand the boundaries of human wisdom, sympathy, and perception. The process is slow-moving but powerful; it may not be fast enough or strong enough to save us from catastrophe, but it is the best means available, and its proper place is at the center of our international relations concerns.

Perhaps the greatest power of such intellectual exchange is to convert nations into peoples and to translate ideologies into human aspirations. I do not think such exchange is certain to produce affection between peoples, nor indeed is that one of its essential purposes; it is enough if it contributes to the feeling of a common humanity, to an emotional awareness that other countries are populated not by doctrines that we fear but by individuals like ourselves—people with the same capacity for pleasure and pain, for cruelty and kindness, as the people we were brought up with in our own country.

If intercultural exchange is to advance these aims—of perception and perspective, of empathy, and the humanizing of international relations—it cannot be treated as a conventional instrument of a nation's foreign policy. Most emphatically, it cannot be treated as a propaganda program designed to "improve the image" of a country or to cast its current policies in a favorable light. Such exchanges can be regarded as an instrument of foreign policy only in the sense that the cultivation of international perception and perspective is—or ought to be—an important long-term objective of the foreign policy of any country aware of its true national interests as inescapably encompassing regional and international self-interest.

The secretary, in his remarks before the Board of Foreign Scholarships, quoted Pericles on the lasting effect of inspiration in terms which could well summarize all intercultural exchanges: the effect "lives on far away, without visible symbol, woven into the stuff of other men's lives."

## ARMIES AND ATOM BOMBS ARE NOT ENOUGH

The security of the United States cannot and should not rest solely on armies or atom bombs, no matter how powerful or destructive. As President Eisenhower has said, "Today it is vitally important that we and others detect and pursue the ways in which cultural and economic assistance will mean more to the strength, stability and solidarity of the free world than will purely military measures." It is for this purpose that the Fulbright Program has been conducted.

ANNALS, AAPSS, 424, March 1976

# Who Participates in Education Exchange?

By WALLACE B. EDGERTON

ABSTRACT: International education has been a growing field in the United States since the beginning of major exchange activity with the establishment of the Fulbright-Hays Fellowships shortly after World War II. In its various aspects in the United States—exchange of American and foreign students, faculty, leaders, and specialists—international education assists a minimum of 250,000 individuals each year to study, teach, or perform research. Worldwide, the number of exchangees is several times this total. Many of the factors that have promoted the growth of large-scale exchange can be expected to continue to promote growth in the future, but there are a number of new elements that will affect the make-up of the exchange population in the future. This article briefly examines a number of these factors and discusses reasons why they can be expected to play a significant role in determining the future of exchange.

Wallace B. Edgerton is the President of the Institute of International Education, a position he has held since 1973. Prior to that time, he was Deputy Chairman of the National Endowment for the Humanities. Mr. Edgerton was educated at Columbia University. In the intervening years between his graduate studies at Columbia and his appointment to the Endowment, he was associated with a private voluntary health agency, acted as the Administrative Assistant to Senator Harrison Williams of New Jersey, and conducted a consultant practice for private organizations concerned with education and foreign assistance.

THIS article will attempt to accomplish two purposes. First, it will review in brief compass the development of exchange in the United States in the postwar era—the period in which international education has experienced its greatest growth in the United States and around the world. The major resource for this information is *Open Doors*,[1] the annual report of the Institute of International Education on the exchange of students and scholars. This document is based on a census the institute conducts each year with the cooperation of United States colleges and universities, the National Association for Foreign Student Affairs, and the American Association of Collegiate Registrars and Admissions Officers, and with the partial financial support of the United States Department of State. It has been the only comprehensive source of information on United States exchange statistics since its inception over 20 years ago.

Second, the paper will seek to identify some of the factors that will determine the future of exchange in the latter half of the seventies and beyond. International education is a rapidly changing field. It has exhibited enormous growth over the last quarter-century, a pattern that can be expected to continue. However, the conditions that have produced this rapid rate of growth are not immutable. There are major forces that could act to inhibit, as well as to stimulate, exchange. These forces will affect both the number and the type of participants in international educational movements.

International education has con-

tributed greatly to the major goal of international understanding by promoting an awareness of the shared nature of most human concerns. Moreover, it has been an unparalleled means of promoting understanding of other cultures, their ways of thinking and their problems, in depth and over time. This "basic value" is worth emphasizing here, because the choices that the "investors" in international education—governments, foundations, universities, corporations, binational, multinational, and international agencies, and hundreds of thousands of private individuals—have made in the postwar period and will be making in the future turn largely upon the varying interpretations they place on the basic value of international educational experience. To develop an example: for many less-developed nations, the great merit of exchange has been the access it provides to other ways of thinking. Specifically, these nations have sought to expose their students to highly developed Western means of organizing thought and knowledge, so that these processes could then be applied to the tasks of national development. For an American social scientist, however, the merit of an exchange experience might be chiefly that the increased understanding of another culture that the experience makes possible provides comparisons to aspects of the American social structure.

Such examples need not be ramified endlessly. The point to be made is that the question of who participates in educational exchanges cannot be separated from the underlying question, "Why do they participate?" Statistical data can tell us something about the "why" of exchange by providing information on

1. *Open Doors: Report on International Exchange* (New York: Institute of International Education, published annually since 1955).

the choices exchangees have made over the years and might be expected to make in coming years, but as in any other complex field, the numbers cannot tell the whole story nor indicate with absolute certainty what the future may hold.

## THE DEVELOPMENT OF EXCHANGE IN THE POSTWAR ERA

*Open Doors* censuses have gathered data on United States and foreign students and scholars for many years—and these are the categories in terms of which most people think about exchange. They are also the categories about which the most is known in terms of numbers, fields, countries of origin, levels of study, and so forth, and this section will focus largely upon them.

However, there are many other types of educational exchange. International education is not necessarily limited to the pursuit of a degree or to a postdoctoral research or teaching fellowship. Numerous international programs exist which have education as a partial component, or which provide an educational experience outside the confines of the classroom and laboratory. The United States Department of State, for example, has offered short-term travel and study awards to up to 1,500 distinguished foreign nationals annually for many years. The International Visitors Program, as it is called, is genuinely educational in intention and result. It brings together professional colleagues and provides opportunities for group study in major international problem areas, such as food and nutrition, urban transportation, and energy. United Nations Educational, Scientific and Cultural Organization (UNESCO) conducts a worldwide program somewhat comparable to the Department of State activity in terms of the types of individuals assisted.

The Agency for International Development (AID) administers a large and rather unique program, the AID Participant Trainee Program, through which men and women from less-developed nations receive an educational experience related to their countries' developmental needs. Although the program has a large academic training sector, it also offers opportunities for study in government agencies, industry, and many other nonacademic institutions. There are also numerous transnational corporations which offer their own internal programs of international training. The list of educational activities carried on outside traditional academic exchange could be extended at some length, and all of these activities offer a real educational experience to their participants.

Academic exchange is of course the dominant focus of international education, and its growth since World War II has been remarkable. Exchange between the United States and the rest of the world received its initial strong impetus after the war, with the establishment of the Fulbright Fellowships, which this year celebrate their thirtieth anniversary. The program continues to be strongly supported by the United States government and serves as a model for effective exchange efforts.

*Foreign students.* By 1955, the first year of *Open Doors'* publication, some 34,232 foreign students were reported on United States campuses, 19,124 of them undergraduate. Nearly 30 percent of the total came from the Far East, 25 percent were Latin American, 15 percent European, 13 percent North American

(Canadian), 13 percent Near and Middle Eastern, and less than 4 percent were African. Less than 25 percent were women. Roughly half of these individuals received all of their support from personal funds, while 19 percent were aided by foundations and other private agencies, 8 percent by United States or foreign governments, with the remainder receiving support from miscellaneous sources. Foreign students tended to concentrate in the major industrial states and in the larger and better-known universities. By far the most popular fields of study were engineering and the humanities, followed by the social sciences, natural and physical sciences, health sciences, business administration, education, and agriculture, in that order.

Ten years later, the foreign student population had more than doubled. *Open Doors* 1965 reported 82,045 international students, 38,156 undergraduate, a significant increase in the proportion of graduate to undergraduate students. Thirty-six percent came from the Far East, 17 percent were Latin American, 14 percent Near and Middle Eastern, 12 percent European, 11 percent North American, and 8 percent originated in Africa. Over the decade the percentages of students from the Far East and Africa increased, while the percentages from Europe, Latin America, and North America decreased. Only 23 percent of 1965 students were women. Forty percent were self-supporting; 23 percent received support from a United States academic institution, 14 percent from foundations and other private agencies, 10 percent from the United States, and 6 percent from foreign governments, with the remainder receiving support from miscellaneous and usually multiple sources. Foreign students continued to cluster in the major industrial states and at a relatively small group of major universities (over 1,800 institutions reported students, but 47 percent of the total were resident in only 42 colleges and universities). The only notable change in preference order of fields of study from that prevailing 10 years before was a sharp increase in the numbers in the natural and physical sciences; a particularly high proportion of Far Eastern students (25 percent) pursued academic programs in these fields.

By 1974, the foreign student enrollment in the United States had further increased to 151,066, 76,946 undergraduate. The largest proportion continued to come from the Far East (35 percent). Twenty percent were from Latin America, 15 percent the Near and Middle East, 10 percent Europe, 6 percent North America, and 9 percent Africa. The proportion of Europeans and North Americans continued a long, slow decline. Far Eastern exchangees retained their primary position in terms of percentage of the total, while the proportions of foreign students from Latin America, the Near and Middle East, and Africa were moderately higher than those of nine years before. Twenty-four percent of international students on United States campuses were women (virtually the identical male-female ratio has prevailed since the first surveys). The largest proportion of foreign students continued to be self-supporting, with the next highest proportion receiving whole or partial support from United States academic institutions. Foreign students continued to study in the greatest numbers in the major industrial states (with the exception of Florida, which has a disproportionate population of Cuban students) and in larger and better-known universities.

The proportions of foreign students in major areas of study have shown remarkable stability over two decades. Some long-term changes are discernible: a slow decrease in study in the humanities, continued primary position for engineering, a peak in interest in the natural and physical sciences in the mid-sixties followed by a slow decrease, stability of interest in the social sciences, fluctuations in interest in business administration and the health sciences, and stability of interest in education and agriculture at the end of the preference order.

*United States students.* Statistics on United States students have also displayed some remarkable consistencies over the years. The highest proportion of United States students have always studied in Europe (52 percent of the 34,218 students in the 1972 academic year, the most recent year for which data is available). The three nations receiving the largest number of American students have consistently been France, Canada, and Mexico. The order in terms of numbers has tended to be Europe, North America (Canada), Latin America (including Mexico), the Far East, the Near and Middle East, and Africa. The order in terms of fields has displayed similar stability: the humanities (44 percent in 1972) have always been the fields in which most United States students study abroad, followed by the social sciences, health sciences, and the physical and natural sciences in secondary positions, while the smallest numbers have studied abroad in business administration, education, engineering, and agriculture.

*United States and foreign faculty.* The largest proportion of foreign faculty come from Europe, with the Far East close behind, followed by Latin America, the Near and Middle East, and Africa, usually in that descending order. The top five countries of origin have typically been the United Kingdom, Germany, Japan, India, and Canada in varying order. The physical and natural sciences have held first position among areas of study for two decades, followed by the health sciences, humanities, social sciences, engineering, agriculture, education, and business administration. Foreign scholars have tended to concentrate in largest numbers at a fairly small group of institutions. (In 1974, more than half of the 10,084 reported were teaching or doing research in just 30 institutions. The top 10 schools in that year were California, M.I.T., Harvard, Wisconsin, Illinois, Stanford, Yale, Columbia, Washington University, University of Washington.)

The United States faculty pattern over many years has been an overwhelming concentration in Europe (59 percent of 6,522 faculty abroad in 1974), with Latin America and the Far East in secondary positions and the Near and Middle East, Africa, and North America following. They have represented the humanities (31 percent in 1974), social sciences, physical and natural sciences, education, engineering, health sciences, agriculture, and business, in almost unvarying order over 20 years.

In the recent past, the numbers of foreign faculty in the United States has been trending downward, after many years of growth. The numbers of United States faculty abroad have displayed no consistent upward or downward movement in recent surveys; their numbers had shown consistent growth over most of the period covered in *Open Doors* surveys.

## THE PRESENT SITUATION

In 1975 the Institute of International Education (IIE) totally revamped its census procedures to correct a problem of under-reporting that had tended to minimize the totals of exchangees reported in several recent years. The process was begun with the census of foreign students, which indeed reported a significantly higher total after the change in information-gathering procedures was instituted. Some 218,000 students were reported, a difference from the year before of over 60,000. The difference was, to a large extent, accounted for by greatly improved accuracy and consistency on the part of academic institutions reporting non-citizen students who were, in fact, immigrants to the United States. The non-immigrant total for the year was 154,588, up from the 125,116 reported the previous year by means of the outmoded statistical procedures.

Statistics prepared by UNESCO for the 1974 World Population Conference in Bucharest[2] projected a world enrollment in higher education of approximately 50 million in 1975. Enrollment in the United States is nearly one-fifth of that total. An extrapolation of 1971 figures contained in the most recent *UNESCO Statistical Yearbook*[3] would sug-

gest that a conservative total of 600,000 foreign students might be included in the world enrollment figures projected for 1975. Foreign students in the United States would represent either one-fourth or one-third of that total, depending upon whether the figure used for foreign students in the United States does or does not include the foreign student immigrant. In either case, the United States is by far the largest recipient of foreign students as an individual nation, and indeed its foreign student population exceeds that of all continents with the exception of Europe (1971 figures, the most recent available, suggest that four-fifths of all foreign students study in developed nations. The 1971 rank order of major regions of the world: Europe, North America [UNESCO includes Central American and Caribbean countries in this region], the Arab nations, non-Arab Asia, Latin America, the U.S.S.R. and non-Arab Africa).

There are obvious reasons for the primacy of the United States in student exchange: the breadth and diversity of its educational system, the wide range of types of institutions, the scope and quality of graduate education, the traditional generosity of United States institutions to the student in need of financial aid, the generally welcoming attitude of United States citizens to foreign visitors, and others. All of these reasons form part of the "why" of exchange mentioned at the beginning of this paper—the motivators for the significant expenditure in time, effort, and funds necessary to support the exchange experience of even a single individual.

It is apparent from *Open Doors* data that these have been particularly impelling reasons for the stu-

2. *Educational Development: World and Regional Statistical Trends and Projections Until 1985* (Paris: UNESCO background paper for World Population Conference, August 1974), E/Conf. 60/BP/10.

3. *UNESCO Statistical Yearbook* (Paris: UNESCO, 1973), tables 2.6, 4.7, 4.8.

dents of developing nations. Year after year, the highest proportion of foreign students have originated in these countries (84 percent in 1974). Moreover, their proportion of the total, as well as their actual numbers, has tended to increase over time. Since the highest proportion of foreign students are (and always have been) self-supporting, it is apparent that these students and their families are characteristically willing to make a large investment in the value of international educational experience. It would seem a fair prediction that the motivating factors noted above will continue to stimulate the growth of exchange between the United States and the rest of the world.

### EXCHANGE IN THE FUTURE

However, there are factors in our contemporary environment which suggest that there may be some changes in the make-up of the exchangee group in the years to come. Those who participate may come for different reasons than they have in the past.

Among the factors which may have an effect on the future of exchange are:

1. *The new wealth of resource-rich nations.* The major change in the international environment in the seventies thus far has been the rise of the oil-rich nations. The Organization of Petroleum Exporting Countries (OPEC) may prove to be only the first of a larger group of nations with greatly increased economic strength based on their control of essential natural resources. OPEC states are making substantial investments in education. Venezuela alone increased its exchange activity with the United States by

over 2,200 students in 1974–75, through the Venezuelan government-sponsored Programa de Becas Gran Mariscal de Ayacucho, a project which is training the personnel this South American nation will need to diversify its economic base. The Institute of International Education is the administrative agency for the program in the United States.

The number of foreign students from the Middle East is also growing, and perhaps even more important, the national governments in the region are developing numerous cooperative arrangements with United States universities which are intended to build institutions or strengthen existing ones in these countries. Such cooperative arrangements may substantially increase faculty movements between the United States and this part of the world.

2. *Worldwide recession and inflation.* However, much of the world in the recent past has experienced severe economic dislocation from the combined effects of recession and inflation. It is to economic pressures from various sources that we largely ascribe the recent stagnation in number of United States faculty abroad and the recent downward trend of the numbers of foreign faculty in the United States. International exchange is not an inexpensive activity, and the costs of "filling-in" for exchanged faculty also continue to mount. Economic pressures are very real to the United States student and to United States universities, but not to anywhere near the degree of constraint they impose on students and institutions overseas, particularly in those nations which are resource-poor.

However, an opposite effect may also occur. Increased economic pressures abroad may push more and more students and faculty toward the industrial nations, where economic opportunities are relatively greater and the prospect of a secure future more hopeful.

3. *Diminished dominance of the United States in international affairs.* This factor is likely to have its effects on exchange only over an extended period of time. As the number of significant political actors on the world scene increases, and as the relative dominance of the United States diminishes, it is entirely possible that the United State's role in educational exchange may increase. As the United States is less and less able to take its primary power position for granted, it may rely more on the persuasive powers of educational and cultural exchange activities to support its values to the rest of the world (a point of view particularly well-stated in the recent report of the Panel on International Information, Education and Cultural Relations, *International Information, Education and Cultural Relations: Recommendations for the Future*).[4]

4. *Political factors in the developing nations and in the Communist nations.* Although the dangers in this area of concern should not be overstated, it is nonetheless true that the political climate in the individual nations of Asia, Africa, and Latin America can have dramatic effects

4. *International Information, Education and Cultural Relations: Recommendations for the Future*, Report of the Panel on International Information, Education and Cultural Relations to the U. S. Advisory Commissions of Information and on International Educational and Cultural Affairs (Washington: Georgetown University Center for Strategic and International Studies, March 1975).

on the exchange of persons. One need only point to the vicissitudes of exchange relationships between the United States and India in recent years, or to the recent improvement of relations with the People's Republic of China, which has resulted in a notable increase in exchange activities.

5. *The brain drain.* "Brain drain" is a two-sided question. For some, it represents a highly unfortunate transfer of needed manpower resources from the less-developed to the more-developed nations of the world. Others point out that there is a very real difference between the number of trained individuals a nation may need and the number it may actually be able to absorb into its existing economic structure at a certain level of integration. For some nations, in this view, the brain drain may be, in fact, a safety valve for graduates who could not be utilized effectively at home. In any case, the policies of nations toward this sensitive issue can be expected to have effects on exchange. It will be interesting to see the results of the recruitment efforts that a number of resource-rich nations have recently undertaken in the West to attract their citizens homeward, where they now can be more effectively used as the result of the greater economic strength of these nations.

6. *Changing attitudes toward education.* Anyone who follows the literature on international exchange notes the increasing emphasis on "mutuality" in exchange relationships. For many nations in Asia, Africa, and Latin America, the institution-building phase of their educational development is rapidly coming to an end. They are now seeking to relate the programs of their institutions more closely to na-

tional development needs and to focus attention on major problem areas. Many educational leaders overseas see an increased role for United States faculty in projects that involve collaborative research on topics of shared concern, particularly in social, scientific, and technological problem areas. Over time they foresee a diminished general role for United States education in the training of their students, as their own institutions are increasingly able to carry the load (particularly in the area of graduate education), but a continued role in providing the more advanced and specialized studies.

One of the strongest movements toward the "indigenizing" of education overseas is that being made under the general title of nonformal education. Many United States educators are already involved in this worldwide movement toward genuinely mass education, and this would seem to be another of the several areas in which there is potential for productive collaborative efforts internationally.

A movement that may have an effect on the shape of exchange in the more distant future is that toward recurrent education—"lifelong learning." There is an increasing awareness that the need for learning never stops. There is also an increasing awareness on the part of educated people that our world has become irreversibly interdependent. It is not impossible that the two perceptions may give rise to a third perception: that one of the more productive uses for an educational interlude in later life might be an international exchange experience. Certainly such an experience would prove useful to the United States manager in an increasingly internationalized busi-

ness environment or to the urban planner seeking new means of organizing services in his city or region.

7. *Changing interests of funding agencies; their leadership role.* It is worth mentioning, in a recital of major factors that will affect exchange, the important role the major United States foundations and other large international funding agencies can be expected to play in shaping international education's future. These organizations affect international education in two ways: (*a*) by the sheer weight of their funds, they can alter the shape of the sectors of education in which they choose to invest; (*b*) perhaps even more important, these agencies are in a position to play a leadership role. They can draw the attention of national government, universities, and private organizations to areas in which international education and research could prove productive, and time and again they have done so. In some cases, the more forward-looking funding agencies are years ahead of their time in drawing attention to an area in which there is need for international research and training, for example, the interest of the Rockefeller Foundation in agricultural production dating to before World War II.

8. *Interdependence.* Interdependence may do more to motivate the growth of exchange, particularly as it affects United States students and faculty, than any other factor. It may also act to shift the focus of United States interest in exchange toward an increased attention to the non-Western cultures. It is apparent that interdependence has its effects on all our lives, but the dimensions of these effects are as yet dimly understood. As an awareness of the

variety—and urgency—of our shared concerns increases, it is predictable that interest in study and research related to the issues and problems of interdependence will increase. One would expect this to be a slowly-developing process, and one would hope that its end result would be a much deeper understanding of other nations (and particularly of non-Western nations) than now typically characterizes educated American men and women.

A number of the factors identified above will materially affect the shape of exchange in the next several years—for example, the new wealth of the Middle East. Some factors are likely to have their effects only over an extended period—for example, interdependence and the changing role of the United States in international affairs. In any case, it is our belief that international exchange has the potential for continued productive growth. There are factors that may change the reasons that men and women seek an international education, but as noted at the beginning of this article, exchange continues to be an unparalleled means of promoting international understanding in sufficient depth to make a difference in perceptions, attitudes, and decisions. The "who" and the "why" of exchange may change in the future, but the basic value of exchange experience would seem unquestionable. Certainly the evidence of 30 years of large-scale exchange activity between the United States and the rest of the world would tend to confirm this view.

# Developing Education v. Education for Development

By KENNETH W. THOMPSON

ABSTRACT: Educators in both the developed and developing countries have approached problems of educational development in one of two frameworks. The traditional approach has put the stress on developing the necessary structures and personnel as part of an indigenous attack on institution-building. More recently the emphasis has shifted to the purposes of education, which in turn would determine the patterns of institutional development. Whatever the differences between these two approaches, the heart of the matter is the identification and preparation of qualified individuals. Staff development remains central and certain lessons are at hand from 25 years of experience in international educational cooperation. A recent review of this experience supported by 12 large donor agencies helps to illuminate the problem. Various models have emerged in South America, East Africa, and in Asia. If there is a desire to learn from the past and not "become famous" in the present, there is a rich body of experience relatively untapped which serious and interested groups may explore.

*Dr. Kenneth W. Thompson is currently Commonwealth Professor of Government and Foreign Affairs at the University of Virginia. During the past two years, he served as Director of a major study of higher education in the developing countries, undertaken by the International Council for Educational Development in New York at the request of 12 of the major national, international, and private assistance agencies. The study is to be published this year (in two volumes) by Praeger. Dr. Thompson's most recent other works include* Foreign Assistance: A View from the Private Sector *and* Understanding World Politics, *both published by University of Notre Dame Press.*

MODERN society has a penchant for gimmickry, and even in fields such as education there are always political leaders, some erstwhile educators, and a few foundation presidents willing to oblige. In philanthropy this means looking for catchy titles for long-standing historic interests or pouring old wine into new bottles. Apparently, public relations specialists believe that the public will be impatient with scholarly endeavors which merely study or improve or reform. The goal must be the conquest of hunger, controlling population growth, or overcoming disease. However, if any of mankind's enemies has surrendered unconditionally to battle cries as ambitious as these, history has yet to record it. By the end of a long campaign, no one recalls the banner under which the war was begun nor the promises by which men and funds were enlisted.

What this has to do with education, particularly in less developed countries, may not be immediately apparent.

Most educational perspectives are long-run, and strong educational institutions are not created overnight. We know certain things about international exchange and the anatomy of university development, although there is much still to be learned. Organized efforts on a considerable scale have been going on for over a century, and those who would transform education ought to reflect on this history. Unfortunately, the overall history has yet to be written; it lies hidden in the records of the organizations, foundations, and public and private agencies for whom international exchange has been a first order of business. Study is complicated and made more difficult by the fugitive character of much of the record. "We are an organization without a memory," declared a respected official of the United States Agency for International Development (AID). Until recently, the archives of organizations as renowned as the Rockefeller Foundation were inaccessible to all but a handful of staff members. The evidence on education and development lies buried in written reports, diaries, and memoranda, and in the living history of devoted officers and staff members who have served at home and abroad.

## THE HEART OF THE MATTER: THE INDIVIDUAL

In the absence of the kind of research and study which would enable the writer to speak authoritatively, a few simple propositions can be made with some confidence. The heart of the matter in international exchange programs, indeed in all education, is the individual. There can be no substitute for identifying and assisting the exceptional individual. On the face of it, this would seem to be the most straightforward part of the enterprise. In practice, it is often the most difficult. The first step is defining the areas in which assistance is to be given. This action, which is a necessary evil given the fact that resources are limited, is also fraught with uncertainty and contradictions. What if the priorities of the grant-making agency clash with national priorities? What if there are no fledgling biologists but a plethora of promising young economists? What if the staff members of the donor agencies are qualified to evaluate the potential of agriculturalists but not social scientists, and it is social scientists which both the donor and the country concerned wish to encourage? What if, for this same example, the network of agency advisors within the country favors agriculture and not social science? How do a country and a donor agency shift gears once their hierarchy of interests and objectives have shifted? Almost any experienced technical assistance officer can offer numerous examples of these and similar problems.

The plain fact is that there are three indispensable ingredients for identifying uniquely qualified individuals, and one or more may be missing: a uniquely qualified grant officer or "ivory hunter," a physical presence on the ground, and a network of trusted and tested national advisors pointing the way to talented individuals. Sometimes the functions of these three distinct activities can be merged; more often they require diverse capabilities and actors. To neglect any one for any substantial period is to court history's judgment that those who came to help with ample resources and good intentions left without having achieved their purposes.

The unsung heroes of private philanthropy—the field I know best—are men and women with a peculiar and unusual knack for discovering talent. The human qualities which comprise their skill are difficult to describe and impossible to quantify. Some are aggressive interrogators and communicators. Others, such as the late Walter Rogers of the Institute of Current World Affairs, leave those they interview baffled by their detachment, informality, and reserve. Rogers had an uncanny ability to light up his pipe, sit back, listen, ask seemingly irrelevant questions, and produce a profile of the candidate which il-

luminated future no less than present talents.

A few are Renaissance men with a universal comprehension that is breathtaking. The example par excellence of this was the late Henry Allen Moe of the Guggenheim Foundation. At the time of his death, a colleague recalled: "He could remember virtually every fellow and what he did, and when one would come back to visit he would be able to ask intelligent questions about the former fellow's work. He kept in touch with them through voluminous correspondence, and always made time to see them when they returned, moving them to feel that the foundation was their intellectual home."

A larger group of "ivory hunters" are thoroughly at home in a specialized field which they pursue with unquenchable zeal and commitment. Drs. Gerry Pomerat, Warren Weaver, and Alan Gregg of the Rockefeller Foundation were such men in the natural sciences, and Joseph H. Willits, John Marshall, Roger F. Evans, Robert Crawford, and Gerald Freund in the humanities and social sciences. It should be possible to draw up an honor role of men of this type who were the professionals' professional, but with a few exceptions such as Moe and Rogers they complete their work, are remembered by those they helped, but otherwise quietly disappear from sight. An all too prevalent assumption is that anyone can do the job, and the selection of talent scouts too often goes to the low man on the organizational totem pole. It is said that too much time and effort can go into the search for individuals. Too much paper work, too many interviews, and too much travel are the three charges leveled at this endeavor, and to this there are few convincing answers when efficiency and economy are the controlling factors.

Diverse as such men and women may be, they have certain distinguishing traits in common. They are persistent and indefatigable laborers in the vineyard. They are good listeners. They know how to use advisors. They focus on both the present and the future. They do their homework. They have the confidence and therefore the ungrudging assistance of professionals in the field. They know where to turn when they reach their limits. They shun the first judgment of a candidate, whether their own or that of another so-called authority. They are content with the nobility of their mission, not forever seeking a wider and more prestigious role. They are magnets attracting information and intelligence that long years of experience help them to sift and sort out. They live vicariously in the achievements of those they have helped advance and progress. They are fulfilled, not embittered, in knowing their candidates and not themselves will gain the Nobel prizes.

A second ingredient of a successful selection process carried on in a foreign country is a physical presence on the ground. It is tempting but illusory to imagine that one can know another country as well as one's own. Not by accident, Moe and Rogers did most of their great work in the United States. They were tuned in and had antennae out that seemingly reached every corner of America. The task is infinitely more demanding and complex in another land. Someone must be in touch not once or twice a year but on a continuing basis. There are tribal, ethnic, and class factors to penetrate, institutional and faculty politics to comprehend, and overall cultural phenomena to understand—all in a condition of flux and change. Someone must feel the pulse of society, not at the moment of selecting an individual, but essentially day by day. Besides all this, there are records to keep, reports to file and collate, and interviews to conduct—when the iron is hot. If this is important in familiar societies such as certain European countries, it is doubly important in Africa and Asia. The singular success of the Rockefeller Foundation fellowships program in Latin America, Africa, and Asia has rested on the ongoing work of its field staff, particularly in its operating programs. Someone must keep up to date.

A third ingredient is a network of trusted advisors who are nationals of the country in which the work is carried out. One instrument can be the country advisor. The late prime minister of Italy and distinguished economist, Luigi Einaudi, played this role in the 1930s and 1940s for the Rockefeller Foundation. More often, donor agencies have found that a group of advisors are best equipped to meet this need. Sometimes rectors or vice-chancellors, other times deans or departmental heads, but oftentimes unique individuals within or outside a faculty are able to serve in this way. All too often, entrepreneurs and intellectual adventurers, whether foreign or local, volunteer and press their claims. While a few, including an extraordinary ambassador or broad gauged businessman, have proven to be invaluable sources, more often they end up being selfish special pleaders. Particularly in science and education, the first need is for professionals who can speak with professionals, whose credentials are beyond reproach. The inevitable jockeying for influence and power within an institution makes it essential that someone be on top who can see the problem as an insider and not as a transient outsider with contacts and alliances providing only fragments of the big picture. Skilled ivory hunters learn how to use the intelligence and judgment of local authorities, checking and cross-checking, interviewing and re-interviewing, and following a changing situation through the eyes of proven and trusted advisors.

### GROUNDWORK FOR SUCCESS: INSTITUTION-BUILDING

A less happy chapter is the failure of well-qualified individuals returning from study abroad to find opportunities commensurate with their growth and development. The files of donor agencies are full of stories of exceptional individuals, well-chosen and well-trained, who failed on returning to use their newly developed skills. The answer in the industrial countries has been to work with institutions to obtain commitments of positions to which individuals might return. In some developing countries, such institutions are lacking, and there the answer is to combine individual support with institution-building.

Institution-building at its most pretentious has viewed outsiders as the prime movers and principal architects of universities in Asia, Africa, and Latin America. More modestly, it sees technical assistance agencies as helping the people of less developed countries to build strong local institutions. It was this viewpoint which prevailed in the 1950s and 1960s. From this experience, certain principles and guidelines have emerged which give direction and structure to educational assistance. We know, for example, that *concentration* by cooperating agencies on a few institutions is superior to scattering efforts. In philanthropy as in baseball, you score runs by bunching hits. Some agencies have assisted 200 or more institutions. My sense is that they might have contributed more by limiting themselves to a dozen or 20.

*Continuity* is another guiding principle. "Rome wasn't built in a day." The Mexican Agricultural Program of the Rockefeller Foundation was launched in 1943. Its major accomplishments occurred in the late 1950s and 1960s. Because Mexico was not abandoned but evolved into, first, a series of country programs in Colombia, Chile, India, and elsewhere and, second, a network of international agricultural institutes, including the International Maize and Wheat Improvement Centre in Mexico, it provided the basis for the "green revolution." It is illusory to believe that miracles are possible overnight. Twenty-year problems cannot be solved with three-year plans and one-year appropriations, yet all too often this has been the pattern of foreign assistance programs.

Finally, the most urgent educational problems are too complex and demanding to be left to amateurs. *Career professionals* and a *career service* for helping educational institutions are needed. Needed, too, are experienced and energetic expatriate educators willing and able to dedicate three to ten years of their lives to working abroad. Short-term visitors have a role to play, but they serve best in association with long-term institution builders. Undergirding all this are the objectives of institution-building: training indigenous educators, building strong faculties and departments, collaborating in research and curriculum building, and attracting public and private support. For all this there are few shortcuts. Developing cadres of well-qualified local leaders is a human task first and foremost, and upon it all future progress is dependent.

There are manifold reasons for moving from an individual-centered to an institution-centered approach. For one, individuals are relatively powerless to guarantee themselves a place in the educational system once they have left their countries. The aphorism "out of sight, out of mind" has application here. If a young scholar is part of an institution, it can undertake to secure and keep open his or her place. For another, the isolated individual returning from advanced or specialized training abroad is unlikely to have much influence. He needs some kind of mutual protection society if his new and innovative ideas are to be brought to bear. Left to himself, he may be written off as a disruptive and troublesome force bent on changing the status quo. With others, he can form a critical mass of well-trained people who wish to introduce new methods and knowledge. Finally, he can be part of past, present, and future if he is linked to earlier programs and joins with others to develop new personnel and programs in areas he hopes to establish and expand.

The key to institution-building is faculty development. If international educational cooperation over the past 25 years teaches us any-thing, it is in the broad area of staff development. Through cultural exchange and private and public fellowship programs, a body of experience has been established. First, we have learned more than a little about staff training. One element which was underestimated in the beginning of cooperative endeavors was *local training*. Institution-building was to remedy this at the undergraduate level. Fellowships at the M.A. and Ph.D. levels or their equivalent, financed both from national and international sources, were seen as corrective at the graduate level.

We recognize now the importance of training within the culture. Loyalties and values are formed on the playing field as well as in the classroom. It is vital that commitments and habits be built both before and after study abroad. One way of fostering this is to enable young scholars to begin their thesis research in their own countries. Another is for the local institution to retain some control over what is studied abroad. Taken together, these factors add up to the localization of staff training.

At the same time, *overseas fellowships* have been and remain a crucial element of staff training. The operational questions are: Where? When? How many? An institution must strike a balance between providing opportunities for enough personnel to constitute a critical mass for educational change on their return and too many returning scholars who may constitute a glut on the market. If those who are trained abroad are not to become part of the brain drain, they need positions and professorships to which they can return. At one level, rather simple administrative devices can help fill this need. Before the Rockefeller

Foundation will grant a foreign scholar an award, it requires the signature of two institutional sponsors assuring that the student will have a post waiting on his or her return. In 1961, the then president, Dean Rusk, who was passionately committed to fellowship training, reviewed a sample of 1,000 fellows and discovered that all but one had returned to his or her own or an equivalent post. When this record is compared with those of short-run airlift fellowship programs, the advantages of a rational, carefully planned, and well-tested program are all too obvious.

The *linking of local and overseas training* is the third important element. Of all elements in faculty development, this is the point of greatest disjunction. An African university in a tropical area had an architecture course for the planning of central heating plants. Medical schools in countries with only rudimentary health facilities have been encouraged to introduce work in open heart surgery. Institutions must look to the future—but how far into the future? A corrective against extravagant innovations of this kind is to insist that the young scholar do thesis research in his or her own country. An African vice-chancellor, taking me on a tour of communities served by his university, pointed out that clean water, and therefore deep wells, was the number one public health need of his area, not population control or psychiatric medicine. Training has to begin where people are now and not where they might be in some indeterminate future.

## GRASSROOTS PURPOSES: EDUCATION FOR DEVELOPMENT

Some changes in the titles of programs are made largely for public relations effects. There has been much of that in the headlong rush to find new captions for old activities: education for life, basic education, and education for development. Ambitious new leaders have, in their own words, looked for ways "to make themselves famous." It is possible, however, in philanthropy as in life, to do the right thing for the wrong reason. Institutions are not ends in themselves, and higher education everywhere, if it is to be deserving of support, must serve urgent community needs. These needs may be local (community colleges in this country), regional (land-grant institutions), or national and international (Harvard and the University of Chicago). The problems may be sectoral or overall problems, but all are comprehended in one way or another under the caption "development."

At this point, the question arises, "What is development?" I would argue that we can know what it is in a given context even when definitions are difficult. In the less developed countries, it is increased food production, better nutrition, health and sanitation, cultural development, rising incomes, jobs and employment, and mass education. The question to ask is whether institutions are contributing to one or more such urgent needs even when measurement is difficult. The search goes on for better indicators—social and economic—but human needs have a way of outrunning the perfection of precise and sophisticated indicators.

Higher education for development has been the subject of a 12-agency review,[1] seeking answers to

1. The World Bank, Inter-American Development Bank, USAID, the foreign assistance programs of the French, British, and Canadians, IDRC, UNDP, UNICEF, UNESCO, and the Ford and Rockefeller Foundations.

the question, "Higher education for what?" in Africa, Asia, and Latin America. It has reviewed what has been learned from 25 years of educational assistance and has sought to project this into the future.

The most important single discovery is the primacy of local and regional leadership. We have come to a moment in history in which "outsiders must be on tap not on top." Time has run out on highly visible expatriate leadership. The future of educational institutions is unmistakably in the hands of national and regional leaders in Africa, Asia, and Latin America. This does not mean that partnerships are ruled out. It does mean that forces are at work in the world—far-reaching nationalistic and world changes —that have old, established patterns. The most striking and least understood aspect of worldwide interdependence is the substitution of mutual dependency for one-way dependency—a change which any nation, any place in the world, at any stage of development, ignores at its peril. We are engaged, in the 1970s, in trying to make ordinary a form of interdependency which in the past was extraordinary but without which man's survival is in question.

The consequence of this historical movement through the several stages outlined above is to change the worldwide context of cooperation for educational development. This change is more profound than an end to imperialism or a simple resurgence of nationalism in the developing countries at a moment when nationalism's demise is being proclaimed in the developed world. It suggests rather a basic moral and political restructuring emerging on many fronts. Good intentions are no longer enough; help must always appear as a response to an invita-

tion. Human nature may not have changed, but the basic necessities have shifted as has the balance of world forces. This is one reason we turned to African, Asian, and Latin American educators and developers to carry out some 20 case studies in our Higher Education for Development study. The time has passed when such studies can or should be conducted from Washington or New York, London or Paris. The moment now is ripe for national educators to review their own institutions for themselves, but also for those who seek to help.

One purpose of looking at higher education around the world is to learn from other systems. Some say that the goal should be models which can be applied across national and cultural boundaries. Others question whether models are possible, given the diversity of cultures and educational systems. In one culture, the obstacle to faculty development may be the iron grip of a single professor: for example, in Brazil the catedrático. In another, the problem may be a lack of full-time faculty positions—whatever the reason. Yet with all the apparent similarities and differences, examples of institutional development in one culture can be helpful to educators in another. For instance, Dr. Monekosso, the head of an extraordinarily successful health sciences program at the University of Yaoundé (Cameroon), told me he had read a paper by Dr. Velazquez, then of Cali, Colombia, and was struck by the similarity of their experiments and innovations despite the fact that they had never met. He suggested that at some stage they might usefully work together.

With this possibility in mind, it may be useful to look at certain examples or models of institutions which have grappled with the central problem of building a cadre of qualified faculty to give leadership in development. No problem has greater urgency, for trained people are always in short supply. When institutions offer few if any incentives for them to choose educational careers, the bottleneck of too few personnel is likely to persist.

One "model" for building cadres of experienced staff who make educational commitments to the future is that of the University of East Africa. The Rockefeller and Ford Foundations provided the funds for a Special Lectureship program, whereby young men returning from study abroad were given interim faculty appointments until established posts became available. Attrition was reduced and young scholars were enabled to remain in academic life until permanent posts became available. For relatively small amounts of money, professional competence was assured for East Africa well into the future.

Another example of effective faculty development has been through what a former president of the Rockefeller Foundation half-seriously called the saturation model. The Universidad del Valle in Cali, Colombia, received approximately $24,000,000 from outside agencies in a decade and a half. Fellowships for study abroad and travel grants for professional development were provided on a scale seldom matched anywhere. In a relatively short period of time, an outstanding faculty with strength in depth was created, particularly in engineering and the health sciences. Venezuela today has embarked on its own crash program for training local administrators and faculty in given disciplines, and Venezuela, Iran, and Saudi Arabia talk of training personnel at home and abroad in the tens of thousands.

Another model is the early nationalizing of a university faculty. The University of Khartoum was established in 1951 as a university college granting external degrees of the University of London. From that date, it set forth on a staff development program with large-scale support from the government of the Sudan. In 1956, no more than 5 percent of the faculty were Sudanese while by 1972–73 the percentage had increased to about 75 percent.

In Nigeria, the University of Ife, beginning in 1966, set aside 10 percent of its budget for the rapid Nigerianization of its staff. Between 1966 and 1970, it recruited more than 120 young graduates from Ife and other Nigerian universities, apprenticed them to an appropriate department or faculty for one session, and then sent them abroad for Ph.D. study. By 1963–64, 43 percent of an academic staff of less than 50 were Nigerian, but by 1971–72, 329 of 415 staff members were Nigerian. The question for these universities and others remains, "What is the best proportion of local and outside staff members?" Admittedly there are differences by fields, but the twin pressures of building an indigenous staff and keeping the university international in its outlook are persistent features of faculty development which must be kept in perspective and balance.

A model at the opposite extreme is that of an international university, of which the United Nations University and the American University of Beirut (AUB), to a lesser extent, are examples. Its problems, as those of the national university, are ones of balance and who decides. It needs a fixed base which the United Nations University appears to be finding in existing institutions and which AUB discovered in Lebanese-American cooperation. It must build on strength—but where is it to find such strength?

A final model is that illustrated by the Catholic University in Chile. Here an outside agency—the International Cooperation Agency (ICA), AID's predecessor organization—was able to help the university do what it wanted to do but was unable to do, left to its own resources. As a condition for funding a broad-gauged fellowship program with awards at the University of Chicago, ICA required that the university create eight additional faculty posts to which young men and women studying abroad could return. In this case, a wise and experienced educator, Professor Theodore Schultz, guided both Chilean national educators and the American donor agency by drawing on his vast knowledge of university life without overstepping the boundaries of the outsider. He made room for young Chilean economists without imposing impossible burdens on the university. He gave intellectual and moral support to those seeking to build a modern economics faculty.

This leaves unanswered the question of whether, somewhere, there is a "model" of a universal faculty development plan applicable to all. So far we have not found one. In its absence, it would seem that "models" or, more precisely, examples such as those enumerated above could be helpful for other nations and cultures.

## THE DEVELOPMENT OF EDUCATION V. EDUCATION FOR DEVELOPMENT

One feels a certain sense of futility and déjà vu in listening to some of the debates in education, especially when they are carried to the point of reductio ad absurdum. Such a debate is the one on whether the goal should be the development of edu-

cation or education for development. It is absurd that anyone would imagine that any of the purposes of education could be served by the nondevelopment of education. Moreover, the noneducated can hardly be expected to demonstrate what education can do for development. Some may for their own selfish interests and purposes say that institution-building is irrelevant to development, but when they do so they prove they know nothing about either education or development. The long road to education for development passes through the development of educational institutions. No one has yet found a shortcut or detour. Trained people working out from some institutional base are essential. It is impossible to ignore or obscure this, whatever one's motives.

Having said this, the argument for focusing on education for development is also strong. Educators must throw the spotlight on development. No one can take the routes to development for granted. If education is to contribute, educators must join with the animators of development in identifying society's most urgent problems. At the Federal University of Bahía, Brazil, a major interdisciplinary approach has been launched to explore every facet of the society's development problems: biologists and agronomists, public health experts, government officials, and economists joining in far-ranging review. The first step in education for development is to determine priorities, as seen by society and as judged by an institution's capacity to help. Inasmuch as the thinking of government officials and national planners must be taken into account, educators and planners must achieve the best possible form of working relationship shaped by the place of government in society.

A second step is for educators to inventory who is doing what about education for development. There is a growing sense in the less developed countries that higher education is part of the total educational system. Especially at such centers as Ahmadu Bello University and the University of Ife in Nigeria, the so-called university in Mali, and at the University of Zambia, the university is engaged in training teachers, preparing new curricula and teaching materials, and organizing summer programs for primary and secondary school teachers. Institutes and centers at universities such as these assume responsibility for coordinating teacher training in the rest of the educational system. At the same time, they come to recognize that other higher educational centers are engaged in worthwhile training programs more appropriate to their interests and purpose. An example is the Ngee Ann Institute in Singapore which trains young people in engineering and business skills, awarding certificates rather than diplomas. Ngee Ann, which had functioned at the degree-granting level, voluntarily lowered its sights to meet urgent manpower needs which universities were not meeting. The Asian Institute of Management and the Center for Research and Communications in the Philippines have similarly reached out to provide neglected forms of training and research in the Philippines.

Third, higher education must find ways to increase acceptance for its product. These may include keeping government and business better informed about its work, bringing leaders from these sectors onto the campus, and providing work study or intern opportunities for students.

The University at Kumasi, Ghana has designed a successful two-way flow of students going out as interns to business and agricultural enterprises and bringing engineers and agriculturalists onto its campus as professors. The experiment has not been free of problems, and points of resistance were present among faculty members, businessmen, and students. By persisting, however, the university has removed many of the obstacles and brought about a rather healthy working relationship.

At Ahmadu Bello University, native artisans come on campus to teach indigenous arts, and students go to the villages where they produce and sell handicrafts and arts. It is possible to draw up checklists of steps that have been taken to bring higher education and the various sectors of the community together, ranging from a rather strict control and identification with government which exists in Tanzania to voluntary cooperative relationships, such as those between government, agriculture, and the National Agricultural University (La Molina) in Peru. Suspicions and misunderstanding are often present, but many universities have found ways to mitigate and resolve such problems. They prove that it is possible to link the world of education more closely with the world of work and public policy.

Fourth, it now seems clear that when education turns its attention to urgent development problems, the motivating power may come from one or more of several directions. In Tanzania, the driving force is the commitment of the government and society to social revolution. Education is seen as but one of several instruments designed to serve this social purpose. A few innovative educators may provide the inspiration, as in the case of a young physician in the Cameroon, Dr. Monekosso, or two prominent surgeons, Dr. Alfonso Ocampo Londoño and Dr. Gabriel Velazquez, at Universidad del Valle in Cali, Colombia. Sometimes the initiative comes from professional schools, which are oftentimes more closely attuned to social problems. It may also come from enlightened spokesmen of the social sciences or businessmen, lawyers, or public officials turned educators. Lastly, an external assistance agency may serve as a catalytic agent to get an institution moving, bringing fresh ideas and flexible funding to spur action. The work of Drs. John M. Weir and Guy S. Hayes of the Rockefeller Foundation at Universidad del Valle illustrates this approach. What all have in common is an awareness that higher education must do more than simply wait for society to come to the university with its problems. It must, through its leadership and mission, be an active and dynamic force in the community.

Fifth, higher education, even when it achieves a certain momentum in serving development, continues to face new and different challenges. Each step forward helps to identify new measures which must be taken. Ironically, a higher educational system based on social equality, such as Tanzania's, has done little to advance the education of women. Those higher educational programs which have done most for increasing food production have characteristically done little for land reform and the needs of the small farmer. When government has taken hold of higher education, it runs the risk of stamping out private initiative. Seemingly every advance has left higher education for development with new problems. It never reaches the stage where its work is done once and for all.

Sixth, the debate which provides the theme of this paper is one that cannot be resolved unequivocally once and for all for one side or the other. Higher education must be more than the machinery for providing services to society. Education involves more than building a system of little TVA's. Even the land grant colleges, which perhaps more than any other institutions of learning were born out of the need to serve an important sector of American society, are in fact full-fledged educational institutions. This is because the various branches of learning are interdependent. Science and medicine strengthen, reinforce, and feed one another and depend in turn on other disciplines concerned with the social and cultural dimensions of society. The main business of universities remains the advancement of knowledge and training young leaders in new knowledge.

A university is part of a worldwide network of learning. It stagnates when it is cut off from the sources of science and learning. In the long run, it is in the training of developers across a broad spectrum of knowledge and knowhow that universities do most for society. This process is a slow and gradual one. It begins, and from one standpoint never ends, in furthering staff development. Lacking qualified staff committed to an ongoing educational mission, an institution is unlikely to train the type of leaders who can respond to successive and diverse challenges. That is why the building of strong, vital, and relevant institutions is essential to education for development.

It is said man never learns from history. If those who express a new-found zeal for education ignore the fact that institution-building and staff development are the crucial steppingstones to development, they will have gained fame, funding, and material resources but lost their souls. They will learn in the end that fame is fleeting, especially when built on sand. Education for development is educational development. In Puey Ungphakorn's telling phrase, "Study is service is study," we have come full circle. The only route to service is the transcending of self-serving attitudes which seek fame for the donor and not those who are served.

Annals, AAPSS, 424, March 1976

# Exchanges with the People's Republic of China: Symbols and Substance

By Douglas P. Murray

ABSTRACT: Since the advent of Ping-Pong diplomacy in April 1971 and the joint U.S.-PRC Shanghai Communique almost a year later, the United States has become one of China's principal exchange partners—despite the absence of formal diplomatic relations. The countries' differing social systems and goals are well reflected in the exchange process and the imbalance in flow of visitors: approximately 10,000 to 12,000 Americans to the PRC and barely 700 Chinese to the U.S. On the U.S. side, two general categories and four specific exchange "channels" are involved: "government-facilitated" exchanges, through direct negotiations and in cooperation with designated private organizations, and private arrangements, ad hoc and through organizations apparently having a "special relationship" with the PRC. Although Americans of all backgrounds and viewpoints have visited China, formal exchanges of scholars have been heavily weighted in scientific and technical fields, and cultural projects in performing arts and sports—reflecting Chinese but not always U.S. preferences. Exchanges cannot be entirely removed from politics despite their avowed "people-to-people" nature, and critical problems remain concerning reciprocity, substantive content, and integrity. Although diplomatic relations might lead to extended student exchanges and cooperative research, the effect probably will be most evident in the form and content rather than volume of activity.

*Douglas P. Murray has been Director of the U.S.-China Relations Program at Stanford University since early 1975. Previously he was Program Director and then Vice President of the National Committee on U.S.-China Relations, on whose board he now serves as Vice-Chairman. He received B.A. and M.A. degrees from Yale and, after several years as a teacher in Hong Kong with the Yale-in-China Association and service with The Asia Foundation as Representative in Singapore, received a Ph.D. in International Development Education from Stanford University. He has published several articles dealing with Chinese education in Southeast Asia and U.S.-China cultural relations.*

I N NOVEMBER 1975, the "senior official" on board Dr. Kissinger's aircraft returning from Peking commented that "the Chinese will do just enough in bilateral relations with the United States as they think they need to give a certain impression to the world—it's a matter of how close they want to symbolize their relationship with us."[1] His statement is an appropriate prologue to any discussion of cultural exchanges with the People's Republic (PRC). On the one hand, the United States has become one of China's major partners, not only in trade but also in cultural relations. On the other, while having an independent life and real problems of its own, the exchange process has been largely a barometer of the peculiar political relationship, continuing as it does without benefit of formal diplomatic ties.

Many have remarked on the similarities, in style and substance, between our cultural relations with the PRC and earlier experiences with the socialist states of Eastern Europe. The parallels are real, but less important than the differences. During the Cold War decades, our exchange partners were countries we officially recognized but considered adversaries; China today, although hardly an ally, is at least far from being viewed as an enemy. Rather than hard-won deviations from a strained formal relationship, academic and cultural exchanges with China in the past five years have been active, joint demonstrations of an important political link—one that has not yet been diplomatically "normalized" because of residual United States interests on Taiwan. Through exchanges, a continued

1. *New York Times*, 20 October 1975.

commitment to the spirit and objectives of the 1972 Shanghai Communique can be signaled, even in the face of specific policy disagreements. Public attitudes in both countries can be cultivated and/or tested. And, as seemed to happen in China late in 1975, if the underlying rationale of rapprochement comes into serious question, the exchange process can be slowed to signal displeasure.

ORIGINS AND OVERVIEW

Both the form and substance of our exchanges with the PRC were importantly shaped in their first year— beginning when the United States removed the last restrictions on travel to the PRC on March 15, 1971. China's startling invitation to the United States table tennis team in early April was followed by Dr. Kissinger's secret July visit and President Nixon's trip to Peking in February of 1972. This first phase, during which several hundred private Americans traveled to the PRC, concluded with the reciprocal United States tour of China's table tennis team in April of 1972. It was a year in which Americans, by the hundreds of thousands, "rediscovered" China, apparently inundating Chinese government offices in other countries and Peking with visa applications; and both Chinese and American officials learned, through Ping-Pong, that PRC citizens could tour this country without serious problems of security or political harassment. Even more important, the Shanghai Communique signed by President Nixon and Premier Chou had inscribed the importance of exchanges in the official guidelines for United States-China relations:

The two sides agreed that it is desirable to broaden the understanding between the two peoples. To this end they discussed specific areas in such fields as science, technology, culture, sports and journalism in which people-to-people contacts and exchanges would be mutually beneficial. Each side undertakes to facilitate the further development of such contacts and exchanges.

Thus, "government-facilitated" exchanges, typified by the two Ping-Pong tours, have been one of the principal categories of our cultural relations with the PRC during these initial, exploratory years. Although only about 6 percent (roughly 700) of the approximately 10,000 to 12,000 Americans to visit China and barely two-thirds of the 700 Chinese to come here fall under this rubric, this is the only channel through which reasonable reciprocity in numbers and kind is possible through prior agreement.

The above figures demonstrate a dramatic though understandable imbalance in the overall flow of private citizens between the two countries. The "essential differences" in the social systems of China and the United States, noted in the Shanghai Communique, obviously include differing policies toward freedom of travel, in the private financial resources that make travel possible and in the fundamental purposes that visits and exchanges serve. For China, where "politics is in command," cultural relations are at the forefront of cultivating world opinion and are a means of obtaining information and insights useful to her own independent development. Our government certainly has similar goals; but official efforts have been almost overshadowed by the activities of private American citizens pursuing their own disparate interests with unbounded enthusiasm and, frequently, considerable frustration. The American demand

for both Chinese visas and Chinese visitors continues to far exceed the supply; while the United States cannot inhibit its own citizens from visiting China, it has had no reason to refuse visas to the relatively small numbers of Chinese applicants. Consequently, China effectively controls the flow of traffic in both directions, generally being able to select whom to send and whom to receive.

## TYPES OF EXCHANGES AND VISITS

Within the United States, two general exchange categories and four distinct "channels" have emerged since the 1971–72 phase. Their respective significance can be appreciated only with reference to the difference between the two societies and to the lack of a formal cultural agreement between the two governments. Pursuing an active exchange program in the absence of diplomatic relations has produced some unusual and often ambiguous distinctions regarding what is "official" and what is "private."

### "Government-facilitated" exchanges

Since all visits in either direction require at least the issuance of visas, some government facilitation is always involved. But several elements distinguish this semi-official category. First, both governments expect all in-country costs to be met by the hosts, with the visitors responsible only for their international travel. Second, special attention is given to the program and general welfare of the guests, which on the United States side has particularly meant providing immigration courtesies, security escorts, and frequent White House receptions. Third, and most important, both governments consider these projects to be both necessary and sufficient conditions for implementing the spirit of the Shanghai Communique in regard to people-to-people contacts. The facilitated exchanges themselves fall under two rubrics:

1. *Exchanges of federal and state officials, arranged and administered directly by the governments.* In practice, "official" exchanges have involved a one-way path toward China, since Peking insists that apart from the diplomats posted to her Liaison Office (Washington) and UN mission (New York), PRC officials as such will not come here as long as the offending Taiwan embassy remains. None of Secretary Kissinger's eight trips to Peking, much less the journeys of Presidents Nixon and Ford, have yet been reciprocated. Through November of 1975, six congressional delegations (both representatives and senators), a group of White House Fellows, and a contingent of state governors had toured the PRC through intergovernmental arrangements. It is worth noting, however, that China also directly invited two congressional delegations and several individual senators and state governors without recourse to the "facilitated" route.

2. *Scholarly and cultural exchanges involving private citizens, arranged by designated United States organizations.* In the private sector, the Committee on Scholarly Communication with the People's Republic of China (CSCPRC)— sponsored jointly by three academic organizations[2] and based at the National Academy of Sciences in Washington—and the National Committee on United States-China Relations (NCUSCR)—an independent educational organization in New York[3]—have been considered the appropriate sponsors of "facilitated" exchanges. In principle, the CSCPRC is concerned with exchanges in all scholarly fields, including the social sciences and humanities; but because of China's strong (and usually prevailing) preferences, exchanges in the natural and physical sciences have predominated in practice. The NCUSCR, with an equally wide span of interests in public affairs, education, performing arts, and sports, has encountered similar difficulties in conducting a balanced and comprehensive program.

Each of these committees was formed in 1966, the CSCPRC specifically to promote scholarly interchange with China (an effort initially thwarted by China's introversion during the Cultural Revolution), and the NCUSCR to stimulate public education and policy discussions on United States-China relations. The latter provided financial and administrative assistance to the U.S. Table Tennis Association during the return visit of the Chinese team in 1972, and from that experience decided to seek additional cultural exchange opportunities. Both organizations sought and developed cooperative working relationships with the Department of State and with Chinese counterpart groups—the CSCPRC with the Chinese Scientific and Technical Association, and the NCUSCR, working through the new PRC Liaison Office in Washington,[4] indirectly

2. Sponsored by the National Academy of Sciences, the Social Science Research Council, and the American Council of Learned Societies. Address: Office of the Foreign Secretary, National Academy of Sciences, 2101 Constitution Ave., Washington, D.C. 20418.

3. Address: 777 UN Plaza, 9-B, New York City, NY 10017.

4. Address: Liaison Office of the People's Republic of China, 2300 Connecticut Ave., NW, Washington, D.C. 20008.

with such organizations as the Chinese People's Institute of Foreign Affairs, the Association for Friendship with Foreign Countries, and the All-China Sports Federation. Both committees receive annual grants and occasional project support from the State Department's Bureau of Educational and Cultural Affairs to supplement their funding from private foundations and other sources. It should also be noted that a new National Council for United States-China Trade (NCUSCT), a private organization based upon corporate memberships, was established in 1973 after close consultation with the Department of Commerce. Both with and without "government facilitation," the council has sponsored several trade-related delegations to and from China, but its interests generally fall outside the concerns of this report.

The two committees annually submit exchange proposals to the appropriate Chinese offices regarding the kinds of groups each hopes to send and review reciprocal proposals from China. Parallel discussions are conducted between the two governments, and from this dual process mutual agreements eventually are reached. These exchanges, like most other visits, have involved relatively short-term (two-to-six, but usually three-to-four, week) tours to a variety of cities and sites rather than extended stays specifically for professional purposes. While the CSCPRC normally serves as sole sponsor of its projects, systematically selecting delegation members or institutional hosts according to academic criteria, the NCUSCR often invites the co-sponsorship of an appropriate professional body in the respective field. Both committees seek to include an academic China specialist in each group they send in order to provide cultural perspective and

language skills, and in part to compensate for the dearth of direct exchange opportunities in Chinese studies.

Through the fall of 1975, the CSCPRC had sent 15 scholarly delegations to China, 11 of which represented scientific or technical fields as diverse as seismology, solid state physics, plant studies, acupuncture anesthesia, and paleoanthropology. It had served as host to significantly more groups (20) from the PRC; all but two of these (librarians and language teachers) were in medical and life sciences (7), engineering and technology (6), or physical sciences (3), or were multi-disciplinary scientific delegations (2). For its part, the NCUSCR had sponsored substantially fewer, but often much larger exchanges: six visits in each direction, including (a) the Shenyang Acrobatic Troupe, Wushu (traditional sports) Troupe, and two athletic teams from China, and (b) delegations of American secondary educators, world affairs specialists, university presidents, and an Amateur Athletic Union (AAU) track-and-field team to the PRC. The NCUSCR also played a major though non-sponsoring role in three other facilitated exchanges, all in 1973: the China tours of an American swimming team, of men's and women's collegiate basketball teams, and of the Philadelphia Orchestra. Roughly half of the participants in facilitated exchanges, in both directions, have been members of athletic or performing arts delegations.

Although China firmly insists on the "people-to-people" rather than official nature of all exchanges with the United States, the operational distinction is not always easy to maintain, even on the United States side. Certain projects. such as the 1973 Philadelphia Orchestra tour, have been of sufficient magnitude and/or delicacy to require direct government assistance to professional organizations other than the two exchange committees. The most complex case was the magnificent Chinese Exhibition of Archaeological Finds (shown in Washington, D.C., Kansas City, and San Francisco between December 1974 and August 1975). Major logistical problems, expenditures and insurance commitments in the millions of dollars, and extremely detailed negotiations required a flexible partnership between governmental and private resources. Although administrative responsibility initially was placed with the National Gallery of Art in Washington, D.C., the gallery worked nominally in association with an ad hoc host committee including representatives from several museums, the Department of State, the National Endowment for the Humanities, and the NCUSCR. Nonetheless, much of the day-to-day negotiations had to be conducted at the governmental level.

*Private visits and
  exchanges*

Reflecting China's policy of promoting "people-to-people" friendship, the vast majority of American travelers have gone to China through entirely private arrangements, at their own or their organization's initiative. But only a handful have been reciprocated by Chinese visits to the United States, and this is hardly an area of true exchange. Less affected by shifts in United States-China political relations per se, private visits are strongly influenced by changing moods within China. The 1971–72 period, when the United States-China relationship was being renewed, was one

of relative domestic relaxation following the turmoil of the Cultural Revolution. During times of "political mobilization," such as the 1974 campaign to "criticize Confucius and Lin Piao," foreign visits to China have dropped sharply. Since the National People's Congress in January of 1975, which appeared to resolve various internal political questions, the influx of foreigners has again increased.

The demand for Chinese visas—informed speculation puts the requests in the millions, and thus the acceptance rate well below 1 percent—has probably astounded even the Chinese authorities. Of the roughly 10,000 Americans who have visited China through private arrangements (only the Chinese know the exact number), a substantial portion (some estimate as many as half) have been Americans of Chinese origin who, in general, are encouraged by the PRC to make fraternal visits.

General tourism has not yet developed, with the rare exceptions of passengers from cruise ships invited to spend several days in Canton or Shanghai, in part because of China's severely limited (though expanding) hotel, transport, and interpreter resources. The vast numbers of applications enable the Chinese to be highly selective; although sometimes hard to perceive, there usually are specific "reasons" for each invitation—to make an important symbolic gesture, gain access to informed views or technical information, cultivate public opinion, or to reciprocate past hospitality, friendships, or support. "Affinity groups" of up to 25 persons representing specific professional or institutional interests have been most common, even though the programs arranged by the Chinese hosts normally involve a broad, rather "touristic" schedule in addition to activities germane to the group's particular interests.

These private visits can be considered under two headings—the third and fourth of the "channels" mentioned above. There are the truly ad hoc arrangements and, increasingly, visits arranged through intermediary organizations which have developed a "special" relationship with the PRC. Although this dichotomy is somewhat artificial, since today's ad hoc visit may initiate tomorrow's special relationship, certain features merit separate consideration.

3. *Ad hoc visits and exchanges.* In the fall of 1970, Chairman Mao had told Edgar Snow that Americans of all backgrounds and viewpoints would be welcome in China, signaling even before Ping-Pong the possible end of mutual isolation. From the outset, this principle seemed alive and well, even though the earliest visitors, naturally enough, were people already known to China's leaders, through personal acquaintance or public reputation, who presumably would be responsible and compatible guests. Journalists from the *New York Times* and *Wall Street Journal*, businessmen, eminent scientists and other scholars, and delegations from ethnic minority and radical organizations such as the Black Panthers, Young Lords, and the Socialist tabloid *Guardian* found their paths crossing in the PRC. Many early visitors subsequently introduced other prospective travelers, and Chinese officials began to indicate, usually privately but sometimes publicly, persons or groups they wished to welcome. Some Americans went as guests with all expenses met, but as the numbers grew and China's hosting arrangements became more systematized after the disruptions of the Cultural Revolution, pay-as-you-go became the rule. The China International Travel Service, the Overseas Chinese Travel Service and, for businessmen, the semi-annual Canton Trade Fair Committee now sponsor the great majority of foreign visitors. Additionally, some groups or individuals representing specific professional fields may be invited by state agencies such as the Chinese Academy of Sciences or, more commonly, "mass" organizations in the respective scientific, professional, or cultural fields—for example, the Chinese Medical Association, the Scientific and Technical Association, the Chinese People's Institute of Foreign Affairs, or the Chinese People's Association for Friendship with Foreign Countries. In a few cases, usually arising from prior associations, a particular university or research institute serves as host; some specialist delegations have been welcomed informally by "journalistic circles" or "educational circles" in the Chinese capital, reflecting the continued absence of professional bodies in these fields after the Cultural Revolution.

The kaleidoscopic range of American visitors to China during these five years is difficult even to illustrate, much less characterize briefly. China's National Day receptions in Washington and New York are probably the most diverse assemblages in recent diplomatic experience, with youngsters in blue jeans, bearded scholars, and Chinese Americans both humble and eminent rubbing shoulders with senators, film stars, and business tycoons; they indicate how well China's Liaison Office in Washington and Foreign Ministry have succeeded in comprehending and relating to the complex mosaic of America's pluralistic society. While maintaining a cooperative and reasonably active exchange relationship at the official level, China has opened up innumerable private options for pursuing cultural diplomacy.

Slowly, the two-track pattern is also being reflected among Chinese visitors to the United States. In 1973, small groups of scientists attended two international conferences on mining and high-energy physics in New York, and a high-level delegation of Chinese journalists was received by the American Society of Newspaper Editors (ASNE), reciprocating a previous ASNE trip to China. COMSAT hosted a small PRC Satellite Communications Study Group that same year. A group of American replantation surgeons (1974), the American Meteorological Association (1975), and the American Institute of Architects (1975) all have had reciprocal visits from their Chinese counterparts. A few Chinese citizens have made quiet, private trips here to see relatives, and a much larger number of technicians—perhaps 150—have come for extended periods of training in American firms as part of trade agreements such as those with Boeing and Kellogg. It seems likely that greater numbers of Chinese will visit the United States sponsored by organizations other than the CSCPRC, the NSUSCR, or the NCUSCT; but whether any of these events will be considered quasi-official fulfillments of the Shanghai Communique remains to be seen.

4. *Visits and exchanges through "special relationships."* Success in arranging either reciprocal exchanges or repeat visits obviously implies a special quality of relationship with the Chinese. The vast majority of trips in each direction have been one-shot affairs; but many individuals, several universities, and organizations such as American Women for International Understanding, the ASNE, and various ad hoc and formal groups from the Chinese community, have arranged second and even serial tours. In a few cases, notably the radical newspaper *Guardian*, the annual regularity of their travels suggests a prior understanding with their Chinese hosts. But among these "special relationships," one American organization has come to stand out in both its geographic scope and level of activity: the United States-China People's Friendship Association (USCPFA), which already has sent a score or more groups, involving several hundred people, to the PRC.

The first local association was formed in 1970, and a national organization was established in September 1974 at a Los Angeles conference attended by representatives from more than 40 local groups and hailed by messages from Peking. By late 1975, associations were operating in some 70 cities across the country, coordinated through three regional associations and a national office in Los Angeles.[5] Principal founders of the first local and, later, the national association included several expatriate Americans long resident in China who had returned home after the inception of Ping-Pong diplomacy.

The association's stated goal is "to build active and lasting friendship based on mutual understanding between the people of the United

5. Address: 2700 W. 3rd St., Room 102, Los Angeles, California 90007.

States and the people of China," through both public education programs within the United States and cultural exchanges. USCPFA activities include "speaking out against distortions and misconceptions about the People's Republic of China"; its magazine and newsletters, eschewing criticism of PRC life and policies, seem largely consistent with China's own published views and perspectives. Although reminiscent of the United States-Soviet friendship groups of earlier decades, the USCPFA is not operating in a Cold-War climate of suspicion and thus is more readily accepted and able to build upon public interest. As a "people's" organization open to "anyone who agrees with our goals," the USCPFA has grown and proliferated remarkably, aided in large part by the ability to arrange tours to the PRC. Each regional association receives an annual "quota" from China, perhaps as many as half a dozen delegations. Although some visits have been organized along interest-group lines, most tours have involved people from diverse backgrounds and, at least initially, membership in the association apparently was not a necessary criterion. But as the "visa power" of the associations increased, so too did the preference that tour participants be members, and the prospect of a China trip has become a strong inducement to join—even for those unfamiliar or uncomfortable with the organization's general tone and posture. Since the regional associations are able to charge a flat amount that usually exceeds the per capita tour charges levied by China, these travels also provide a means of subsidizing their other activities.

Thus far, the USCPFA either has not sought or has not succeeded in arranging an "exchange" program, since no Chinese groups have visited the United States under its auspices. Many local chapters, however, have actively participated in hosting Chinese delegations coming under other sponsorship, notably those through the government facilitated route, and regularly seek to arrange receptions or banner-waving throngs at airports. An interesting question, given the exchange patterns outlined above, is whether the association might eventually emerge as an "alternate channel" for Chinese visitors to this country.

## ISSUES AND PROBLEMS

Having started from base zero less than five years ago, exchanges between the United States and China have progressed remarkably. Certainly their effect on American public attitudes and perceptions, warped by decades of Cold-War rhetoric, has been profound and the impact on the people of China may well be no less important. The information gained about the workings of Chinese society and about areas for potential long-term cooperation is proving invaluable, despite obvious limitations. Yet, critical problems remain—regarding reciprocity, substantive content, and integrity—none of which can be entirely separated from the realm of politics.

1. *Reciprocity and mutual benefit.* Presumably, neither the signers of the Shanghai Communique nor anyone else expected the flow of visitors between the two countries to be even approximately equal. "Reciprocity" was desired primarily in the facilitated exchange arena. It quickly became apparent, however, that the term meant different things on each side of the Pacific.

For China, with its highly centralized planning, it has meant an overall balance in the number of facilitated delegations, including those in the trade field and others not sponsored directly by the designated American committees. For the American committees, reflecting their private and independent status, it has meant seeking a balanced annual program for each of them. The greater problem, however, has involved the nature of the exchanges themselves. The NCUSCR, and to a lesser extent the CSCPRC, expected a reasonable balance within each broad field—in performing arts and sports, civic affairs, science and technology, the social sciences and humanities—and also the right of each side to determine the composition of each of its delegations. For the Chinese, however, reciprocity seemed to mean accommodating each side's *differing* fields of interest, while emphasizing the need for detailed approval of each delegation by the host country. Since the United States has consistently sought a larger and more diverse program, China has been free to accept and propose only the minimum needed to properly "symbolize their relationship with us." The result has been a program shaped primarily by Chinese views: an almost annual imbalance in the programs of each United States organization; cultural exchanges primarily of performing groups and sports "spectaculars" to enhance public opinion rather than projects in education or civic affairs that might deepen understanding of specific issues; scholarly exchanges predominantly in the sciences rather than in the more politically sensitive social science and humanities fields; and among the social science,

humanities, and public affairs groups, a relatively greater number going to China than coming here. The persistence of this pattern has become a source of increasing frustration and unhappiness in the respective American scholarly and civic constituencies.

The question of reciprocity has also taken on strong political overtones in the context of individual exchange projects—most notably two that were canceled at the eleventh hour in 1975. In March, barely two weeks before a large PRC performing arts troupe was to arrive in the United States, China insisted on adding several program items, including a highly popular new song entitled "The People of Taiwan Are Our Brothers" which included the lyrics "we must liberate Taiwan." Seeing this as a potential source of great embarrassment to local host groups across the country, and possibly a direct attempt to test American policy, the NCUSCR and the State Department opposed the program change. The impasse resulted in cancellation of the tour, to great mutual regret. In the Chinese view, the United States had violated the spirit of the Shanghai Communique regarding the status of Taiwan and had wrongly elevated a purely internal matter—Taiwan— to an international political issue. In the United States view, the Chinese had introduced a political element into a strictly cultural exchange and, especially since the Philadelphia Orchestra had carefully tailored its 1973 program to Chinese wishes, had failed to reciprocate by respecting the wishes of the host. In September, a delegation of American mayors, scheduled to visit China through the NCUSCR and the U.S. Conference of Mayors, was canceled because of China's last-minute request that the mayor of San Juan, Puerto Rico (who was also president of the National League of Cities), be excluded. This time, it was the Americans who saw a political intrusion into an "internal matter," and the sponsoring organizations held firm.

2. *Substantive content.* As suggested above, there is an implicit tension between "form" and "substance" in the selection of exchange projects. And within those exchanges that do take place, there are differing concerns regarding substantive content. American organizations, and the scholars and other publics they represent, have steadily pressured not only for "more" but "better." The PRC has seemed concerned primarily with giving foreigners a comprehensive overview of life in the new China through short-term tours, rather than opening specific facets of her development to close scrutiny. In contrast, American hosts tend to "show and tell all" and to expect reciprocal treatment. Private American proposals for bilateral discussions of world problems have elicited few signs of interest from the PRC. The quest of Americans for longer stays in fewer places, in-depth professional visits, and cooperative research ventures has met with only minimal success, although there are encouraging signs of change. Members of Chinese scientific delegations occasionally have given lectures or papers at scholarly meetings here and generally are showing greater willingness in this regard. Several American scientists of Chinese origin have spent two or three months conducting collaborative research in Chinese institutions. A number of other Americans, such as Yale biologist Arthur Galston and Berkeley China Specialist John Stewart Service and their wives, have made second visits to China of several months' duration. But for most Americans, visits in either direction —however delightful and generally informative—have been less than completely rewarding in professional terms.

Efforts to establish student exchanges, even in regard to language training, have been similarly unproductive. Several American students of Chinese origin have spent a year or more at universities and language institutes in Peking, but they are exceptions explained by personal acquaintanceship and/or ethnicity. Although hundreds of students are exchanged annually between China and other Western countries, there seem to be no immediate prospects for student exchange programs with the United States; and, as with long-term scholarly exchanges and cooperative research, the reasons are partly political. The Chinese imply that with hundreds of Taiwan students and teachers on American campuses, and an embassy in Washington to support them, PRC students and scholars residing here might face awkward and embarrassing situations. In the interests of reciprocity, until the way is paved for their citizens to come for extended periods, China considers the reverse process equally "inconvenient." These circumstances have not, of course, precluded Chinese technicians from training in United States firms (though admittedly in cloistered circumstances) when important national needs were involved. Much of China's reluctance even to experiment in this area surely reflects a disinterest in symbolizing the United States relationship more substantially.

3. *Integrity*. The "opening" to China unfortunately spawned a "visa culture" in some quarters. China specialists who for years had written freely about "Communist China" worried that their publications, past and future, might prejudice chances for the pilgrimage to Peking; many people wondered how "complete" they should be in their applications, especially regarding past visits to Taiwan; and private citizens serving as officers of exchange-related organizations often strained to avoid offending the Chinese in articles and speeches without, at the same time, compromising their own or their institution's integrity. The problem was heightened for successful applicants, since the Chinese presumably would be especially interested in public reports about their trips, and some visitors became more sensitive to Chinese reactions than there was need to be. But the sense of prior restraint with which many Americans approached China, coupled with the vital and impressive society they saw (albeit superficially), resulted in a remarkably good press for the PRC. Premier Chou En-lai actually felt obliged to caution one group of American journalists about presenting an overly rosy picture, and a Harvard China specialist warned of the "Marcopoloitis that paralyzed American critical faculties in the early 1970s."[6] Never the dominant mood, the "visa culture" and the uncritical analyses it generated subsided as the new relationship became a more normal part of the international landscape; but it

probably will never disappear altogether.

A more serious issue involves Chinese attitudes to events held in the United States, particularly those cultural exchanges having great public visibility. Major concern has been expressed about the media; film and TV coverage occasionally has been curtailed when hosts could not provide adequate assurance that it would truly "promote friendship" —or, understandably perhaps, when it seemed the product would be used for "commercial exploitation." Writing of an incident in December 1974, Jerome Cohen noted that:

The forced cancellation of the press preview of the magnificent Chinese Archaeological Exhibition in Washington brings to the surface some of the implications of United States-Chinese exchanges in our country. Actually, China's interference with free communication goes beyond its refusal to accept journalists from South Korea, Taiwan, South Africa, or Israel at the preview. The Chinese insisted upon, and were granted, the power to determine not only the intellectual content of catalogs and all public statements, but also even the books to be sold by the National Gallery Bookstore![7]

How far American hosts should go in accommodating Chinese wishes about what Americans see and hear, while seeking a constructive relationship with a radically different society, is a question that undoubtedly will endure. There will always be some who do not stand up for their principles, others who make matters of principle out of issues that are not, and mutually exclusive principles which occasionally but inevitably produce conflict between the two countries. To pursue ex-

6. Jerome A. Cohen, *New York Times* (18 December 1974), Op Ed page.

7. Ibid.

changes with complete integrity, Americans will need an equal store of patience and wisdom.

## FUTURE PROSPECTS

By mid-1975, earlier thoughts that President Ford's impending fall visit to Peking might result in diplomatic recognition—and thus increased cultural relations—had begun to wane. China's apparently cool reception to Dr. Kissinger in October, and dire warnings about United States efforts toward detente with the USSR, suggested that United States-PRC relations were at the chilliest point in their brief span. Early indications were that at least "government facilitated" exchange activity would be frozen at or below previous levels; and the apparently ceremonial nature of the presidential visit in early December stimulated no greater hopes. But within any possible scenario, the prospects for substantial improvement in either quantity or quality do not appear bright, constrained in large part by China's already crowded and internationally competitive travel market. Without diplomatic recognition, a sizeable increase in Chinese visitors to the United States seems most unlikely; and private American visits to China will certainly remain highly selective and could reflect even greater Chinese emphasis on cultivating public support and key opinion leaders rather than on deepening learning opportunities.

Diplomatic relations could, of course, come at any time—within months or not for years. When it does happen, the effect will probably be most pronounced on the form and substance of exchanges, rather than on the volume. The doors would be opened for students (especially in the language field), though it would be overly optimistic to expect more than a few dozen per year in each direction. A few selected scholars might engage in joint research for several months, and several journalists might be stationed in each capital. But even diplomatic relations are no guarantee of such developments, which will surely depend on China's judgments about the terms and implications of the formal tie. For the United States, at least, the government would have a freer hand to sponsor and conduct exchange activities as it wishes without having only to facilitate the work of others; a formal exchange agreement might clarify the mutual interests of the two parties and establish useful guidelines; and some of the political clouds that occasionally have dimmed specific projects would be dispelled.

Our exchange relationships with China will never be entirely free from politics. For the PRC, a skilled practitioner of cultural diplomacy, politics will remain "in command," and both governments will continue to view the exchange process as an instrument of national policy—for good reason. Several years ago, Dick Wilson, the respected British journalist and scholar, wrote of

the vastly larger drama which is about to unfold, namely, the political consequences for the world as a whole of the "great divide" between the Chinese culture which has dominated half of mankind at earlier periods in history, and European culture which is the commanding influence in our present day world.[8]

The political consequences will, of

8. *New Nation* (Singapore, 24 March 1971).

course, be critically important, not only for United States-China relations but also for the larger international order. Yet it is easy to overlook the basic cultural, even moral, foundations of this "great divide" and the vast gap in mutual comprehension between American and PRC citizens that remains after five fruitful, but largely experimental, years of serious contact. Despite many serious problems, exchanges have become an invaluable bridge for humanistic and scientific learning. The stakes are too large to treat them as only an accessory to politics or to let politics bar their steady evolution.

# Institutional Linkages: A Key to Successful International Exchange

By RALPH H. SMUCKLER

ABSTRACT: As we approach a new era of international relations, institutional linkages—planned, long-term agreements between universities to cooperate along mutually beneficial lines—should form the basis for expanded and increasingly valuable international exchange. From an institutional perspective, there are various types of exchanges, each with its own purpose, clientele, and use. Institutional linkage encompassing these exchanges can take various forms. Linkages offer advantages by encouraging planned use of resources and, particularly at unit levels within universities, drawing on new resources of support. They can add to the quality of both faculty and student exchange. In relations with some non-Western countries, institutional cooperative agreements based on gain for both sides are an appropriate and timely replacement for assistance contracts and can help to correct past deficiencies in exchange programs. While other bases of expanded exchange programming exist and should be encouraged, the institutional focus provides advantages of size, diversity, and resources which give it advantages in the foreseeable future. There is a study now in progress to appraise various means of encouraging productive higher educational relations between the United States and other countries. One alternative being examined is the proposed new Association for International Cooperation in Higher Education and Research (AICHER) which would assist in the formation of institutional linkages.

Ralph H. Smuckler is Professor of Political Science and Dean of International Studies and Programs at Michigan State University. He has served as Vice President of Education and World Affairs, Representative of the Ford Foundation in Pakistan (1967–69), and is presently Chairman of the Research Advisory Committee of the U.S. Agency for International Development, and a board member of the Institute of International Education (New York) and of the Midwest Universities Consortium for International Activities.

HIGHER educational institutions and, hence, the societies of which they are an integral part benefit from a well-established flow of knowledge and scholars across national boundaries. As problems become increasingly complex, even global in nature, this movement of ideas and people will greatly increase in significance and, in some instances, take on critical importance; therefore, international scholarly exchange which embodies this flow should be encouraged, expanded, and made as productive as possible. These assertions are seldom contested in serious discussion. They are rooted in the nature of science and the growth of knowledge about man and his environment. They form the basis for the comments which follow and which stress the need for broadening the institutional role in exchanges of the future.

From a university perspective, the international exchange of persons means many things and has a different ring to some people than to others. There are a number of categories of exchange which have consequence for institutional programs and plans. Each category has its own clientele group, serves distinct purposes, and poses a set of issues or problems somewhat different from others. It is useful to distinguish among them if one is to plan effectively to meet institutional program needs.

## CATEGORIES OF EXCHANGE

The first broad division which runs throughout all of the categories separates exchanges with institutions in advanced countries, primarily Western Europe, from those with economically less developed countries. The flow of American students and faculty to and from Western Europe is more traditional, has a long history, and seems more natural; it requires far less encouragement. It takes place under an infinite array of circumstances and frequently at considerable sacrifice or financial loss to individuals involved. In contrast, exchanges with the economically less developed world require careful arranging and must overcome economic and cultural barriers which are of much less consequence in West European exchange. Each type of exchange can usefully be viewed as it operates in respect to advanced, Western countries on the one hand and to areas of Asia, Africa, the Middle East, and other non-Western areas, on the other.

In the full range of exchanges, including those with traditional and with non-Western areas, one can group programs according to purposes and clientele to be served. Foreign students studying at American institutions comprise the largest and, perhaps, most significant category. From the university perspective, the main purpose is to provide education to persons who for one reason or another do not or cannot study at home. An auxiliary or secondary purpose is to provide a cross-cultural, more lively and worldly atmosphere for United States students. The foreign student phenomenon which has grown so large in this country during the post-World War II era has had a far-reaching impact on individuals and institutions abroad and in this country.

In more recent years, foreign scholars on postdoctoral fellowships or appointed as visiting professors at American institutions have formed another category of exchange. These exchanges serve to add quality to our teaching or research efforts and, frequently, to provide advanced training or experience to the visiting scholar.

Groups of United States undergraduates studying abroad—mainly in Europe—comprise another significant category. These programs vary in duration, location, purpose, and in many other respects. They differ in quality and seriousness from academic tourism at one extreme to specialized study in a stimulating foreign setting at the other. There are also many individual programs abroad for American students. These are frequently tied to advanced graduate work, primarily dissertation research; but undergraduates, too, fall within this individualized category.

There is a full range of exchange arrangements through which American faculty members study or teach in foreign settings. This broad category includes senior Fulbright scholars; professors who have served under development assistance contracts sponsored by foundations, government, or multilateral agencies; and foundation grantees. It includes as well the professor on sabbatical leave who chooses to spend time abroad at his own expense. The range of faculty members working or studying abroad on their own or through institutional arrangements seems infinite in variety. Within the range are those faculty members, few in number, who are exchanged through a direct person-for-person understanding, one institution borrowing a faculty person from a university abroad which has in turn borrowed from it. From the university perspective, all of these exchange programs serve

to add to the quality of professorial performance and to bring an international and comparative perspective to the classroom or research laboratory. In the case of assistance contract programs, the university is also fulfilling a broad service function in line with its own philosophy and definition of institutional purpose.

These six or seven different forms of exchange programs are all a part of American higher educational relationships with other societies. Each has its purpose and operates with varying degrees of success. Most commonly, these arrangements, through which our institutions tie in with institutions of other societies and our students and faculty members relate to counterparts in distant parts of the world, progress with little institutional planning and advanced coordination. Although much individual planning occurs, rarely do we find institutional ties developed between a university in the United States and one abroad which encompasses in a planned way the various forms of exchange, placing each in the perspective of institutional goals and purposes. And yet, as our nation enters a new era of international relations, including those between educational institutions, such "linkages" will probably become—and it is my thesis that they should become—the basic underlying structure for a wide range of educational exchange, encompassing the various categories and blending them in new, productive ways.

## THE CONCEPT OF INSTITUTIONAL LINKAGE

Without detracting from the momentum and significant benefits of individualized and ad hoc exchange programs, we need far more planned linkage arrangements to undergird exchange in the future. What is the meaning of "institutional linkage"? Ideally, a university—or a department of a university—in the United States works out an agreement with an institution in another country which sets forth the goals and purposes of working together over the long run. Each party from its own perspective, indicates the purposes to be served and the means to accomplish its purposes through exchange and other cooperative efforts. Each states its intention to devote resources over a number of years to the relationship. Financial resources may be modest and the pace of the program may be conditioned on their availability. Following an agreement, a variety of exchanges occur on a planned basis, with each side perceiving the understanding to be serving its interest and, therefore, justifying the expenditure of its energy and funds. Such arrangements might include cooperative research activities, exchange of faculty, undergraduate study programs, access to facilities for graduate research, exchange of materials, and many other types of cooperative endeavor. If built upon a clear appraisal of short- and long-term gain and established so that resources can be sufficient to cover essential costs, both parties to the agreement are strengthened over the years.

Linkages of this sort are probably best established between units of institutions rather than universities as a whole. A college of business at a university in the United States might well decide to associate with a similar college or school in Western Europe, gaining easy access to research opportunities within the Common Market and providing access to the study of American management techniques for foreign visiting professors. An institution concerned with rural development issues and processes on the subcontinent of Asia may affiliate closely with those components of an American university similarly committed, and in the process both may gain expertise and access to training opportunities and knowledge. Institution-wide agreements may provide encouragement and a framework, thus facilitating work between specific units; but unless departments or colleges are intimately involved and see the advantages to be gained, opening doors merely through institution-wide arrangements probably will result in less than optimal gain.

There are many variations on the institutional linkage theme. Several institutions in one country may link up with one university abroad. Consortia may be formed to establish and maintain effective ties, thus broadening access on both sides. A network of relationships may be in order as a means of avoiding too narrow an exchange or the weaknesses of inbreeding or exclusivity. Agreements may be formal and detailed or quite informal. In all cases, however, linkage should be based on clear understanding of purposes to be served and backed up with necessary financial understandings. Linkage should be perceived and operate as a two-way street. Although the relationships may form slowly and the flow of persons initially may be small or one-sided, the program ought to be monitored and planned so that the value to both sides can be enlarged as experience justifies expansion.

## THE VALUE OF INSTITUTIONAL LINKAGE AS A BASIS FOR EXCHANGE

It is my thesis that institutional relationships along these lines form the most promising underpinning for educational exchange of many types in the future. While we should protect the range of individual or ad hoc exchange programs, planned institutional relationships offer certain distinct advantages which will probably become increasingly important and ought to receive more attention.

First, institutional linkages offer the best prospect to improve the exchange flow between the United States and economically less developed countries. Exchange with the non-Western world has been deficient in a number of ways. Numbers have been relatively small. While many students have come from these areas to the United States, our students have studied there far less than in Europe. For various reasons, Fulbright program appointments in the less developed areas have been hard to fill, and some positions have remained vacant. In the past, a good share of the movement of faculty to institutions in some non-Western countries resulted from assistance or development contracts incorporating the flow of American experts to aid institution-building efforts abroad. Since the development tasks were usually perceived narrowly, and mainly related to technical fields, the range of contact was narrow. Large segments of the American faculty who could have gained much had little exposure.

It is generally recognized that our nation's relationship with the "third world" must now take a new form, and the same applies to academic exchanges. American university relations are coming out of an era of tutelage. In many situations, the assistance contract of the past generation is obsolete. There are now institutions in countries where such relationships existed which ought to be approached on the principle of equality and the basis of long-term, mutual gain. As we establish new forms, we ought to be able to correct former imbalances.

Institutional linkages permit full acknowledgment of the principle of mutuality which is increasingly important in international educational relations. Agreements should include plans for joint research, opportunities for students, access to laboratories and to research sites and data. Institution by institution, we should be forging the types of ties with colleagues in Asia, Africa, Latin America, and the Middle East which will serve our needs as well as theirs over the long run.

Exchanges and relationships with institutions in the Soviet Union and Eastern Europe leave room for much improvement. Here too, it is important for us to establish our purposes and needs as we work out agreements with institutions in the Socialist countries. We know from recent statements of Russian educational leaders that agreements through which planned institutional exchange can take place are perhaps the only basis on which institutions in centrally planned economies can work with us. Thus, we must agree on the important fields in which university links should be built—and these should not be limited to only those of importance to others—and proceed to establish the planned flow of people that will be of benefit in both directions. In some cases, individual institutional linkages will not be possible and broader groupings on each side will be necessary. This may be less manageable, but such consortia fit within the same general mold and ought to be made workable.

Another important consideration favoring the institutional linkage pattern is that it permits better planning within the American institution. In so doing, it offers the opportunity for impact on programs of a broad nature. It can be placed on a long-term basis. Faculty members can plan activities during sabbatical leaves, taking into account opportunities created through agreements. Curricula can be developed which take advantage of new study-abroad opportunities for undergraduates. Dissertation research planning is placed on a more secure footing. Important area study programs can help to determine the regional focus of the institutional ties and benefit accordingly. In general, the academic program of the American institution—and the university abroad—can proceed in a more deliberate fashion.

As a corollary, programmed exchange relationships permit long-term joint research endeavors. In most fields this is a necessity if the research is to be of consequence. Long-term linkages would assure the flow of information and the availability of equipment during research sojourns abroad. It would encourage and facilitate the meeting of minds which is a forerunner to successful cooperative research. A professor at either the American or foreign institution could send graduate students to work in a laboratory abroad under the tutelage of a professor with whom he shared a laboratory the previous year and have some confidence that the quality of work and the necessary level of supervision will meet his standards.

One great advantage of the linkage concept is that it encourages and permits a more rational use of funds. Institutional ties which are planned over the long run should be of sufficient value to justify use of university funds on each side. Funds from outside sources can thus be stretched to cover more exchange activity. While these non-university funds will always be important, they should not be the sole basis on which institutional exchange interests are fulfilled. University international exchange programs cannot, in view of their importance to quality educational programs, be left to support only from outside sources. If there were a complete accounting, we would probably find that most funds for international exchange today come from educational institutions, in one way or another, rather than through foundation grants or government subsidies. These outside sources could continue as valued allies, effectively providing the "mortar" to hold the institutional "bricks" together.

Carefully worked out, mutually beneficial arrangements offer the potential of bringing forth more funding on a more stable basis than in the past. The establishment of linkages on the basis of mutual benefit, department by department and college by college, would mean that departmental and college funds could maintain the visiting professor and support faculty leaves or graduate assistantships which are at the base of exchange programs. Within most American universities, the focus of year-to-year budgetary power on these matters is at the department or the college level rather than residing in the central administration. Teaching or research assistantships are controlled at the operating levels of the university for the most part, and decisions on who is to fill the assistantship are made there. Visiting professors are selected at the department level. Leaves are initiated by departments and legitimized at higher levels. If a chemistry department establishes a valued relationship with a university in Germany or in Iran, it probably can allocate some funds in partial support of its relationship because, in fact, it is the point of actual control of such funds.

As a corollary, institutional linkage agreements would put funds now expended on international exchange to more advantageous uses. The visiting professor or the groups of students would be integrated within the department or college more effectively. Too often, when support is provided entirely from higher levels or outside sources, the visitor is kept on the fringe of academic affairs and only through perseverance or good fortune contributes to full capacity.

There are also a number of important but lesser advantages to be served. Recurrent exchange between two institutions eliminates some of the rough edges on personal arrangements. Routine matters, such as housing and dormitory facilities, can be dealt with more thoroughly. Unattended, these essentials can partially offset the gains of international exchange. Through advanced planning on an institutional basis, there would be fewer openings remaining unfilled in the more remote institutions. It may be true that from time to time persons of less experience or talent may come into the exchange relationship, but there is no reason to believe that this would be the general case, nor more prevalent in the future than at present. Furthermore, under a planned institutional arrangement, even those who on their own would be less successful exchanges would in fact be incorporated more productively through a systematic use of talent. Over the years, the level of frankness on personnel matters could be expected to increase, so the exchange program would improve in value on both sides.

## THE INSTITUTION AS A FOCUS

The above advantages of a program and financial nature are real. There are also certain potential problems. The most basic relates to the assumption that the institution, as such, is the appropriate and useful unit for planning and leading in the direction of more effective exchanges in the future. There are other alternatives, for example the individual scholar or student, the professional or disciplinary association, national organizations, or the department within the institution. There are reasons to place the university ahead of these others during the period ahead, not in ways to weaken their importance, but, instead, to augment the institutional role by comparison.

First, the institution controls resources to make planning effective, including not only financial resources but structure and talent as well. The purposes to be served by exchange relationships can be placed within broader goals and a long-term perspective. Put another way, the university is the point at which the various strands of exchange converge — student programs, faculty efforts, cooperative research, study abroad, and so on. It is the logical point for planned use of resources and opportunities to take place.

Second, the university offers a good opportunity for a residual effect. It has the quality of permanence. Individuals and associations may come or go, but the university continues to educate, to absorb and reflect new movements, and to relate to its environment. An international dimension well established through linkage relationships will have a long-term effect on programs.

Third, in contrast with disciplinary or professional associations, a university focus permits a combination of approaches — multi-disciplinary teams or programs — which are increasingly in tune with the reality of today's problems. Furthermore, the institution is large and diverse enough to permit one unit or department to benefit from the experience of another. This assumes institutional memory and internal communication, but such are not beyond reach in most institutions.

Finally, institutions abroad seem to want to relate to universities in this country. The pattern of operation and of institutional leadership in many other countries calls for negotiation or discussion with parallel units here. Governments abroad may be more involved than in the United States, but usually the institution is in a position to negotiate and deal as necessary with the authorities.

The growth of a base of institutional linkages underpinning other exchanges in the future should not be construed to eliminate or weaken other avenues. Indeed, in many ways it strengthens the others. We should, in any case, protect the pluralistic approach we now have. As mentioned above, the institutional role in no way replaces departmental or college involvements;

indeed, it strengthens and depends on them. Each of the alternative means — from the individual scholar approach to the national organization which encourages and facilitates exchange — contributes in its own way. However, because of the advantages outlined above, the institutional base should now be expanded in significance.

## HOW TO EXPAND INSTITUTIONAL LINKAGE

If institutional linkage ought to be the underpinning for expansion of exchange programs in the future, how can we proceed to promote such relationships? We need, at the institutional level, an awareness of the importance of the development of these types of ties and their value. They ought to be actively promoted in line with institutional goals. These goals ought to be made more explicit. On the national scene, we need a means of facilitating the building up of long-term inter-university relationships. An organization to accomplish this was foreseen in the proposal to establish the Association for International Cooperation in Higher Education and Research (AICHER).

The proposed association is the product of a task force established by the six major higher education associations based in Washington — the American Council on Education, the American Association of Universities, the National Association of State Universities and Land Grant Colleges (NASULGC), the American Association of State Colleges and Universities, the American Association of Colleges, and the American Association of Community and Junior Colleges. The six asked NASULGC to take the lead in outlining and developing the new association, which would be essentially an outgrowth of the six domestically oriented higher educational associations. These encompass among them all elements of American higher education.

A new association based on this broad membership would be a first attempt to provide a clear entry point to American institutions for the many universities and organizations abroad which seek relationships in the United States. AICHER would provide not only an entry point, but also a source of information, a base for providing technical assistance on the formation of institutional cooperative relationships, a point for monitoring the network of relationships, and a facilitating mechanism for promoting institutional ties. Operating with a relatively modest budget, it could provide funds to help establish and, on a limited basis, sustain agreements between institutions based on their own perception of institutional advantage and goals to be attained through cooperation. By far, the largest funding over the longer run in all such relationships would not come from AICHER, but from the institutions themselves or from funds controlled by them. AICHER, however, would gather enough support from government and private services to sponsor occasional seminars, provide the basis for meetings between institutions, provide "topping up" funds, and generally take steps to promote institutional linkages of a long-term, mutually beneficial nature.

A study beginning during 1976 is intended to examine the value and feasibility of the proposed AICHER scheme and various alternatives. Through a grant from the Agency for International Development and funding from other sources, the six association Task Force led by NASULGC is reviewing and examining the costs and benefits of alternative arrangements to promote interinstitutional ties. Views and insights from many sources will be collected and reviewed. The product of the year of study and feasibility testing will be presented toward the end of 1976. We may then see more clearly what national mechanism would best serve to encourage institutional relations internationally.

The steps being taken on the national scene are in no way a substitute for the individual institutional momentum which does exist at the present time. At the meeting of the International Association of Universities in Moscow in August 1975, the need for increased institutional cooperation was affirmed by spokesmen for universities in many countries of the world. The need for this international cooperation among universities was one of the major themes emerging from the congress. The statements made by Soviet institutions along this line have encouraged American universities and others to take steps toward establishing institution-to-institution relationships which would be of mutual benefit. From one month to another, requests for new international ties are received at institutions in the United States. There is good reason to believe that in the era ahead, the variety of ad hoc exchange relationships which we now have will be joined by a strong network of institutional ties which will be based on mutual benefit and sufficiently planned and financed to assure the type of flow of knowledge and people which is so essential to the advancement of science and the enhancement of the quality of life.

# Exchange of People among International Companies: Problems and Benefits

By SUSAN S. HOLLAND

ABSTRACT: As international companies have expanded throughout the world, they have increasingly served as an important vehicle for the transfer and exchange of people. However, the extent to which these exchanges have led to improved understanding and forging links of friendship and cooperation, or, conversely, to increased suspicion, resentment, and distrust, depends largely on the participants' ability to understand and adapt to each other's perspectives, goals, and cultural backgrounds. This ability can be developed through adequate special training prior to and during the exchanges. However, adequate training of this type has not been provided by international companies to personnel involved in exchanges. Other factors affecting the outcome of such exchanges include the willingness of the people involved to integrate into and become active members of the host community and the companies' policies concerning the hiring, training, compensation, and promotion of the host country nationals on the same basis as parent company managers. On the other hand, benefits resulting from these exchanges include training of host country employees and transfer to them of productive management, marketing, and financial knowledge, creation of new jobs, and increased productive capabilities of the host countries. Especially important, given the training and sensitivities of the people involved, is the ability of international company managers to stimulate among people of diverse backgrounds and outlooks a cooperative working relationship.

---

*Susan S. Holland is currently the Director of Operations and Planning for the Council of the Americas and Corporate Secretary and member of the Board of Directors and Executive Committee of the Fund for Multinational Management Education. She has coedited* Changing Legal Environment in Latin America: Management Implications, *volumes 1 and 2, and written an article on "Ancom Organization and Institutions." She was a member of the Board of Editors of* Journal of International Affairs *and of the Society of the School of International Affairs.*

THE spread of foreign investment has served as a vehicle for a rather extensive exchange of persons throughout the world. As international companies (ICs)[1] have expanded overseas, international executives and experts have followed to manage and direct them. Further, ICs have drawn nationals of host countries into their operations and have sent a number back to the parent headquarters for training and exposure. However, the extent to which these exchanges have stimulated improved understanding and cooperation or resentment and distrust among people involved in the exchanges throughout the world depends on a number of factors and conditions which this paper will attempt to examine briefly in the space permitted.

## THE GROWTH OF THE IC

The existence of these ICs is certainly not a new phenomenon. Their origins have been traced by some authorities back to the early international financial companies that sprang up around the Mediterranean during the fourteenth and fifteenth centuries, while others attribute their origins to the international trading companies that evolved in the seventeenth and eighteenth centuries to secure both raw materials and markets for their countries' exports. Whatever their birthright, ICs did not rise to prominence until their major expansion after World War II. For example, it is estimated

that United States direct foreign investment alone amounted to a book value of about $7 billion in 1940 and since World War II has grown from almost $12 billion in 1950 to $78 billion in 1970 and to almost $119 billion in 1974.[2]

And, of course, United States companies are not alone in their foreign thrusts. Japan's foreign direct investment mushroomed from about $283 million in 1960 to $3.3 billion in 1970 and to $12.7 billion by March 1974.[3] Comparable overseas direct investment figures are difficult to obtain for European countries; however, according to one source, outstanding direct overseas investment by the European members of the Development Assistance Committee (DAC, including Belgium, France, West Germany, Italy, the Netherlands, Sweden, Switzerland, and the United Kingdom) rose from $39.6 billion in 1967 to $52.3 billion in 1973.[4]

According to the same source, total overseas direct investment by all of the DAC countries (including the European countries plus the United States, Japan, and Canada) rose from $104.2 billion in 1967 to $176.7 billion in 1973. Thus, although these figures do not include all investor countries, we can begin to appreciate the magnitude of overseas activities of ICs.

1. The term international company is used here to include multinational or transnational corporations or enterprises, international holding companies, and so forth, and no distinction is made among them for the purposes of this paper. The generally accepted criteria for qualification as an IC of at least $100 million sales and 30 percent of income generated abroad are applied here.

2. An official at the U.S. Department of Commerce.

3. "Japan's Direct Investment Overseas," *Keidanren Review*, no. 30 (July 1975), pp. 5–10; Gene Gregory, "Japan's Changing Industrial Structure: Challenge and Response," *Columbia Journal of World Business*, spring 1975, p. 97; and an official of the Japanese Consulate in New York.

4. "White Paper on International Trade," Ministry of International Trade and Industry (MITI), Japan, 1975; the source stresses that the information is based on inconsistent data sources, making exact comparison difficult.

And this growth trend seems to be continuing, although, according to preliminary and incomplete data, the Organisation for Economic Co-operation and Development (OECD) reports that there has probably been a slight slowdown in world-wide foreign direct investment. There has been a decline in the rate of increase of the flow of United States foreign direct investment since 1972, although not of the total amount,[5] and a falling off in Japanese direct investment flows from $13.5 billion in 1973 to $12.7 billion in 1974.[6] Also, there has been a shift in that, especially since the major currency devaluations and revaluations that occurred throughout the world in 1971, there has been less outgoing investment from and more flowing into the United States from abroad. In the future, however, it is estimated that United States ICs will continue growing at significant rates but European and especially Japanese ICs will outpace their growth. And although under present economic conditions the growth rates of both ICs and governments have slowed somewhat, still it has been estimated that ICs are growing at about double the rate of purely domestic companies as well as of most governments. And it is further estimated that by 1980, ICs will be responsible for about 50 percent of the world production.[7]

5. An official at the U.S. Department of Commerce.
6. "Direct Investment Abroad Slow in Fiscal 1974," *Bank of Tokyo Weekly Review*, vol. 29, no. 34 (8 September 1975).
7. An official in the Invisible Transactions and Capital Movements Division, Organization for Economic Co-operation and Development, Paris, 1975; John H. Dunning, "The Multinational Enterprise: The Background," in *The Multinational Enterprise*, ed. John H. Dunning (New York: Praeger Publishers, 1971), p. 19.

*Reasons for spread overseas*

The reasons for this remarkable overseas investment by ICs are many and complex. A number of these can be grouped as defensive strategies, such as preventing a competitor from preempting a market, overcoming tariff or trade restrictions, diversifying risk, home market saturation or declining home market for products, and currency overvaluation at home or undervaluation in the host market. Other reasons include availability of raw materials, transport costs, labor cost advantage, incentives offered by host and/or home country.

But whatever its motive for going abroad, the distinguishing factor of an IC is that it is more a concept or strategy of decision-making and organization than an actual "institution"; it is characterized by a worldwide perspective. Its decision-making process organizes management, technology, know-how, capital, labor, and resources on a global basis, disregarding boundaries, to achieve the most efficient production and distribution of goods and services.

## THE IC AS A VEHICLE FOR EXCHANGE OF PEOPLE

And just as the IC has been an important vehicle for the transfer across national boundaries of capital, material resources, technology, and goods and services, so too has it been responsible for massive transfers, exchanges, and contact among the world's people. The number of United States managers of ICs living and working abroad in 1971 was placed at about 40,000 to 50,000[8] and their

8. Source: James A. Skidmore, Jr., President of Handy Associates, as cited by Gerd Wilcke, "Multinational Managers: Overseas

families probably bring the total to 150,000 or more.

These figures do not take into account technical experts sent overseas by ICs or consulting firms for short periods of time, nor the significant numbers of nationals in the host country (hereafter referred to as host country nationals — HCNs) who are brought to the parent headquarters in the United States for training or for work assignments.

But despite the significant numbers of United States employees abroad, incomplete data seems to indicate that, while total foreign direct investment by United States firms has been increasing significantly, the number of United States expatriates employed abroad by these firms has probably not increased at the same rate. The employment practices reported by a number of United States ICs seems to substantiate this trend. It would appear that the reason for the slower increase of United States expatriates relative to foreign investment is that more and more companies are attempting to replace United States expatriate staff in their overseas operations with HCNs or, to a much smaller extent, with third country nationals (hereafter referred to as TCNs).

Japanese companies and affiliates abroad, according to Business Asia, in an article discussing a recent study by the Dodwell Marketing Consultants, are estimated to employ almost 120,000 Japanese expatriates.[9] The larger numbers of Japanese expatriates overseas with ICs are most likely due, in part, to the different personnel policies of Japanese firms which, on the whole, do not employ as many HCNs and depend more on parent country nationals (hereinafter referred to as PCNs) to run their overseas affiliates.

Although comparable data are not available for the rest of the world, since the United States and Japan account for a major portion of total overseas investment and, therefore (it can also be assumed), a substantial portion of overseas personnel, we can at least appreciate what the magnitude of the exchanges brought about by ICs must be. These exchanges of persons are a potential stimulant to greater understanding and cooperation among peoples from different countries. International managers and executives are in a position to play an important role in furthering and promoting or obstructing the development of harmonious relations among nations and peoples of the world; they increasingly have the potential to help forge cooperative links and communities of interest throughout the world or, on the other hand, to discourage such cooperation.

The extent to which exchanges generated by the ICs lead to increased, in-depth understanding among the expatriate executives and their families depends on many factors. Central to such understanding are: the preparation of the expatriates for the cultural and other differences they will encounter; the ability of the participants in the exchange to communicate effectively on a variety of levels; the extent to which the HCNs are integrated into the operations of the IC in the host and home countries; and the extent of contact experienced

---

Positions No Longer a Dead End," New York Times, 12 March 1972; Spencer J. Hayden, "Personnel Problems in Overseas Operations," Personnel, vol. 45, no. 3 (May–June 1968), p. 14.

9. "Japanese Direct Foreign Investments —Past and Future," Business Asia, 4 April 1975, p. 107.

by the expatriates outside of their work environment. The failure of an expatriate to understand the people and culture of a host country can lead to grave misunderstandings, disappointment, suspicion, and cultural shock, all of which make it difficult for him to perform effectively.

### PROBLEMS AND POTENTIALS FOR GREATER UNDERSTANDING AND COOPERATION

#### Cross-cultural exchanges

For any meaningful understanding and communication to occur, the businessmen involved in the exchanges need to be able to understand and deal effectively with the differences they will encounter. Such differences will be found in each other's cultures (in the broad sense of one's patterning of behavior, including one's attitudes toward work, leisure, and learning), languages (spoken and nonverbal), social structures and customs, values, beliefs, civilizations, and modes of living. These must all be considered, as well as the more obvious differences in each other's concepts of management and business structures, governments, and legal systems.

It is the responsibility of the international manager to spearhead the process whereby such understanding may be attained. He must acquire a broad cross-cultural understanding if he is to promote among people from diverse environments cooperation and teamwork fundamental to the successful conduct of business. The ability to achieve this is what Pieter Kuin called "the

magic of multinational management."[10]

#### Sociocultural differences

Now admittedly, achievement of such an integrative function is no mean task, given the significant differences that exist between the diverse sociocultural and business environments around the world. People's values and cultures are an integrated part of their being, and one must first understand one's own sociocultural background before he can understand how it differs from those of other countries. That is, he must be able to understand how his own attitudes, values, objectives, methods, and expectations differ from those of the HCNs so that he can understand how the HCNs react to him. With this understanding, he should then be sufficiently flexible to be able to adjust and modify his values and expectations to the extent necessary to make his perspective and goals understandable and acceptable to the HCNs so that an effective working relationship can be established to permit the achievement of the desired results.

Thus, even if he feels that his method of doing business is best, he needs to be able to communicate this to the HCNs in terms and language that they can understand and in terms of what is good for the host country and not only what is good for the parent company. He needs to strive to adapt his methods to the local business methods and institutions rather than trying to force the use of his own business methods on

10. Pieter Kuin, "The Magic of Multinational Management," *Harvard Business Review*, vol. 72 (November-December 1972), p. 89.

them. The ability to do these things will make the exchange with his host country colleagues a positive and fruitful experience. However, there are basic conflicts and outright contradictions in the values of different areas of the world which make integration and cooperation among businessmen quite difficult.

## The United States

For example, the United States international manager is conditioned by a socioculture that generally values objectivity, totally depersonalized decision-making, accuracy, directness and openness of communication and relationships, pragmatism, practicality, egalitarianism, problem-solving, competition and competitive self-advancement, individual responsibility, initiative, and so forth. And these values are reflected in the management systems of United States executives in that they delegate authority and expect their subordinates to assume responsibility and to make decisions; are expected to work in team or group relationships which are very open; are openly competitive within certain limits. Promotion is based on the demonstrated ability to assume responsibility and achieve a desired goal.

However, these values and the actions and behavior patterns they elicit can make it very difficult for a United States businessman to relate effectively to HCNs with contradictory sociocultural behavior patterns. This may be especially true in dealings with businessmen in the developing countries, who may place value on subjectivity, for example, or on abstract ideas rather than scientific formulas; or who cannot accept methodology and systematization and whose society may maintain personalized and hierarchical or vertical, family-oriented systems of human relationships.

## Latin America

For example, in Latin America, many of the above characteristics exist. Its socioculture is generally characterized as hierarchical, authoritarian, paternalistic, socially stratified, family-oriented, humanistic, intuitive, personalistic, and not achievement oriented. For example, where a United States businessman believes it is important to be very open in a relationship, a Latin American prefers to keep relationships at arm's length and believes that to be open is to abdicate one's manliness and to be weak; it means the loss of tactical advantage.

These values are reflected in management systems that are family oriented and conservative, that favor the maximization of immediate personal income and luxury consumption rather than longer-term expansion and profit maximization. The Latin American may expect and want the United States manager to be an authoritarian leader who demands obedience and respect and who gives orders rather than delegating responsibility or trying to be "chummy" with his subordinate. And yet, he is also expected to be interested in the personal affairs of his subordinate in a paternalistic manner. Since the United States businessman's values and culture are so different, it becomes very difficult for the United States and Latin businessmen to work together effectively unless each can understand the other and adapt his ways of doing business to achieve a cooperative compromise.

### The Asians

In Asia, the sociocultural values and structures are generally quite different from those in the United States, resembling somewhat those in Latin America and the developing world. Generally, the sociocultural environment in Asia is characterized by: the family as the central social unit with formalized and controlled interpersonal relationships and identity based on the family, rather than the individual—which provides the individual with a sense of security; paternalistic and rigid hierarchical or vertical relationships and societal organizations; reverence for the elderly and vestige of authority and decision-making in the hands of the elderly or head of the organization—and thus follows respect for formal authority as well as seniority, loyalty, and obedience to the system; reliance on formal rules and procedures; indirect and vague or circuitous verbal communication stated in generalities that are acceptable and inoffensive to all; subjectivity; intuition; humanism; ritualization of relationships; dislike for disagreement or differences of opinion or any type of confrontation, dislike for interpersonal competition and preference for group cooperation.

These values are reflected in the Asian business environment in that industrial enterprises are generally run by families and the system of control and management is generally vertical, with all power vested in the head. It is difficult for businessmen from these countries to comprehend the concept of delegating control to individuals. Also, less priority is placed on obtaining profits than on securing a share of a market or maintaining family integrity or company prestige.[11]

In Japan, these values are clearly demonstrated in the management system of Japanese companies, which guarantees concurrence and cooperation of all the middle managers involved in a decision and precludes individual responsibility. This decision-making process, known as "ringi seido," requires all managers to concur in a decision by signing a document known as the "ringisho" which is circulated horizontally and vertically throughout the firm. Although this system is slow and cumbersome, it allows the signers to participate in the decision and is an excellent tool for communication among the managers.

It is not surprising, then, that a Japanese manager often has great difficulty in fully understanding a United States boss who tries to implement United States concepts of management. Unless each understands the other's cultural heritage and concepts of management, great frustration and disharmony could occur between the two, and both might emerge from the experience more suspicious and wary of the other than when they first met.

Similarly baffling to businessmen from other cultures is the Japanese custom of remaining with the same firm for life and the system of basing promotion not on individual productivity or performance but on seniority. The insularity that results from this practice, combined with the homogeneity of the Japanese,

11. Todayashi Yamada, "Managerial Problems of Multinational Enterprises," *The New Role of Management: Innovation, Integration, and Internationalization: Proceedings of the 15th CIOS International Management Congress* (Tokyo: Kogakusha Company, Ltd., 1969).

the unique characteristics of their management system, and frequently the almost exclusive use of the Japanese language, is reflected in the manner in which the Japanese invest overseas or form joint ventures at home. Japanese firms do not permit non-Japanese personnel to participate in their decision-making processes, nor do they give non-Japanese employees significant management responsibility. Thus, joint venture attempts between Japanese and non-Japanese firms are often not very successful and have been fraught with problems of misunderstanding, frustration, and resentment. The exceptions to this have been those companies that have made painstaking efforts to establish effective communication and understanding.

It is interesting to note in passing, however, that at lower corporate levels—for instance, the labor force or lower level HCN managers—Japanese ICs are often able to establish good working relationships with their workers. This is because of the similarity between the Japanese socioculture and that of many parts of the world, particularly the developing countries. There are overlaps, for example, in the customs of paternalism and close company-worker relationships. Thus, in overseas operations, in the instances where language permits, the Japanese managers will usually make a point of personally getting to know each employee and of frequently working on the production lines with them to establish good working relationships and good worker morale.[12]

12. The sources for this section include: *The Role of Japan in Latin America* (New York: Council of the Americas, 1973); Todayashi Yamada, "Managerial Problems"; Ehud Harari, "Morale Problems in Non-American MNCs in the U.S.," *Management Interna-*

## The Western Europeans

Although it is more difficult to generalize about a Western European socioculture, some similarities can be identified, including the reflection of a combination of the traditional and the new. Thus, a continuation of the historical orientation toward family and social standing is reflected in somewhat hierarchical social structures, paternalism, elitism, individuality—all of which are partially tempered by the value placed on capability and performance. Enterprise, productivity, ambition, and competitive self-advancement are valued, but these are balanced by a greater orientation toward leisure, public service-oriented activities, and the family. Rationality, reason, humanism, and socialism are also valued, while less value is placed on the profit motive.

These characteristics are reflected in European management practices and business formation, in that European enterprises, especially the smaller ones, tend to be family, or at least, social-elite-biased, with greater weight in terms of hiring and promotion given to social status and family than to performance or capability. Organizational and management structures tend to be vertical, with most decision-making authority centralized in a few hands and with little delegation of authority. This system produces rather conservative management policies that aim to avoid risk that might jeopardize family wealth.

*tional Review*, vol. 6, no. 43–53 (1974); *The Role of American and Japanese International Corporations in a Changing World Economy: A Dialogue* (Boston: Edward R. Murrow Center of Public Diplomacy, 1974); S. Prakash Sethi, "Japanese Management Practices: Part I," *Columbia Journal of World Business*, winter 1974, pp. 94–104.

On the other hand, European paternalism, growing out of the feudalistic past, is reflected in a greater sense of social responsibility for labor, to the extent that, in some firms in some countries, management is more willing to give labor a voice in the management of the firm.

Many European firms tend to attach greater importance to full employment and preservation of family control than to growth and profits. And they place less emphasis on competitive self-advancement or promotion, as was illustrated by a European manager employed by a United States IC who, because of the firm's policies on promoting HCNs, had a chance to try for the position of vice-president at parent headquarters. When queried about that opportunity, he responded that "the European mentality is not the same. In the U.S., a promotion in a man's work is considered a single goal for life. For me, life is too pleasant for this. Once a person has achieved a certain economic situation, he should turn to the spiritual and cultural things."[13]

Thus, United States and European managers might find it difficult to compromise and adapt their different outlooks and concepts of management to achieve an effective working relationship. However, like the Japanese, European managers may find it easier to relate to employees in developing countries than do United States expatriate managers because certain sociocultural similarities exist. Also, the Europeans have had a longer history of overseas investment than most United States firms and were the first to recognize the value of hiring,

training, and promoting HCNs to key management positions. Also, many Europeans, according to Pieter Kuin, long ago recognized the importance and need for cross-cultural understanding and exchange and have attempted to train their managers in this area, while at the same time training HCNs to understand the parent firm's philosophy.[14]

## Need for cross-cultural training

Thus we see in these limited examples of sociocultural differences that real understanding and effective communication and cooperation among businessmen from one socioculture operating in another can be very elusive without adequate training. Unfortunately, however, such preparation of expatriates by ICs is inadequate in the United States and Europe, and almost nonexistent in Japan and other Asian countries. This is lamentable, since this kind of training can spell the difference between success or failure in the ability of an expatriate businessman to establish friendly and cooperative relationships with his overseas counterparts.

As important as training for the expatriates is training for the HCNs with whom they will be working. Such training should cover not only the business and management skills they will need, but should also include cross-cultural training for all of the reasons stated above. As many of the HCNs as possible should be sent to parent headquarters for on-the-job training (OJT) as well as cross-cultural exposure. In addition, experts

13. "How to Develop a Multinational Executive (Eaton)," *Business Week*, 12 June 1971, p. 88.

14. Pieter Kuin, "The Magic of Multinational Management"; Todayashi Yamada, "Managerial Problems"; Alison R. Lanier, *Your Manager Abroad: How Welcome? How Prepared?* (New York: American Management Association, 1975).

from the parent should be sent to the field to provide on-site training. The transfer of the HCNs and the dispatch of short-term training missions to the field increase and broaden the exposure of all of the businessmen to each other and help solidify a sense of cooperation and common goals among all of them.

## Corporate training programs

Existing corporate cross-cultural training programs leave something to be desired, although more and more ICs with extensive overseas operations are establishing their own special training programs for their international managers. Some managers in the United States and Europe do receive limited training or orientation courses that include the law, politics, business practices and conditions, language, and perhaps a little bit about local customs and manners. But few companies offer courses for either PCNs or HCNs that cover the cultural norms, values, beliefs, and customs of the countries involved.

A few examples of existing programs include the special training center established by Westinghouse in Pittsburgh to provide cross-cultural training for its United States international managers and their spouses. Pepsico and IBM also have set up special training institutes; IBM's provides training for not only PCNs but also for its HCNs. Shell and Unilever also emphasize the importance of providing cross-cultural training for their international managers. DuPont recognizes the importance of providing cross-cultural training for its PCNs and is planning to institute in 1976 an in-depth, 10-day training program for PCNs and their spouses who work in their Iranian subsidiary.

The three-part program will cover what an American is (what are his motivations); what an Iranian is; and how to operate in Iran.

However, a substantial number of other ICs still do not provide adequate training for their managers. Instead, many send their managers to outside training centers such as the Business Council for International Understanding or the Overseas Briefing Association.

In the case of Japanese businessmen, little training has been given them concerning foreign business or cultures, although, increasingly, such programs are being developed. The Japanese have generally preferred to introduce Japanese management techniques and philosophies into the host country, and some Japanese firms have provided training for HCNs at parent company headquarters in Japan. For example, in order to indoctrinate its United States employees with the Japanese parent company's corporate techniques and "spirit," the YKK Zipper Company in Macon, Georgia, sent several United States graduates from Georgia engineering and technical schools (without their spouses) to the parent headquarters for a three-month total immersion course. The program was designed to provide technical OJT and to inspire and instill cross-cultural understanding in the trainees of the Japanese devotion to the company "spirit" and to make them good "company men."[15]

## Integration into the host community

Cross-cultural training can also help PCNs to more easily integrate into the host country community where they are stationed. Corporate

15. Louis Kraar, "The Japanese Are Coming—With Their Own Style of Management," *Fortune*, March 1975, pp. 116 ff.

policies vary on the importance of this issue, but certainly the greater the degree of integration of the PCNs and their families into the local communities, the greater the opportunity to strengthen cross-cultural understanding and ties.

The degree of integration by PCNs varies by company and country of origin. Increasing numbers of United States and European firms encourage their international managers where possible to avoid living in foreign enclaves or "ghettos" and encourage them to take an active role in the host community. However, at the same time, many provide fringe benefits and cost of living adjustments which permit the international manager to live on a higher standard than his national counterparts, sometimes causing resentment on the part of the HCNs. More and more United States and European ICs are organizing special orientation programs for the spouses and families of international managers.

On the other hand, Japanese socioculture and employment practices, compounded by significant differences in language, have on the whole discouraged the Japanese from integrating into host communities. Japanese expatriates usually keep to themselves and live in Japanese enclaves. This practice is understandable, given the nature of the Japanese concept of the company as the only community he knows and his strong sense of loyalty to both company and country.

This insular behavior is encouraged by parent company managers, who consider close identity with and assimilation of foreign cultures by Japanese expatriates to make reassimilation after repatriations more difficult. However, some Japanese

top managers recognize the problem of isolation of the Japanese executives and are beginning to change their attitudes on this matter and to encourage the managers to integrate.

Given these obstacles, where Japanese PCNs have succeeded in integrating into the local host community, it is especially remarkable. One such example in the United States is Mitsubishi Aircraft in San Angelo, Texas, whose executives have joined the local country club and whose wives were assisted by United States wives to become active members of the community. Usually adjustment of Japanese wives to a foreign host community is one of the greatest problems for Japanese PCNs, since the wives normally are not provided with language training or orientation to the new environment. However, as one United States-based Japanese executive put it:

"Even if we try to live by ourselves, the Americans don't let us. The Americans are very friendly; they just come at you. Recently, I had to rescue my wife from a group of ladies at a cocktail party. They wouldn't let her go until she promised to join their Japanese flower arranging club."[16]

Thus we can see how integration into the community can lead to significantly increased understanding and friendship among the PCNs and HCNs in many countries of the world.

Integration of the Japanese children into foreign host country education systems has also presented some problems, according to Yataro Yoshido, an executive of Mitsui in Houston, Texas. He pointed out that because the Japanese children were

16. Ibid.; Philip Shabecoff, "Japanese Businessmen in the U.S. . . . ," *New York Times*, 12 November 1972.

not prepared for foreign schooling, particularly because of a lack of knowledge of the English language, some Japanese companies have had to provide special teachers to provide remedial assistance to those children to ease their assimilation into the United States school system.

### Access of HCNs to top management positions in ICs

Another area, mentioned earlier, which influences the extent to which exchanges of businessmen lead to greater cooperation and understanding, concerns the policies of ICs on permitting HCNs to assume meaningful, top management positions in the host country subsidiary and even the parent company. Failure by ICs to hire, train, promote, and compensate HCNs on an equivalent basis with PCNs leads to resentment by HCNs, who feel they are being treated as second-class citizens. More and more ICs, including some Japanese, are realizing that there are many benefits from staffing subsidiaries with HCNs, and many United States and European ICs already staff their overseas operations with more than the legal requirement of PCNs. According to the National Foreign Trade Council, in 1970, over 95 percent of the personnel employed by United States ICs were nationals of the country in which they worked.[17]

ICs are increasingly sending technical and management experts from the parent to the overseas subsidiary for limited periods to train HCNs to assume responsible management positions and then are bringing the PCNs home. And an ever increasing number of United States and Euro-

pean ICs are giving HCNs the right to be eligible for top management positions in the parent company, as demonstrated by Eaton Corporation, which in 1971 abolished the position of Vice-President International, pledging to operate as if there were no boundaries—which opened the path for promotion of HCNs to top positions at parent headquarters.[18] Other examples of United States ICs with Europeans now as the head or in key top-management positions include IBM, with Jacques Maisonrouge, a Frenchman, formerly as the president of IBM World Trade Corporation and IBM senior vice-president, and now as chairman of the board, IBM World Trade Europe/Middle East/Africa Corporation and IBM senior vice-president. At Schering-Plough, Willibald Conzen, a native of Germany, is now president. At AMAX a Frenchman, Pierre Gousseland, is executive vice-president and group executive.

On the other hand, as pointed out earlier, Japanese firms continue to fill top management and senior technical positions in their overseas subsidiaries primarily with Japanese nationals, as confirmed by Ishikawajima-Harima, Mitsubishi, Mitsui, and a number of others. This policy has reportedly led to greater resentment by HCNs toward Japanese PCNs and ICs than toward European or United States ICs overseas. However, the Japanese are beginning to recognize the need for change.[19]

### BENEFITS OF THE EXCHANGES

Having examined the potential problem areas, let us look at some of

17. *National Foreign Trade Council Inc. Bulletin*, no. 3399 (7 October 1970).

18. *Business Week*, 16 June 1971.
19. Shabecoff, "Japanese Businessmen"; Harari, "Morale Problems."

the potential benefits and positive contributions to improved understanding and development that can and have resulted from exchanges of persons among ICs and their affiliates throughout the world.

### Improved human capabilities through know-how transfers

The training that has been provided to HCN employees by the managers and technical experts sent to the subsidiaries, as well as to HCNs who have been brought to parent headquarters, has been very extensive and has substantially raised the levels of management and technical know-how of the HCN employees. Although it is difficult to measure the total amount of training provided to HCNs in this manner, extrapolation and generalization from a few case examples could give us some idea of the magnitudes of these transfers. According to some case studies that have recently been developed but have not yet been published by the Fund for Multinational Management Education, in order for a United States pharmaceutical firm, Pfizer, to provide ongoing support for one subsidiary in Brazil, in 1974, it provided training to Brazilian employees of management and technology know-how amounting to a total of 8,648 mandays of training, including formal training, OJT, ongoing training, and foreign trips or visits. During the same year, ITT provided know-how and technology training through its Mexican subsidiary amounting to 129,644 man-days.

The total number of man-days of training provided by ICs to their subsidiaries may vary according to the kind and size of company. However, even assuming a rather conservative total of man-days of training for each subsidiary, if we were to multiply that number by the estimated number of subsidiaries that exist throughout the world to which such know-how training is provided on an ongoing basis, we might begin to comprehend the magnitude of the transfers provided by the exchange of persons among ICs per year. The total would be staggering; and this does not include the know-how and technology training that is provided through manuals and designs, nor the training that is provided to HCNs who are brought to headquarters.

### Socioeconomic contributions

Many businessmen have learned that they can enhance their companies' economic position and reap other benefits by assuming a responsibility for helping the host country achieve its economic and development goals. This type of attitude is important in view of the rising nationalism and expectations of the communities where ICs are operating.

One of the most important contributions that IC managers can make to socioeconomic development is to help establish in a host country a business enterprise that is efficiently run in a manner that takes into account the host country development goals and that can effectively mobilize capital, people, technology, and know-how to achieve productivity. Such an enterprise becomes a contributing member of the society by providing jobs, training, know-how, and technology, and by helping to establish concepts of thought and behavior among the HCNs that can contribute to the welfare of the host country—such concepts as productivity, efficiency, responsibility, cost-effectiveness, and in some more backward societies the whole concept of a money economy. In addition, an efficiently run business enterprise often leads to the establishment by other HCNs of auxiliary services and suppliers which provide additional employment for HCNs not employed directly by the business enterprise. Many consider that the management and technology know-how brought to host countries by IC managers and embodied in effectively run business enterprises are more important inputs for development than capital, since the possession of capital alone will not provide a developing country with the means for production.

## Increased understanding and cooperation across borders

However, one of the most important benefits of the exchange of persons between ICs is increased understanding and cooperation among peoples of sometimes exceedingly diverse backgrounds, outlooks, values, and behaviors. As we have seen in this article, the role of an effective international manager is to forge links; to bridge barriers, be they geographic, cultural, linguistic, philosophical, or other; to minimize and accommodate tensions and potential conflicts; and to meld people with different outlooks into an effective cooperative working relationship to achieve a given set of goals. Thus, they are in a sense diplomats or peacemakers. Or as Dimitris Chorafas put it:

They must think and act like statesmen . . . men who have wide appreciation of business and of the cultural problems that exist around the world . . . men willing to engage in lifelong learning and who have empathy for different points of view, culture, and civilizations, and who are able to see and appreciate local resources.[20]

And indeed the IC, through its extensive overseas operations, has mobilized a growing cadre of such IC statesmen who serve the IC throughout the world and to whom citizenship in a particular nation state is perhaps less significant than citizenship in a world of international business—thus a global citizenship.

As Arnold Toynbee put it, "The businessman of the future, I believe, will be one of the key figures in a world civil service . . . whatever their official labels may be, most of them in the next generation will be employed in building up and maintaining the new world order that seems to be our only alternative to genocide."[21]

Eldridge Haynes, former president and now chairman of Business International, also believes that the IC can serve as a force for peace:

There are at least two practical reasons why international companies' growth and profits depend on peace. First, the international company must have open trade routes to get its raw materials. It must be able to move its components and finished goods from one subsidiary to another and from one market to another, for it has built an international network of interdependent units. It must be able to move people and money as well as goods—to move them at will and with speed. It must have constant and uninterrupted . . . communication.

20. Dimitris N. Chorafas, *Developing the International Executive* (New York: American Management Association, Research Study 83, 1967), p. 15.
21. Peter Parker, "Management and Its Internationalization," *Proceedings of 15th CIOS*.

Second, the international company needs customers—at home and at work —not in foxholes. It needs workers trained in producing and marketing.

To an international company, a frontier is worse than a nuisance. Differences in currency exchange rates are worse than a headache. And differences in national laws and regulations are sometimes impossible to observe. . . .

Utopia for international companies would be world government. A world without frontiers. Absolute freedom of movement of people, goods, ideas, services, and money to anywhere from anywhere.[22]

Courtney Brown, former head of Columbia University Graduate School of Business, also noted this potential of ICs and their managers to harmonize relations throughout the world when he referred to ICs as "a new world symphony . . . the hoped-for force that will eventually provide a means for unifying and reconciling the aspirations of mankind."[23]

Although the statements by these men may seem to be somewhat idealistic, the managers of ICs around the world do have the potential of helping to bridge and reconcile the differences among peoples. However, the extent to which these international corporate statesmen succeed in developing worldwide cooperative networks among people will depend to some degree on the levels and adequacy of cross-cultural training they receive and the degree to which they are able to be open and sensitive to the values and goals of their colleagues from other countries.

22. Eldridge Haynes, "The International Corporation and the Nation State," ibid.

23. Courtney C. Brown, ed., *World Business: Promises and Problems* (New York: MacMillan Co., 1970), p. 3.

ANNALS, AAPSS, 424, March 1976

# Study and Training Abroad in the United Nations System

By WILLIAM D. CARTER

ABSTRACT: The United Nations and its Specialized and Associated Agencies have, since their foundation, provided fellowships, study tours, training courses, and workshops to enable specialists from their member states to obtain further training and to exchange experience on problems of mutual interest. Such programs have played a major role in the work of the United Nations system in the developing countries. The present article describes the main features of these programs over the past three decades, some of the problems they have faced, and how they have developed in response to changing perspectives and needs of the member states of the organizations. Some notable developments in these programs during the past five years are discussed, for example, the increased contribution of international, regional, and national training institutes in the organization of training programs and their researches on program content and methodology; new departures in the field of evaluation; the co-ordination of international training programs situated in the developing countries and the potential role of technical co-operation among the developing countries.

---

*William D. Carter joined the UNESCO Secretariat in 1947; he organized and administered its research program and advisory services on Exchange of Persons and its fellowship programs until 1965. He originated UNESCO's publication:* Study Abroad, International Handbook of Fellowships, Scholarships and Educational Exchange. *Since 1965, he has been a consultant to the State University of New York, the United Nations Development Program, and UNESCO. In 1969, he completed a survey of the international programs of the State University of New York, the* International Dimension of the State University of New York. *In 1973, the International Institute for Educational Planning, Paris, published his monograph,* Study Abroad and Educational Development.

PROGRAMS of international fellowships, study tours, training courses, and workshops have long enabled specialists from the member states of the United Nations and its Specialized Agencies to obtain further training and to exchange experiences and ideas on problems of mutual interest. The place of such activities in the program of each agency varies according to their functions and objectives. For example, the training program of the World Meteorological Organization to build up weather services in its member states differs in scope from the wide-ranging training activities of the Food and Agriculture Organization aimed to improve world food production or those of the World Health Organization in the education of doctors, public health workers, and the development of medical schools and medical research.

To describe the whole range of international training activities of all the agencies is obviously beyond the scope of this article. This presentation will attempt to cover some of the broader characteristics of the international educational and training activities of the agencies over the past three decades, some of the problems which have been faced, and how such programs have responded to the changing perspectives and needs of their member states. Certain activities and programs are covered in some detail to illustrate interesting methods and techniques, many of which may be found in the programs of other agencies.[1]

1. The following agencies of the United Nations system are engaged in various types of international study and training activities: the United Nations Department of Economic and Social Affairs; the United Nations Industrial Development Organization; the United

## INTERNATIONAL DEVELOPMENT

The education and training activities of the whole United Nation's system assumed greater importance and impact in 1950 with the establishment of the United Nations Technical Assistance Program for Less Developed Countries. Supplementing programs already being undertaken by the specialized agencies, the United Nations initiative greatly augmented funds available for technical aid while coordinating the work of the agencies which provided their expertise in the planning and administration of projects through recruitment of experts and the development of training and fellowship programs.

In the mid-sixties, the United Nations Technical Assistance Program became the United Nations Development Program as increased financial resources enabled it to fund larger scale projects which, through such assistance, might become viable for longer-term investment. So that by 1974 the United Nations Development Pro-

Nations High Commissioner for Refugees; the United Nations Relief and Works Agency for Palestinian Refugees in the Near East; the International Labor Organization; the Food and Agriculture Organization; the United Nations Educational, Scientific and Cultural Organization; the World Health Organization; the International Civil Aviation Organization; the Universal Postal Union; the International Telecommunications Union; the World Meteorological Organization; the Inter-Governmental Maritime Consultative Organization; the International Atomic Energy Agency; the International Bank for Reconstruction and Development; the International Monetary Fund; the United Nations Institute for Training and Research; the United Nations Conference on Trade and Development; the United Nations Environment Program. Source: *Study Abroad*, vol. 20, and *Report of the Administrator of the United Nations Development Program, 1974* (DP/111).

gram and its network of agencies were administering funds contributed by 136 governments for work in 117 developing countries and territories. This expansion of resources was also accompanied in the mid-sixties by the increasing interest of the World Bank in the needs of the developing countries, not only in conventional investment fields, but also in such areas as education, agriculture, and population control, development of which could provide an essential foundation for larger investment activities. As these areas required considerable technical assistance, whether through expert services or training programs, the total "pre-investment" activity of the whole United Nations system was further expanded.[2]

2. Owing to the variety of programs, different reporting systems, and sources of finance, it is not possible to provide an accurate overall figure of the number of individuals benefiting in any one year from study grants provided by the various agencies. The following information is indicative of the numbers in certain programs. In 1974, funds provided by the United Nations Development Program financed the studies of 5,343 nationals from 143 countries in 120 countries. In 1974, the World Health Organization made 3,712 fellowship awards of which 2,795 were financed by its own budget, 495 from UNDP funds, and the remainder from other sources. In addition, 1,340 grants were made for attendance at courses and workshops.

The Food and Agriculture Organization (FAO) reports 773 individual awards in 1974, mostly financed from UNDP funds. In 1974, 1,601 individuals took part in 174 group courses, financed for the most part by contributions from 20 governments, outside of their contributions to the regular FAO budget in the Organization's Government Co-Operation Program. Present trends indicate expansion of group training programs and a lessening of individual fellowship awards (1972–73, 1,601).

The World Meteorological Organization reports that of 366 individual fellowship awards, 209 were covered by UNDP project funds, 125 by its Voluntary Assistance Program, and 32 by its regular budget. The 185

## THE MULTI-LATERAL FRAMEWORK

A feature of the international training activities of the United Nations system, which distinguishes them from the more numerous bilateral programs of governments and most national agencies, is the multinational framework in which they take place. In this, the secretariats of the agencies are the organizing and administrative focal points which bring together the intellectual and financial resources of their member states to provide programs for training for those who need them. This provides flexibility in meeting a great variety of training requirements whether for studies in the most technically advanced countries or in areas where conditions or projects are more comparable to the local situation of grantees and so lessening difficulties of language and cultural adjustment. While studies pursued in "high technology" areas have not decreased in many fields, as training facilities in the developing countries themselves have increased in numbers and sophistication, there has been a notable trend

awards made by the International Atomic Energy Agency (IAEA) in 1974 were financed by 29 of its member states. This does not include grants for attendance at the IAEA Trieste Institute.

With respect to the World Bank, it is not possible to estimate the number of individuals studying abroad, as distinguished from the total number receiving training under bank-financed projects. According to the bank's *Sector Working Paper on Education* (December 1974), in the period 1969–73, the bank made loans in the education sector amounting to $947,000,000; in 1974–78 it is expected that this figure will be increased by 14 percent. While a large portion of these funds covers the cost of experts and advisers, considerable funds are included for direct training of instructors, trainers, and administrators, many of whom undertake study and observation in countries other than their own.

in certain fields for studies to be undertaken closer to home.

For example, the World Health Organization reports that of 3,712 awards made in 1974, 2,269 grantees studied in countries located in the same region. The regional office of the World Health Organization in Africa reports that in 1972, 82 percent of its fellows were receiving basic medical training in institutions within the region as compared with 7.2 percent in 1962.[3]

## GROUP TRAINING

While the majority of grants for study abroad have been made by the agencies for individual programs, an increasing number of training activities have been organized for groups, either at international or regional institutes established by the agencies or through collaborative arrangements between the agencies and national training institutions.

## INTERNATIONAL INSTITUTES AND CENTERS

Through the years, certain fields have been identified as requiring special training facilities which are readily available in specific member states. This has resulted in the establishment of a number of international training institutes and centers. From its earliest days, United Nations Educational, Scientific and Cultural Organization (UNESCO) has operated such centers in Mexico and in the United Arab Republic in literacy and fundamental education. The World Bank

3. See Jean Jacques A. Guilbert, *Contribution of the World Health Organization to the Evolution of Medical Education in the African Region, 1962–72* (WHO Document HMD/STT/74.4).

has, for almost 20 years, provided training courses for senior officials in financial and economic planning and related fields in its Washington-based Economic Development Institute. The International Labor Organization's International Center for Advanced Technical and Professional Training in Turin, Italy, has provided a systematic program of courses and workshops in training methodology, management, and technology, adapted to the conditions of developing countries. The UNESCO-sponsored International Institute of Educational Planning has built up a continuing program to provide educational planners, administrators, and teachers with the necessary interdisciplinary knowledge required for educational planning.

The training provided by such centers, which are staffed by permanent groups of specialists from different countries and by visiting experts, has been supported by continuing programs of research, comparative field studies, and evaluation activities to devise suitable training materials and curricula. The institutes have acted as a base for a continuing dialogue among their faculties and trainees from many countries whose own professional experience and needs have played a crucial part in the research and training work of the centers.

As this dialogue has grown in depth and variety, many institutes have organized a growing number of courses, seminars, and workshops in the developing countries themselves in collaboration with regional or national training centers.

The president of the World Bank reports that, in 1975, the bank's Economic Development Institute conducted 17 courses for 452 participants in member countries of the bank, while 11 courses with 265 participants took place in Washington. "This preponderance of overseas courses" the report continues, "reflects the fact that the Institute cannot alone meet the constantly growing demand for the training it provides; it is therefore anxious to maximize its scarce resources by building up training capabilities in member countries themselves . . . to this end it has adopted the possibility of "training trainers"—i.e. including in its courses an increasing number of officials responsible for training in their own countries, who after participating in E.D.I. courses will themselves be able to organize training programs."

## Collaboration with National Institutions for Group Courses

It is impossible to detail the great variety of courses organized by the agencies in collaboration with national institutions which offer their facilities—intellectual, physical, and financial—under what has been termed "multi-bilateral" arrangements. Some examples of such courses are of interest.

In the industrial field, the United Nations Industrial Development Organization has developed its In-Plant Group Training Program in collaboration with corporations, financial institutions, and manufacturing enterprises. These short-term courses aim to provide a combination of theoretical discussion with concentrated periods of practical work. Since 1965, 108 such programs in 33 different fields have been arranged for over 2,000 participants.

During the last 10 years,

UNESCO has developed a program known as the UNESCO University Courses. These courses take place in institutions with recognized international scientific status and are open to participants from the host country, from the developing countries, and from the developed countries in the proportion of one-third from each group. In many cases, repetition of the same course over a period of years enables a number of individuals from the same research unit in their own country to attend, thus encouraging the creation of research groups with similar interests. Participants are required, during the courses, to work on research projects related to their home research. A feature of many of these courses is the "follow-up" assistance, which may include provision of a small piece of equipment for the returning participant, payment for travel for attendance at a scientific meeting, or subscriptions to scientific journals. In 1974, 13 courses took place in nine countries, attended by 450 students from 45 countries including 250 from 34 developing countries.

Another notable program in the scientific field has been established by the International Atomic Agency, which in 1964 set up the International Centre of Theoretical Physics at Trieste, Italy, for advanced research and training in that field. The Trieste Institute, staffed by an international faculty, has developed cooperative relations with some 20 research centers in all parts of the world, to encourage exchange between faculty and participants in the work of the centre. The centre also endeavors to break down the sense of isolation of a number of scientists on their return home, through a system of "associateships" whereby former participants are enabled to attend subsequent courses for a period of five years, to update their experience and to take part in further discussion and exchange with their fellow scientists.

## IMPROVING THE EFFECTIVENESS OF INTERNATIONAL TRAINING PROGRAMS

At the end of the sixties, the whole problem of technical and financial aid to developing countries was reviewed by the United Nations to assess the requirements of the Second Development Decade.[4] In urging an increasing flow of financial aid, these reviews also stressed the need for continuing assistance to developing countries to build up their technical infrastructure in trained manpower, research, and technical capabilities. The United Nations Development Program itself undertook an intensive review of its operations and its capacity to deliver a more extensive and effective program.[5] In this appraisal, the total training effort underwent searching criticism on the ground that its dispersion lessened its potential contribution to development objectives. This dispersion was explained in part by the fact that many countries, receiving outside assistance from many sources, had difficulties in coordinating these offers with their own development plans and training programs. This led, in some countries, to difficulties in recruiting qualified individuals for the opportunities which were being offered.

4. See *Partners in Development*, Report of the Commission on International Development ("The Pearson Report") (New York: Praeger Publishers, 1969).

5. See United Nations, *A Study of the Capacity of the United Nations Development System* (DP/5, 1969) ("The Jackson Report"), vol. 2, pp. 68–9.

In response, the United Nations Development Program organized a series of consultations with a number of United Nations agencies with long experience in international training, to discover ways whereby the training component of its program might increase in impact and effectiveness. From these consultations, a number of ideas emerged which were summarized in a paper presented by the United Nations Development Program (UNDP) to an International Committee of Experts on Training Abroad Policies at UNESCO in 1971, which was attended by a number of training officers of the agencies and UNDP. The committee's report confirmed the dispersion of much international training activity as well as the need for greater integration of such programs with national education programs. The UNDP paper defined a set of measures which might (as the paper put it) "form a program of action in improving the effectiveness of training for development."[6] These measures stressed the need: (1) to promote greater recognition of the centrality of training in development programs; (2) to improve knowledge of training activities and thereby assist in coordination and suggest new approaches in the field of training; (3) to improve awareness of ways whereby needs and priorities in training could be identified more effectively; (4) to improve planning of training programs in general and the training component of specific projects; (5) to improve the capacity of international experts and trainers of trainers to perform their roles as communicators of knowledge and skills; (6) to improve the training of national experts or "counterparts" on projects; (7) to improve the

6. UNESCO (ED71, Conf. 8/5, Annex 6).

quality of the administration of international training (fellowships, study grants, training courses) at the national, regional, and inter-regional levels.

As these measures represented a broad consensus of the experience of the agencies as to what needed to be done, they can provide a useful framework for discussing some of the trends in international training in the United Nations system since 1971.

## The centrality of training in development

The emphasis placed on the need to highlight the key role of training in development projects — even though training had always played an important part in the work of the agencies — stemmed from past experience in development programming which tended to make the provision of expert services the keystone of projects and operations. Not enough attention, as the Capacity Study pointed out, had been given to the equally essential requirement of planning and implementing the training component of projects.

Since the consultations took place, there is evidence that the centrality of training in development cooperation is now well recognized. As the concept of integration of international training with national educational programs has become more widely diffused, project-oriented training is more related to national training programs. Furthermore, the shift of initiative in project planning to the developing countries themselves has helped in relating internationally assisted projects more closely to national programs. The Food and Agriculture Organization, in a *Review of Field Programs*,

1974–75 presented to the 1975 World Food Conference, discussing the future orientation of international assistance, foresees a greater demand for training: for more advanced training on behalf of certain developing countries as well as the need for new approaches and techniques in training for the least affluent of the developing countries.

## Information and coordination

The studies and other research activities of the agencies related to education and training have supported this integration process. For many years, all agencies have conducted worldwide surveys of educational facilities in their particular fields. In administering many thousands of study abroad programs, great experience has been accumulated on the capacities of institutions to meet particular needs, both of individual grantees and of group courses. Efforts have been made by a number of agencies to systematize this information. The World Health Organization has, for many years, published surveys of the curricula of medical schools; the United Nations Office of Technical Co-Operation has published annual inquiries on special training facilities in public administration and social work; the United Nations Industrial Development Agency has circulated studies of training facilities in industrial fields of particular interest to developing countries. More recently, UNESCO has initiated a series of studies on training facilities and institutions in various regions in its field of competence, the first of which covers the African Region. To assist governments in the coordination of international training programs, UNESCO has for many years published its periodic survey

*Study Abroad* which provides information on many thousands of international fellowships and courses. The twentieth edition of this publication, covering the years 1975–78, recently appeared.[7]

Following the recommendation of its Committee of Experts, since 1970 UNESCO has offered fellowships and expert services on the administration of international training programs. It has held a series of regional workshops to review all aspects of study abroad programs. It has published a series of studies by a number of its member states to review their experience as senders and receivers of UNESCO and other fellowships. In these ways, many of the problems brought up in the consultations of the United Nations Development Program have been discussed in the light of the experience of the member states themselves.

A major contribution to this work of coordination has been the decision in 1974 of the Governing Council of the United Nations Development Program to promote greater technical cooperation among the developing countries.

Following studies by a Committee of Experts on the extent and methods of such cooperation—in which training needs and facilities played an

important role—a special unit has been established in UNDP to promote further technical cooperation among developing countries. This unit will provide an information system, so that developing countries can make known their needs and capacities as a basis for increased mutual cooperation; this will be supplemented by a series of regional workshops to define ways whereby developing countries may increase their cooperation among themselves. In this, training and exchange of skills will play a major role.

*Training needs and priorities*

Many agencies have, for many years, conducted inquiries on the specific needs for specialists in their particular areas of competence. Of special note has been the work of the World Health Organization in which its advisory services focused on the identification of needs in medical education. This has not only provided guidance on the organization of health services in the countries concerned, particularly with respect to training programs, but has also assisted 'the organization itself in defining the nature of particular assistance which it provides to its members.

On a broader basis, the World Employment Program of the International Labor Organization has stressed the role of manpower and employment planning as well as the identification of training needs. The economic surveys of individual countries conducted by the World Bank have had the assistance of experts from the Specialized Agencies in the educational and social sectors who have identified broad manpower and training needs.

Some results of these efforts are

7. From 1950, UNESCO has made surveys of numbers of students studying abroad in institutions of higher learning, which have been published in various editions of *Study Abroad*. In 1971, a separate study, covering the period 1962–68, was published by UNESCO entitled *The Statistics of Students Abroad, 1962–68*. The survey covers enrollments in 118 countries, fields of study of foreign enrollees, student movements between "developed and developing countries." Selected tables of the study are included in the appendices of a monograph by William D. Carter, *Study Abroad and Educational Development* (International Institute for Educational Planning, 1973).

reflected in a recent report by the British Council, which for many years has been responsible for the programming of fellows of the international agencies in the United Kingdom. Commenting on the experience of the past five years, the British Council report notes an

increasing use, both by donors and recipients, of the techniques of manpower planning which have led them to identify particular hiatuses to be filled by qualified personnel and to prescribe with increasing exactitude the training programs necessary to fill the gap.[8]

## The planning of training

The British Council's report further states:

there has been a marked growth in the demand for more sophisticated and specialized training. . . . Governments have become accustomed to express their requests for training in more detail than was formerly the case and have been encouraged to do so by the agencies offering awards.[9]

Some of the factors contributing to this trend have already been suggested. Certain further elements have also played a part. The increased number of training centers in the developing countries have helped in identifying individuals requiring further specialized training while the international institutes have been able to provide guidance on the training side. The United Nations Development Program has sponsored projects to enable representatives of national training institutions to meet on an intraregional basis to exchange experience on curricula problems, training methods, and innovations. In addition, large-

scale projects financed by the World Bank have, in a number of cases, been provided with training experts responsible for the overall training plan of the project as well as for its systematic implementation.

## The expert as trainer

The greater emphasis on the transfer of knowledge and know-how adapted to the conditions of the developing countries has in many cases changed perspectives on the role of expatriate experts. In the early years of assistance programs, many experts, in addition to their advisory duties, found themselves performing direct planning and administrative tasks on behalf of their host governments. This day is past. Experts who are not recruited for training assignments as such, are now required to provide more guidance on the ways whereby their technical knowledge can be adapted more directly to the conditions of their host countries. This is illustrated by the increasing number of experts who are recruited from the developing countries themselves, as well as a trend to the recruitment of shorter-term experts.

## Counterparts—a new role

The changed role of the experts has posed new challenges to their associates or "counterparts" on projects. In addition to being recipients of the know-how and knowledge provided by the experts, counterparts are called upon to provide guidance on the ways whereby the "imported" knowledge can be adapted more effectively to local needs. At the same time, the concept of the counterpart has been broadened, so that a greater number of individuals can be attached to projects, thus increasing the "multiplier

8. *The UNESCO Fellowship Programme in the United Kingdom* (British Council, 1974), pp. 3–5.

9. Ibid., p. 9.

effect" of the training aspect of projects.

## Administration

The increasing complexity and scale of training activities has inevitably resulted in reforms in the administrative machinery in program operations. In addition to streamlining of procedures, the greater emphasis on studies within regions themselves has been accompanied by locating more administrative procedures away from agency headquarters. The World Health Organization, with its formal regional structure, has pioneered this pattern of administration and is providing an example to other agencies.

Another factor is the increasing attention given to evaluation. Evaluation of training has, from the earliest days of these programs, generally been concerned with the satisfaction of individual grantees with their programs so as to assist agencies in assessing the adequacy of their own procedures. Efforts to ascertain the use of training following study abroad after the return of grantees have met with rather uneven success.

Recently, such evaluation exercises have grown in depth and intensiveness. The international and regional institutes have conducted "built-in" inquiries to judge not only the adequacy of the content of their courses, but also their subsequent impact.

The Food and Agriculture Organization has set up a continuing inquiry to monitor its extensive program of courses to provide a set of operating procedures to judge content, organization, and eventual use. The procedures of this inquiry are intended to provide course organizers with systematic tools to guide their own work as well as to provide headquarters and governments with something more substantive than the customary, and frequently partial, reports of course organizers and have drawn attention to new ideas and experiments, which, too frequently, have been lost in more general reports of courses.

In the past, there has been an inadequate distinction between what is termed evaluation and follow-up. The greater depth of evaluation activities has served to highlight the limitations of what has been learned about the results achieved. Increasing emphasis is now being laid on the studies of such results.

### SOME CONCLUSIONS

This review only provides a partial picture of the total international training effort of the United Nations system. The progress which has been described since the consultations of 1970 is based on study of documents together with informal consultations on the current state of affairs with many of those associated with the original consultations. Recognizing these limitations, some broad conclusions may be useful.

1. It would seem that some of the negative judgments made in 1970 have been met with positive responses.

2. There is evidence to show that international training is now more closely related to development objectives, while the greater variety in the content of programs reflects deeper understanding of project needs as well as the needs of individuals associated with them.

3. The development of training centers—whether at headquarters or in the developing regions and countries—has helped expand the

impact of training and improved, in many cases, the content of training programs.

4. There has been considerable progress in the role of evaluation, especially as a means to judge and improve the content of programs.

5. The increase of programs undertaken "within the region" has provided greater opportunities for exchange of common experiences among individuals from the developing countries themselves. The initiative of the United Nations-Development Program to promote greater cooperation among developing countries is a crucial factor here.

## FUTURE TASKS

These tentative conclusions represent areas of unfinished business. As the 1974 *Report of the Administrator of the United Nations Development Program* states, much of what has been reported throughout the years in the development area is a recital of "inputs" and the contribution of international agencies themselves to the vast problem of developing countries. Not enough is known of the results of this effort. While there is much evidence on the judgments and satisfactions of individuals concerning the benefits they have received, information on outcomes, both individual and institutional, is not well enough known. As the administrator further states: "now development is perceived in terms of the individual countries' requirements and the impact of technical co-operation is perceived more by internal results achieved than by external inputs supplied."[10] How this frame of judgment will be filled in and how it will broaden the impact of development cooperation is the main challenge now and in the future.

10. United Nations Development Program, *Report of the Administrator for 1974* (DP/111), p. 9, para. 21.

# International Exchange in the Arts

## By Joan H. Joshi

ABSTRACT: Artists through history have needed and benefitted from the stimulation of cultures new to them, and, indeed, their art has been influenced by the milieu in which it was created. The great centers in which artists of a similar persuasion have gathered have provided the special stimulus of competition as well as the opportunity to share technique. The creative and performing arts are presented as inherently international despite efforts of nationalists to promote the distinction of their own culture and even to bend it to particular political or religious beliefs. The choices facing would-be patrons of the arts and the type of programs abroad best suited to the artist are considered, followed by a review of the Institute of International Education's recent activities in the cultural area. Finally, a call is made to the international corporate community to shoulder its share of the funding burden.

*Joan Hatch Joshi is currently Vice President for Exchange Programs at the Institute of International Education where, among other responsibilities, she has administered the Institute's annual national competition for grants to American students for graduate study abroad under the Fulbright-Hays Program and programs sponsored by foreign governments, universities, corporations, and private donors. A graduate of Cornell, Mrs. Joshi attended the London School of Economics and lived and worked in Germany for a number of years.*

Quite early in his life, Pieter Paul Rubens decided he must go to Rome; his maitre had raved about the works of Raphael and Michelangelo. Rubens had seen one of the Florentine Madonnas Raphael had produced in quantity, to fill orders coming in from all over Europe; Rubens was not impressed with her. He had heard, too, how Raphael had pushed everyone out of his way to become the darling of the Vatican, and he was convinced that Raphael was more salesman than artist. Rubens entered the Stanza della Segnatura, the papal chamber of justice at the Vatican, and quickly changed his mind. There were the "Disputà" and the "School of Athens." Life and sublime truth seemed to emanate from the perfect geometry of space, and seemingly minor details in the pictures played significant roles in conveying intangible truth—the bit of bread in the Eucharist, because of its location in Raphael's "Disputà," for example, did seem to become divine. Rubens was convinced that it was not the competent craftsman in Raphael alone that had produced these great paintings; such miraculous iconographs could only have been inspired in the spiritual and intellectual matrix of Vatican Hill.

Not long ago, the Institute of International Education (IIE) received a regular report from one of its grantees who had gone to Spain to study painting. Among other things, the young man wrote that he had been indoctrinated to represent only that which could be seen in nature. He had been upset, therefore, by the extreme scale changes or distortions of space that occur in El Greco's work, until he saw nature in Spain. There he "learnt to expect the most surprising phenomena from the inter-action of the sky and the earth . . . [and] to accept as natural, for example, the liberties taken by certain clouds as they rest far below the tip of a mountain one moment, and then serve as visual extensions of the mountain's peak the next," creating a fantasy landscape. Could these fantasies of nature explain the mystery of the distortion of space in El Greco, whose images are "often most powerful, precisely because of these plastically strange juxtapositions or even contrived situations which become believable through the artist's presentations"?

### New Stimuli

Thus, for both Rubens and his twentieth-century counterpart, locale became a vital component of the training process. All of us need a change in scenery from time to time. An artist's needs in this respect are even greater, not only that he may appreciate in full the works of other artists, learn new techniques, but also for the provocation such sojourns offer to an artist's psyche. Artists are sensitive folk who need the continuous stimulus of exposure to variegated sights and sounds and smells. And what is true of painters in the above cases is also true of others in the creative and performing arts.

Friedrich Nietzsche once wrote that, as an artist, a man has no home in Europe save Paris. One could say that La Scala is home for an operatic singer; or Vienna for a composer of classical music. Albeit such centers shift periodically for political and economic reasons, they serve as secure enclaves in their season for the artists consonant in their enterprise. With the Counter Reformation, Rome was lost to artists; so was Paris later with the advent of Hitler.

But if Rome had not been there, Rubens would not have been able to elicit inspiration from Raphael, Michelangelo, and Titian. Nor would Van Dyke have been able to carry away the Titian technique of Rubens to London from Antwerp; nor would Watteau have turned the technique into the Rococo.

These centers were useful to the artists not only to study technique, but also to compare, to criticize, to envy the works of their contemporaries. Yes, to envy. The jealousy between Raphael and Michelangelo is a legend; Shubert was not much pleased, either, to have Beethoven around in Vienna. Nonetheless, it was Shubert's determined effort to free himself from the overwhelming shadow of Beethoven that gave us the former's romantic songs. Even Beethoven had to admit, "Truly he has the divine spark." Envy and jealousy—those, too, are stimuli for an artist to work even harder, with art the gainer. These centers have some mundane utility as well; as a group of artists of similar persuasion congregate, the purveyors of services and supplies particular to their trade also follow.

Nonetheless, while it is inspiring and educational for an artist to spend some time in such centers, there is danger of his being too removed from the rest of society for too long. Lest his art become stagnant, he must eventually leave the comfort of the company of his fellow artists and strike out along his own trail, both geographically and artistically. Picasso did it more than once; he was not a Cezanne impressionist all his life, neither did he live in Paris all his life.

## ART AS A UNIVERSAL

A nation's artistic achievements are not mere national possessions; they are international wealth for the joy and employ of the whole world. The nations hold them in trust for humanity. To defend their cause, champions of nationalism hold that art will always be national. True. The difference lies in the intention. It is not nationalistic to include a phrase of a "Ländler" in a composition as Beethoven did, nor a gypsy tune as Bartôk did, nor an American Indian melody as Copland did. No one can help inheriting certain national feelings; it is when an artist loses a sense of proportion and propriety, it is when he tries to impose a national idiom on a basically international concept, that his art becomes nationalistic. Worse yet is when the idiom happens to be the official policy of the regime or the religion that governs the artist.

There was an "International Style" in fifteenth-century art, for example, a grassroots movement of sorts. It amounted to artists turning away from Gothic monstrosities to smaller works of a softer cadence. But the Pope and the Holy Roman Emperor were the masters of Europe; and the feudal lords, the patrons of the arts, favored Madonnas and her Child. Indeed, that was the better part of wisdom on their part, if they meant to keep their castles. The artists? They only wanted to survive, and the international movement lost out to the strong spirit of Gothic Mannerism.

There was a sort of universalization of music during the period usually called ars nova, a century earlier. A different kind of politics was involved in the failure of its international spirit. The folk of Europe enjoyed the minstrels who journeyed from country to country, singing the news and mocking those in authority. Government after government passed ordinances prohibiting these itinerant musicians from encouraging social and political revolt; they were too close to the mark for their lordships' comfort.

Sadly, even today states and churches goad artists into toeing the official line, threatening them with excommunication or exile.

Fortunately, such efforts to make art subservient to national interests, however frequent in history, have succeeded neither well nor long; for art is inherently international and universal. Take painting, for example: it is a fact that all children of the world have a common language—painting—a language that is taught to them by no one. It is well known now that a child reared in complete solitude makes use of the same drawing vocabulary as does his more urbane contemporary, a language of rudimentary scribbled signs. The beauty of it all is that this language has not only existed unchanged and untouched since the beginning of mankind, but continues to be understood by children all over the world. That a child loses the ability to use and understand this language of signs at a certain age is a baffling and unhappy dilemma.

Although not in the same strong vein, there is a vocal language the children of the world intone. The nursery rhyme "Hickory Dickory Dock," for example, is an adaptation of an ancient gypsy jingle "Ek kury do kury dok," designed to teach children the multiplication tables (incidentally, the gypsy jingle means one times two is two). One can hear the rhyme from India to Iceland, from Africa to Siberia. The words change, the rhythm lingers on. What is more, even the most isolated children continue to hum it, even when their vocabulary is limited to sounds rather than words. It has often been suggested that

children need international travel the least of all; conversely, therefore, perhaps the older one grows, the more one needs an infusion to remind him that he is but one among billions of human beings on this planet.

## CHOICES

Who should travel abroad in the arts is one of the questions we would rather not face at IIE, though face it we do year in and year out. The professionals who help us screen the candidates are as divided on this point as we are. Should we send the undeveloped, untrained student? Should we send the underprivileged, unendowed hopeful from our minorities? Should we send a professional to absorb new techniques and new insights? Should we send a master to display our achievements or a group of performing artists to introduce our culture to the folk overseas?

By the same token, who ought to come to our shores and for what purpose? Of course, it would be gratifying to be able to help all of them. But even the richest nation in the world has its economic limits, as we are soberly reminded so often these days. Each class of candidates has its merits and its justification for travel abroad. What the institute can do and what it does do is play a balancing act, assisting as broad a range in as large numbers as stretched funds will permit.

Another set of questions the institute must wrestle with time and again has to do with what kind of program to tool out for an artist. Should the program be a formal one, involving attendance at a foreign institution with a fixed curriculum? Should it be a grand tour as was once the fashion? Should an artist be given a free reign to formulate his own program?

Answers to all of these questions hang on basic differences between the educational needs of an artist and those in other fields of endeavor, such as engineering and medicine. At any stage, even at a student level, the artist needs more freedom to arrange his activities. Academic affiliation with an institution abroad is often not necessary, perhaps not even desirable for the fulfillment of an art student's objective, and sometimes very difficult to arrange. Then, the financial needs of these students vary more widely than those of academic candidates; their equipment, their trips to important sites, their private tutors all cost money.

Perhaps more crucial is the time an artist needs to assimilate what he has observed from his master. Wrote one music grantee,

I have never before had time to explore scores to my satisfaction in this way as there has always been the reality of performance, and the external pressures of schoolwork and teaching have left only enough time to concentrate on the very practical aspects of preparation. Although it may seem paradoxical, the condition of having more time and fewer external pressures has enabled me to increase my efficiency in learning what music is both doing and saying, in that I am sufficiently immersed in it to be able to relate, more productively, insights derived from the study of one score to others, resulting in a greater solidification of ideas.

Counterpoint to that is the fear of those who make grants available. How can one justify letting artists just "bum around"? How can one be sure they are learning their craft, if there isn't an institution or authority to countersign their progress? It is, indeed, difficult, and especially difficult to convince those whose grants

we administer. Nonetheless, our experience has been encouraging with artists subjected to a rigorous selection process designed to measure achievement and motivation.

The institute's activities on behalf of the arts date back to 1930, when IIE, then a little more than a decade old, sent 20 students to study art in Paris under a grant from the Carnegie Endowment. These were followed by young American musicians heading for study at the great German music academies and by German musicians coming here to attend Juilliard. As IIE grew and its role in international education exchange expanded and diversified following World War II, so, too, did its cultural programs. In recent years, these have fallen into four principal categories: fellowships to individuals, representation at music competitions abroad, conferences, and general patronage of the arts.

The institute has recruited and screened thousands of United States artists and sent hundreds for short- and long-term study abroad under a variety of programs. These have included the prestigious Kress Fellowships in Art History; the CINTAS Fellowships for artists of Cuban citizenship or descent; awards offered by the German, French, and other European governments; and, especially, the binationally-sponsored Fulbright-Hays Program, which has enabled students of all the creative and performing arts to spend a year in pursuit of their individual goals. With private funds, IIE has also been able to aid in these years young Americans who wished to audition or fulfill engagements in Europe, participate in art exhibits abroad, take summer master classes, or attend conferences.

IIE has served foreign artists by

arranging admission to United States art institutes and conservatories and by organizing individual travel and study programs which enabled them to visit schools and art institutions across the country, to meet their colleagues and exchange ideas, under the sponsorship of the Ford Foundation, the Fulbright-Hays Program, United Nations Educational, Scientific and Cultural Organization (UNESCO), the JDR 3rd Fund and other smaller programs.

The participation of between 15 and 30 young American musicians each year in international music competitions abroad has been made possible by IIE with funds from the Department of State. The program aims to insure that American musicianship is fairly represented in these contests, and indeed IIE-supported contestants have carried off 150 prizes. The 22 first-place winners among them have included Van Cliburn and Jane Marsh.

The institute held its first conference specifically devoted to the arts in 1956, and sponsored another in 1970, featuring the participation of numerous alumni of IIE-administered grants. In addition, IIE has organized seminars and meetings at the request of other sponsors. For example, in 1966 IIE administered an International Congress for PEN, the worldwide organization of writers, which attracted 500 delegates from 40 countries to New York. With IIE support, a like number of delegates attended the International Music Congress in New York and Washington in 1968, and the following year a group of 200 from 23 countries visited New York, Boston, and Washington in connection with the Congress of the International Federation of Theatre Research.

In further patronage of the arts,

IIE administered the Kaufman International Design Awards for consistent records of achievement in creative design, sponsored recordings of contemporary music by foreign and United States composers, and, in honor of its own fiftieth anniversary, both commissioned a cantata by the noted Argentinian composer Alberto Ginastera and organized an exhibit in New York (it later toured the United States for two years) of 44 paintings and sculptures by IIE-related artists. Another exhibit of Fulbright alumni opened at the Union Carbide Building in New York in 1975 under institute auspices, while IIE's own headquarters building on United Nations Plaza features numerous works of art by its successful alumni painters and sculptors.

## FUNDING PROBLEMS

The needs are great, the opportunities waiting, the students, eager to taste a new culture and, indeed, ready to imbibe it for the artistic gain of our own culture, are many. Yet, finally, there is always the problem of funding. There is never enough. As has been pointed out, no nation, however great, can afford—financially, politically, or otherwise—unlimited funds to export its culture abroad or import that of others. As in all things, the private sector must carry a part of the burden. The private foundations are doing their share. But big business?

To be sure, for years well-known United States corporations have given generous support to the arts and artists in the communities in which their plants are located; some have supported even national institutions and right now are buttressing some that are fast becoming national treasures. Philanthropy, social responsibility, the prospect of a tax rebate might be some of the reasons for these donations by industry.

Perhaps a more significant reason might be their own enlightened commercial interest—promotion of their products or their services, not to discount the corporate image-building potential of every dollar invested in supporting artists, for their work is more apparent, more visible. There is nothing wrong in that. However, it would seem whatever moved them out of the local scene onto the national one ought to propel them still further onto the international landscape. There is hardly a major corporation listed on the Big Board today that is not multinational in character. And it behooves business, therefore, to go international in its support of the arts. Some firms have already begun.

The International Telephone & Telegraph Corporation (ITT), for example, has sponsored a substantial fellowship program for the last three years. The program has included a modest number of grants for artists and has supported the two students quoted earlier.

Hopefully, others will follow. If it were not for the art of putting one word after the other to write a memorable message, if it were not for the art of putting one note after the other to create an unforgettable jingle, if it were not for the art of drawing lines that leave an indelible image on one's mind, there could not have been the internationalization of Coca-Cola or Colgate, of Singer or Nestle. For the arts are not *only* for the joy of the aesthetics in life, they are for the employ of the commerce of living as well.

# The Military Assistance Training Program

By ERNEST W. LEFEVER

ABSTRACT: The Military Assistance Training Program has been and is a low-cost, low-risk foreign policy instrument that has served the United States interest in interstate stability and has provided a valuable channel of communication and influence with a significant elite, especially in the Third World. In the past 25 years, the program has reached over 450,000 officers and men from 70 allied and friendly countries. Most of them have been trained in the United States, in more than 2,000 different skills from auto mechanics and bookkeeping to computer sciences and advanced management. The program has advanced the efficiency, professional performance, and readiness of the recipient military services. Perhaps more significant, it has established a continuing link between United States and host-state military leaders, many of the latter being in positions of political responsibility.

---

*Dr. Ernest W. Lefever, a Senior Fellow in Foreign Policy Studies at the Brookings Institution, has traveled widely in Asia, Africa, and Latin America. He is currently studying U.S. policy toward nuclear arms in the Third World. His books include* Arms and Arms Control *(1966) and* Spear and Scepter: Army, Police, and Politics in Tropical Africa *(1970).*

Dr. Lefever's article is based upon a study he has made at the Brookings Institution, but here he speaks only for himself.

ONE OF the least well known and least expensive per capita leadership training programs conducted by the United States government is also one of the largest and most consequential. I refer to the Military Assistant Training Program (MAP), which over the past 25 years has provided United States training for more than 450,000 men and officers from 70 different friendly and allied countries around the world. Never before in history have so many governments entrusted so many men in such sensitive positions to the training of another government. (The number of MAP trainees from 1950 to 1973 by participating country is given in table 1.)

This far-flung program which has averaged more than 17,800 trainees a year has become increasingly controversial, but not as controversial as the overall United States program of providing military equipment and arms by grant or sale. In all transfers of military hardware, the United States or the manufacturer provides specialized training for its use. MAP training may or may not be directly related to the skills needed for a particular weapon or aircraft. The program has made available to foreign military personnel more than 2,000 courses, ranging from jeep maintenance and jet flying to computer technology and general staff training.

The program is consequential because almost half the men it has reached in Asia, Africa, and Latin America are officers and, as is well known, military officers play a significant political role in these regions. MAP may be seen and judged as one form of security assistance, but with equal justification it may be seen and evaluated as one of the larger United States leadership training efforts.

As the United States continues to reduce the size and visibility of its military presence on foreign soil in the immediate future and concurrently encourages allied and friendly states to accept a greater responsibility for their own security, what should be the role of MAP training? In the effort to foster self-sufficiency in national security among friendly and allied states, should Washington increase or decrease MAP training? Given the trend from grant aid to sales in military hardware, should the character or administration of the training program be altered?

To answer these questions, I have sought first to understand the nature of the program and then acquainted myself with the varieties of training offered before I attempted to assess its effects in the participating countries. I have visited more than 20 United States military training facilities, including the Army, Navy, and Air Force Command Schools in the United States; the Army and Air Force schools in the Panama Canal Zone for Latin Americans; and the Army Pacific Intelligence School in Okinawa (now defunct). I visited Panama, El Salvador, Guatemala, Liberia, Morocco, Iran, Thailand, Indonesia, the Republic of China, and Japan to interview members of our military training and advisory missions, United States Embassy officials, and military officers of the host country, including men who have had command-level training in the United States. (As of mid-1970, some 3,264 officers had received United States command

## TABLE 1

### SUMMARY OF STUDENTS TRAINED UNDER MAP—FY 1950–1973

| COUNTRY | UNITED STATES | OVERSEAS | TOTAL | COUNTRY | UNITED STATES | OVERSEAS | TOTAL |
|---|---|---|---|---|---|---|---|
| Afghanistan | 332 | — | 332 | Libya | 429 | 41 | 470 |
| Argentina | 2,654 | 865 | 3,519 | Luxembourg | 63 | 113 | 176 |
| Austria | 405 | 11 | 416 | Malaysia | 341 | 27 | 368 |
| Belgium | 3,768 | 1,430 | 5,198 | Mali | 69 | 5 | 74 |
| Bolivia | 441 | 3,029 | 3,470 | Mexico | 432 | 232 | 664 |
| Brazil | 7,001 | 882 | 7,883 | Morocco | 918 | 1,104 | 2,022 |
| Burma | 775 | 19 | 794 | Nepal | 34 | — | 34 |
| Chile | 2,678 | 2,622 | 5,3000 | Netherlands | 4,744 | 1,553 | 6,297 |
| China (Taiwan) | 20,086 | 4,221 | 24,307 | Nicaragua | 718 | 3,771 | 4,489 |
| Colombia | 2,402 | 3,109 | 5,511 | Nigeria | 462 | — | 462 |
| Costa Rica | 33 | 496 | 529 | Norway | 4,042 | 1,386 | 5,428 |
| Cuba | 307 | 214 | 521 | Pakistan | 3,830 | 530 | 4,360 |
| Denmark | 3,836 | 811 | 4,647 | Panama | 53 | 3,531 | 3,584 |
| Dominican Republic | 699 | 2,572 | 3,271 | Paraguay | 349 | 921 | 1,270 |
| Ecuador | 1,561 | 2,839 | 4,400 | Peru | 3,133 | 2,978 | 6,111 |
| El Salvador | 212 | 1,173 | 1,385 | Philippines | 9,200 | 5,545 | 14,745 |
| Ethiopia | 3,143 | 130 | 3,273 | Portugal | 2,208 | 673 | 2,881 |
| France | 12,600 | 1,742 | 14,342 | Saudi Arabia | 1,122 | 204 | 1,326 |
| Germany | 1,190 | 434 | 1,624 | Senegal | 18 | — | 18 |
| Ghana | 152 | — | 152 | Spain | 7,899 | 1,290 | 9,189 |
| Greece | 11,980 | 2,164 | 14,144 | Sri Lanka | 39 | — | 39 |
| Guatemala | 676 | 2,048 | 2,724 | Sudan | 119 | 8 | 127 |
| Guinea | 4 | — | 4 | Syria | 23 | — | 23 |
| Haiti | 444 | 60 | 504 | Thailand | 9,538 | 4,011 | 13,549 |
| Honduras | 270 | 1,922 | 2,192 | Tunisia | 346 | 169 | 515 |
| India | 504 | 33 | 537 | Turkey | 15,932 | 2,575 | 18,507 |
| Indochina | 408 | 26 | 434 | United Kingdom | 3,719 | 148 | 3,867 |
| Indonesia | 3,648 | 583 | 4,231 | Upper Volta | 26 | — | 26 |
| Iran | 9,018 | 1,789 | 10,807 | Uruguay | 1,075 | 1,172 | 2,247 |
| Iraq | 372 | 32 | 404 | Venezuela | 1,552 | 3,354 | 4,906 |
| Italy | 8,144 | 1,219 | 9,363 | Vietnam | 23,675 | 9,879 | 33,554 |
| Japan | 9,642 | 5,637 | 15,279 | Yemen | 5 | — | 5 |
| Jordan | 791 | 34 | 825 | Yugoslavia | 625 | 219 | 844 |
| Khmer Republic | 435 | 62,959 | 63,394 | Zaire | 310 | 266 | 576 |
| Korea | 22,144 | 9,386 | 31,530 | International Agencies | 465 | — | 465 |
| Laos | 1,830 | 34,176 | 36,006 | General & Regional | 31 | — | 31 |
| Lebanon | 268 | 1,188 | 1,456 | | | | |
| Liberia | 517 | 2 | 519 | | | | |
| | | | | Worldwide total | 232,914 | 195,562 | 428,476 |

SOURCE: *Foreign Military Sales and Military Assistance Facts* (Washington: Office of the Assistant Secretary of Defense, 1974), p. 11.

training. See table 2.) My comments are directed more to a description of what is than a prescription of what ought to be, though my analysis is not without implicit advice.

## MAP TRAINING HAS TWO MAJOR OBJECTIVES

Since its inception shortly after World War II, MAP training has

TABLE 2

FOREIGN ALUMNI OF U.S. COMMAND AND GENERAL STAFF COURSES: 1946–1970

| REGION | ARMY | AIR FORCE | NAVY | MARINES | TOTAL |
| --- | --- | --- | --- | --- | --- |
| Europe (and Canada) | 492 | 235 | 123 | 64 | 914 |
| Latin America | 386 | 241 | 107 | 31 | 765 |
| Asia | 765 | 480 | 122 | 62 | 1,429 |
| Africa | 70 | 41 | 3 | 0 | 114 |
| Australia and New Zealand | 27 | 2 | 7 | 6 | 42 |
| Total | 1,740 | 999 | 362 | 163 | 3,264 |

NOTE: The above information was compiled by Ernest W. Lefever for a study on MAP training at the Brookings Institution.

The United States Army, Air Force, Navy, and Marines each provide command and staff training for officers of allied and friendly states as follows:

1. U.S. Army Command and General Staff College, Fort Leavenworth, Kansas
2. Air University, Maxwell Air Force Base, Alabama
3. U.S. Naval War College, Newport, Rhode Island
4. Marine Corps Command and Staff College, Quantico, Virginia.

The Air Force Command and Staff Course started in 1946 and the Naval Command Course began in 1957.

been designed to support two major United States foreign policy objectives: first, our security interest, by promoting stability within and among participating states and by enhancing their capacity to defend themselves; second, our larger political interest, by strengthening the bonds of mutual understanding through a person-to-person program that has introduced thousands of actual or potential foreign leaders to American life and institutions. People differ as to whether the more limited security objective or the broader political objective should be the primary rationale for the program. In my view, both objectives have validity, because all United States training has inescapable security and political implications. The utility of a particular program for any country must be determined by its results in view of the weight attached to these two basic objectives and the significance of that country to larger United States interests.

WIDE VARIETY OF TRAINING EXPERIENCES

Approximately 11,800 men and officers a year have been trained in the States in more than 175 different military facilities. English is the usual language of instruction. These foreign trainees study side by side with United States students. More than 5,000 have been trained overseas, most of them in the U.S. Army and Air Force schools in the Canal Zone, in Spanish. Thousands of additional men have received short-term instruction in their own country from United States Mobile Training Teams.

All types of training involve a great deal of person-to-person communication between foreign and American military men, but the trainees in the United States naturally have a deeper and more sustained contact with American culture. The significance of this contact depends upon the length of their stay and the extent of their opportunity to see the country. My study of the various training experiences suggests several observations:

1. Generally, the students have been well selected and highly motivated. Consequently, they have generally performed well during the training period.

2. MAP training has been characterized by a high professional quality on the part of both the instructors and the trainees.

3. The content of the technical or doctrinal instruction for foreign and U.S. trainees is the same. Stateside MAP students use the same manuals and training facilities as United States trainees. In the higher professional courses where there are occasional classified lectures, foreign students are excluded. In the Canal Zone where the instruction is not in English, regular United States manuals and materials are used in translation.

4. Most stateside facilities serving MAP students have an information program designed to acquaint them with American life and institutions. While varying widely in comprehensiveness because of the length of the training period, the number of trainees, and the location, the program has generally been well received by the students. Not a single charge that this program has presented a distorted picture of the United States, either overly favorable or overly critical, has come to my attention. Arrangements are made for most trainees to visit military and civilian homes, churches, museums, farms, factories, sports events, places of entertainment, government offices, and other sites. Students who have had several training tours in the United States gain considerable first-hand knowledge of America.

5. English-language facility for stateside training, although not always achieved, opens the door to a wider world of information and communication far beyond the trainee's immediate military needs.

## EFFECTS ON MILITARY PROFICIENCY

MAP training is designed to improve the professional quality and performance of the trainee and thus upgrade his branch of the military service. The extent to which this is achieved depends upon the initial quality of his service, the number of men trained, the level and character of training, the impact of domestic political forces upon the armed services, and other factors. Granting this, several observations may be made:

1. The newly acquired or improved skills of the returning trainee are generally well utilized, especially during the first two years. United States training is generally a positive factor in his military career.

2. Generally, United States training helps the assisted military service to become more self-sufficient in training. Though there is some resistance to the requirement that returnees, when feasible, become instructors for about two years, a great many of them do so, even at some risk to their chances for promotion. MAP training, therefore, has a multiplier effect. Trainees with encouragement from the United States military mission have established many indigenous training schools and facilities from the command and general staff level on down.

3. If the pace toward self-sufficiency in feasible types of training

has been too slow in some countries, this can be attributed not to deficiencies in MAP training, but rather to internal military, political, or economic factors.

4. The armed services in countries with major United States training programs have significantly improved in proficiency and readiness.

5. For training to be effective, it must be supported by appropriate military hardware (arms and equipment). Generally, the hardware-training balance in MAP assistance has been satisfactory, whether the equipment is acquired by grant or sales.

### EFFECTS ON SECURITY AND STABILITY

A major MAP objective is internal and regional stability. In general, this goal has been well served by training, though many political, economic, and other factors bear upon internal security and interstate peace.

1. The increased proficiency of the military establishment resulting from training enhances its capacity to deter or counter internal or external threats.

2. There is no evidence that United States training, or associated military advice, ever induced a participating government to undertake a military adventure against a neighbor. On the other hand, United States training and advice cannot prevent a government from going to war. This is dramatically illustrated by the clashes between India and Pakistan and the short war between El Salvador and Honduras in 1969 which were caused by local grievances, not by the fact that both sides had received MAP hardware and training. Had these four governments heeded United States advice, there would have been no war.

3. Available evidence suggests that MAP training has not stimulated arms races. On the contrary, the net impact of MAP aid, including hardware, has generally had a moderating effect upon the acquisition of arms by the participating countries, thus contributing to stability and arms control in the region. While some types of training may stimulate an appetite for new and unnecessary arms, this factor is usually offset by United States military advice against so doing. If the United States military aid stops, it loses one important channel for exercising a restraining influence.

### EFFECTS ON INTERNAL POLITICAL DEVELOPMENTS

Assuming that in all states internal political developments are largely determined by internal forces, available evidence suggests several observations about the political effects of MAP training:

1. United States training has little effect one way or the other on the political role of the armed forces, a role deeply rooted in the history and culture of a country. To the extent that training may have an impact, it is usually in the direction of a more professional and less political military establishment, because the training itself is essentially professional and nonpolitical, reflecting the United States tradition of civilian supremacy and the instrumental rather than the policy role of the military.

2. Under "normal" circumstances, United States security aid, including training, tends to reinforce the government in power. This is also true of diplomatic recognition and economic aid.

3. MAP training has had no significant effect on the character or frequency of military intervention,

though quiet United States military advice associated with training may have had a slight net effect in deterring or preventing some coups. These extraordinary events are determined almost wholly by internal forces. There is no evidence to support the assertion that MAP trains military officers to overthrow constituted civilian authority.

4. The essential political neutrality of MAP training within a state is demonstrated by the continuity of such aid during periods of internal disruption and over several successive regimes. United States training of Brazilian officers, for example, has continued practically without interruption, despite a series of regimes of various political complexions. There is no evidence to support the assertion that MAP training favors "dictatorial" over "democratic" regimes. MAP has provided training to a great variety of friendly governments, allied and nonaligned, from Austria to Upper Volta, from Afghanistan to Yugoslavia, with the assumption that a more professional army would be more likely to perform a responsible security role than a less professional army.

5. MAP training makes no attempt to mold the political philosophy of the student, much less tamper with his political loyalty. The program does not attempt to control his political beliefs or behavior. If any American officer has ever sought to do so, he was violating fundamental MAP regulations.

## EFFECT ON INTERNAL ECONOMIC DEVELOPMENTS

MAP training has had little effect one way or the other on internal economic developments.

1. Since its cost to the participating government is negligible, it has not diverted resources from other sectors of the economy. Even if the program were costly, one would have to prove that the expenditure was nonessential to prove the charge that it was unwise.

2. By introducing modern military technology and increasing the pool of skilled manpower, training has had a modest positive effect on the economy. It has also stimulated military civic action projects that have, in turn, encouraged economic development. MAP-trained personnel have been active in building roads, bridges, and other engineering projects in Latin America and elsewhere. Some trainees have engaged in sanitation, health, and literacy projects for the civilian population.

## THE MILITARY TRAINING AND ADVISORY MISSION

In the great majority of MAP countries, there is some kind of United States military mission, called by different names, whose function is to facilitate the transfer of hardware, both grant and sales, and to advise on the training program, including the selection and utilization of students and the creation of indigenous training facilities. MAP training cannot be carried on without some kind of competent United States military group in the participating country. Within the past five years, the size of most of these missions has been significantly cut, reflecting the smaller MAP budget and, on a deeper level, a response to the renewed emphasis on self-sufficiency.

The inclusion or exclusion of a particular country from the MAP program is essentially a political decision for the United States government. But once a country is included and the character of the program is determined, the mission should be adequately staffed. In terms of the existing MAP objectives in the African and Asian countries I have visited, several observations about the military missions there occur to me:

1. In all countries, there was good rapport between the United States military advisors and their local counterparts.

2. The responsible host military officials in all countries wanted the training program and the military mission to continue at the present level, and in several countries they wanted more training and a larger mission. They said a drastic cut in present MAP personnel would jeopardize the quality of the program.

3. Every reasonable effort was being made by military missions to adjust to the personnel cutbacks ordered by Washington.

### TRAINING AS AN INSTRUMENT OF U.S. POLICY

MAP training should be undertaken only when it serves the interests of the United States and the participating country and when the benefit is in line with the cost. On our side, this may be more difficult to ascertain than on the other. We have global interests, wide-ranging commitments, and limited resources. We have decided to reduce the size and visibility of our military presence abroad. This decision has affected foreign military bases and military aid. Both hardware and training assistance have been under increasing criticism at home, sometimes for reasons unsubstantiated by evidence.

Given these circumstances, it is imperative that the multiple objectives of MAP training be reexamined and clarified to determine under what circumstances the more spe-

cific security objective of enhancing internal and regional stability should take precedence over the broader political objective of promoting face-to-face contacts with potential leaders when deciding whether to initiate, continue, enlarge, reduce, or terminate a program. If the security goal is uppermost, the decision will be easier than if security and political goals are given equal weight. The security of a friendly country can be enhanced by the United States in a limited number of ways—by an alliance, by the presence of an American military force, or by security assistance. Our larger political objective of keeping channels of communication open with current and future leaders—can be pursued by a variety of military, diplomatic, and economic means.

Regardless of the comparative weight given to security and political factors, some countries are clearly more important to us than others because of their strategic location, size, or political orientation. These should have the first claim on strictly security assistance, including military training and advice. If there are sufficient resources to care adequately for pressing security needs, MAP training can be extended to other friendly countries as one additional means to lend our support and one additional channel to influence their foreign policy.

Assuming continuing pressure on the MAP budget, these guidelines suggest that the bulk of our security assistance be allocated to states that are vital to our interests and face an external threat, such as Turkey, China/Taiwan, and South Korea. States where the threat is not as immediate, but which are strategically located and are prepared to play a constructive security role in an important region, should also merit serious attention. Iran, which is in a position to exert a stabilizing influence in the Persian Gulf, is an example.

The willingness of the state in question to help itself is another positive factor. Taiwan and Iran have shown such a disposition. And Iran has the added asset of oil, which enables it to pay for virtually all its hardware and training needs.

Military training is different from hardware in several respects. It costs less. It has little visibility. Since it is an investment in persons, it need not pass as rigorous a security test as hardware assistance. Consequently, a modest training program in a small land-locked country in a nonstrategic area may be a wise investment in two-way communication, regardless of how much it contributes to internal and regional stability. Such a program might be justified by invoking some of the criteria applied to the leadership exchange program.

The United States interest in helping friendly states to maintain internal stability is another factor that needs clarification. It is easier to make a case for United States military aid to help a country deter or repel external aggression than a case for such aid to deal with indigenous or externally supported insurgents. Assisting a regime to fight guerrillas may be construed as "taking sides in an internal conflict," and this is literally true. But usually United States diplomacy, supported by a variety of instruments, tends to uphold the existing government. United States support for this objective is generally regarded as a legitimate exercise of American influence, as long as the aid is requested by a widely-recognized government. But to peo-

ple at home or abroad who sympathize with the insurgents, the United States is supporting "the wrong side." These critics, therefore, oppose all forms of United States support, and particularly security assistance. No attempt will be made here to resolve this perplexing issue which underlies some of the more impassioned criticism of MAP training.

If we are interested in encouraging self-sufficiency, a good case could be made for expanding the United States training program over the next five or ten years. By training more instructors and pressing more vigorously for the creation of indigenous training facilities, the burden on us for training would be eased more rapidly.

TOWARD A MORE EFFICIENT
TRAINING PROGRAM

Recognizing that the extent and character of United States military training in a particular state must be determined by a complex political calculus involving consideration of possible alternative ways of achieving the same objectives, I turn in conclusion to the question of how United States training programs, however many or few, large or small, may be more efficiently carried out. I am equally interested in quality and economy.

1. There should be no arbitrary limitation on the total number of MAP training openings in the United States or elsewhere. A fixed ceiling introduces rigidity into a program that needs to be flexible and responsive. In my visits to Central America, Africa, and Asia, the most frequently heard criticism from United States and foreign officials was directed against the "Fulbright

Amendment" that limits the number of MAP trainees in the United States to the number of foreign students in the United States during the previous fiscal year under the Hays-Fulbright Act. If the Congress wants to curtail MAP training, it should do so by limiting appropriations, leaving the details of implementation to the administration operating under legislative guidelines.

2. To provide an agreed volume of training at less cost, every reasonable effort should be made to speed up the development of indigenous training facilities, to increase the use of United States Mobile Training Teams, to provide on-the-job training with United States forces in places like Turkey or South Korea, and to expedite third-country training.

3. At the same time, a substantial portion of the training should be continued in stateside facilities for two chief reasons: (a) much of the higher level instruction, such as pilot training and command and staff courses, can be provided only in the United States, and (b) a stateside experience has certain benefits not associated with overseas training, such as the first-hand contact with many Americans in their home environment, the chance to improve English-language competence, and the opportunity to train side by side with United States and other foreign military personnel.

4. Recognizing that there must always be a certain minimum level of technical training connected with the acquisition by grant or sales of United States military hardware, there should be increasing emphasis in MAP training on the more advanced courses, including those providing technical, administrative, personnel management, defense planning, and command skills.

5. The so-called VIP tours to the United States should be continued for carefully selected military leaders and groups. They are relatively expensive, but no more so than their civilian counterparts sponsored by the State Department. Such tours, whether civilian or military, must be justified in terms of developing ties with actual or potential leaders in other countries. Evidence suggests that these leadership experiences, especially if they follow or precede one or two actual training periods in the United States, have served United States interests well.

6. MAP-administered training should not be terminated in a particular country because it develops to the point where it can pay for most or all of its military hardware. When the contacts and communication related to the acquisition of grant equipment come to an end, it may be even more important to maintain a nonequipment-oriented training program. Any sound sales arrangement provides for the necessary technical training related to the hardware being purchased. But most armed services, including the more advanced ones, can profit from the higher level courses. Japan and Iran, for example, pay for their American equipment, and they both have developed military establishments, but their defense leaders still insist upon the continuation of nonequipment training.

7. Since even a minimal training program requires some kind of United States military advisory group in the country, it is essential that the personnel be selected with great care. There has been a substantial enrichment in the quality of these staffs in the past 10 years, but there is always room for improvement. The courses at Fort

Bragg designed to train such personnel are to be commended. Our missions need more senior officers who are fully qualified in the local language. Further, as the size of the mission is reduced, the higher ranks should not be phased out. In fact, a case could be made to upgrade the rank in order to symbolize our partnership with the host government and its armed forces. I have heard it said: "Our generals are getting a bit tired of taking advice from American captains." This may be an exaggeration, but it is a wholesome expression of the self-respect so essential to self-sufficiency.

In conclusion, it may be said that MAP training, by whatever name, is perhaps the single most valuable instrument the president has to encourage local and regional initiative in defense and security. A sustained training program leading to greater self-sufficiency and self-respect will have the effect of relieving the far-flung military burden of the United States. Military training is a low-cost and a low-profile program. More important, it is a low-risk instrument. A training program, as such, has never involved the United States militarily in a foreign conflict. We have provided training for more than 70 countries and we became involved in combat in only two—South Korea and South Vietnam (including Cambodia)—not because we had previously trained Koreans or Vietnamese, but because five presidents believed vital United States interests were at stake.

# Citizen Diplomat: The Community's Role Today

By ALICE REYNOLDS PRATT

ABSTRACT: As community groups serving international visitors look toward the twenty-first century, they can be justly proud of their growth and accomplishments during the past 25 years. The citizen diplomat today is more sensitive to the needs of visiting leaders and students and has more expertise in receiving them. Many relationships are emerging which result in long-term involvements in cultural and business contacts. Over 561 U.S. cities are twinned with 703 cities abroad, adding yet another dimension to the informal exchanges between the U.S. and other countries. National coordinating agencies, with the support and assistance of the Bureau of Educational and Cultural Affairs of the Department of State and the Agency for International Development, provide solid leadership and good liaison between groups. State and municipal governments, with some exceptions, need to devote more attention to protocol for visits of high-ranking officials who are adding more U.S. cities to their itineraries. States and cities where Consular Corps members are located have a special obligation to these representatives of foreign governments. The nationwide network of volunteer community organizations provides a unique experience for visiting foreigners, and the programming compares favorably to other nations where more centralized control is exercised.

---

Mrs. Alice Reynolds Pratt, who is Southern Regional Director of the Institute of International Education, has helped to organize many community groups serving international visitors and students in the Southwest since she joined IIE in 1952. She served two terms as national chairman of COMSEC and was on the board of COSERV. Currently she is State Representative for Sister Cities International. A graduate of the University of Oklahoma, Mrs. Pratt has been decorated by the governments of Belgium, France, and Germany for her work with international students and visitors. Her office serves as protocol office for the city of Houston.

A HANDSHAKE in space.[1] This symbol of friendship thrilled millions the world over, but even more spectacular are the thousands of handshakes on earth which occur every day between United States citizens and the international students and visitors who are in our country. From California to New York and from Michigan to Mexico, warm-hearted Americans are opening their homes and their minds to international visitors.

These guests include students, doctors, businessmen, judges, diplomats, engineers, social workers, writers. Students from all over the world—218,401[2] of them—are in this country to pursue their academic goals as well as to see the United States. Short-term visitors are here for a period of weeks or months. They travel under various private and governmental auspices. Some come by invitation of the Department of State; others are sponsored by Foreign Consulates, the agencies of the United Nations, city administrations, U.S. Departments of Labor and Health, Education and Welfare, the army, navy, and many private agencies. Some of the visitors are tourists who call the numbers listed in directories available at embassies overseas for the "Americans at Home" program.

Thirty years ago, even 15 years ago, no one would have prophesied that Americans in such great numbers would become so intelligently involved in the cultural and educational exchange of persons.

Why are United States citizens interested? What is in it for them and how does the foreign student or visitor benefit from this experience?

## HISTORICAL DEVELOPMENT OF COMMUNITY GROUPS

In the *National Directory of Organizations Serving Short-Term International Visitors*, published by the National Council for Community Services to International Visitors (COSERV), over 88 organizations in as many United States cities are listed as official contacts for agencies programming international visitors; the National Association for Foreign Student Affairs (NAFSA) lists 2,000 names of individuals and communities on its mailing roster, according to Hugh M. Jenkins, Executive Vice President of NAFSA. The Town Affiliation Association (Sister Cities International) lists 561 cities in the United States which have sister city affiliations with 703 cities abroad. In addition, there are dozens of agencies and groups sponsoring programs which foster nonofficial contacts and friendships with persons from abroad.

In the late forties and early fifties, as the numbers of foreign visitors and students increased, many communities realized the need for an organized effort to meet these visitors. Early pioneers were church groups; the Committee on Friendly Relations Among Foreign Students, now International Student Service (ISS); the Institute of International Education (IIE) and its regional offices; World Affairs Councils and the National Association of Foreign Student Advisers, now the National Association for Foreign Student Affairs (NAFSA). Leaders during the period were Katherine C. Bang Donovan of the Cleveland Council of World Affairs; Ruth H. Purkaple of the Committee on Friendly Re-

1. Apollo-Soyuz—17 July 1975.
2. *Open Doors*, Report on International Educational Exchange, Institute of International Education, 1975.

lations Among Foreign Students; Marita Houlihan of the Department of State; Kenneth Holland and Pearl Purcell of IIE; Dr. Joe W. Neal of the University of Texas; and many more.

Organizations were formed independently by many communities to provide a central clearinghouse for international activities within the community. They were called by various names—friendship councils, hospitality committees, international service committees—but all performed a similar function, hospitality and service to the international visitor and to international students if a university was nearby.

Dozens of handbooks were published by individual communities on the "dos" and "don'ts" of entertaining international visitors. Pamphlets were made available to foreign visitors explaining the customs of the United States. Volunteers sponsored orientation sessions for United States citizens as well as foreign students. There was zest and enthusiasm, and the recruitment of volunteers often was preceded by the story of the hapless foreign student who went for a whole year from the classroom to the laboratory to the dorm without ever meeting a single person in the community or being invited to a home for dinner.

The students, too, told each other about this new American phenomenon. A student from India humorously gave the following advice to new students if they should be invited to an American Sunday dinner!

1. Ask your hostess if you may help set the table.
2. You may take off your coat and tie (not your shoes).
3. Your host expects you to sit first at the table, so don't wait

for the hostess because she may be in the kitchen getting things ready.
4. Look out for plates or bowls that may be coming from either left or right.
5. Pass on any plates coming to you . . . from any direction. . . .
6. Don't put too much of each kind of food on your plate because you will find in no time that you have a heap of everything in front of you that will be impossible to finish. Your hosts may think that you have not eaten for at least a week.
7. Start eating when you hear the hostess say . . . "Well, we are all set now. . . ."
8. Use paper napkins as you like . . . you cannot imagine how much the economy of this country depends on the waste of paper.
9. Talk while eating, but do not try to look others in the eye . . . because everyone stops eating and then it will never finish.
10. To save yourself the trouble of talking most of the time . . . ask the hostess how she cooked the chicken . . . fish or apple pie . . . and this will keep everyone else quiet until the end of the dinner. . . .

Red flags soon were hoisted telling the dangers of exploiting the foreign student; proselytizing the foreign student; encroaching on his study time; overselling the United States; wet-nursing the foreign student. Volunteers and professionals were told to listen, to speak slowly, to be knowledgeable about the United States and the student's own country, to read up on the students' or visitors' background.

At NAFSA's tenth anniversary conference in Michigan in the spring of 1958, foreign student advisors and community volunteers devoted seven sessions to discussion of the community and community organizations in the service of overseas visitors and students. At about the same time, the Governmental Affairs Institute called a meeting in Washington of community leaders throughout the country to discuss the short-term visitor or "foreign leader" program.

As the individual community organizations proliferated, all going their different ways, it was recognized that central coordinating agencies—separate ones for students and for short-term visitors—would be beneficial. Both COSERV and the Community Section of the National Association for Foreign Student Affairs (COMSEC) were formed in 1961.

## WHO IS WHO

COSERV, with offices at 1630 Crescent Place, N.W., Washington, D.C., is a non-profit agency founded to facilitate communication between the national agencies that send short-term visitors to United States communities and the local organizations that receive these visitors. It also contributes in a valuable way to raising the standards of local community groups. As an example, communities cannot be listed in its national directory or have membership in COSERV unless the following criteria are met: Community Organization (identified as a "receiving" organization) is a non-profit, local community organization concerned with community services to international visitors, meeting the following standards:

1. Has a purpose that is in conformity with the stated objectives of COSERV, and neither represents nor conveys any special political, social, or religious interest.

2. Is willing to receive visitors without distinction as to race, nationality, or creed.

3. Has a responsible governing board providing continuity and composed of individuals within the community who have access to those organizations and institutions within the community that represent potential resources for a well-balanced program for visitors.

4. Gives evidence of consultation with major community organizations, of having the confidence and support of such organizations, and conforms to the basic principles of sound coordination.

5. Has a community base for contacts and local operations, an understanding of needs of visitors, a diversified body of volunteers necessary for the functioning of the program, and the resources essential for sound operation.[3]

The Community Section of NAFSA (COMSEC) has many of the same objectives as COSERV, but its efforts as a national coordinating and information agency are directed primarily to international students enrolled at United States institutions, whose time in this country may lengthen into several years, and to associated volunteers.

Among its purposes: to further the relationship between campus and community in a mutual concern for foreign students; to promote the most effective service to foreign students by groups and individuals in the community; to develop and maintain a high professional standard in such service; and to serve such groups and individuals in the community by providing means for an exchange of information, by en-

3. *National Directory of Community Organizations Serving Short-Term Visitors*, 8th ed. (COSERV, 1975–76).

couraging and sponsoring conferences, and by initiating such publications as will be helpful in developing community programs.[4]

Both of these organizations have been of enormous help to individual communities. Each organization consults with communities on request, holds workshops, publishes materials, and serves as the vehicle for volunteers from all over the country to get together at national and regional meetings and learn from one another.

Other than setting forth constructive standards of performance, neither COSERV nor COMSEC tries to make all local groups fit the same mold. Each organization offers suggestions, guidelines, and experience from which the communities may draw.

At the local level, COSERV and COMSEC may meld. Community groups often belong to both organizations since, in fact, many cities have one volunteer group serving both students and visitors, rather than dual organizations. This is obviously preferable in smaller cities or in "university towns," where a large university with its international students and university-oriented short-term visitors dominate the international scene. Even some metropolitan areas with strong educational resources, such as Houston, Texas, find it efficient and economical to combine COSERV and COMSEC affiliations and functions in one organization.[5]

The question naturally arises: do the two agencies duplicate each other? The general consensus is that at the national level they do not.

4. *Guide to Community Services* (National Association for Foreign Student Affairs, Community Section).

5. Houston International Service Committee.

Each brings volunteers together with a different body of professionals: in COSERV, the staffs of government-related programming agencies; in NAFSA/COMSEC, the international officers and foreign student advisers of colleges and universities. Each is concerned with a different group of internationals, and the differences are far deeper than length of stay—the mature "leaders" drawn from government, business, and the professions of other countries (COSERV) and the 218,401-strong group of foreign students on college compuses across the country, widely disparate among themselves, from the most timid and untraveled to the highly sophisticated. COSERV and COMSEC each has a defined area of activity, though there is commendable cooperation between them. Community leaders sometimes serve on both boards simultaneously, for example.

Still another aspect of international exchange is the concern of Sister Cities International. Like COSERV and COMSEC, it is a coordinating agency for community groups which draw people from every walk of life into the international sphere. Organized in 1967, and growing in strength and influence, this agency encourages United States cities to form lasting ties with cities in other nations through exchanges of people, ideas, and a variety of things covering the entire community spectrum. Although sister city affiliations are set up at the mayoral or city government level, the activities are carried out by citizens' groups.

The sister city concept grew out of a White House Conference called by former President Dwight D. Eisenhower in 1956. Sister Cities International has its headquarters at Suite 202, City Building, 1612 K

Street, N.W., Washington, D.C. 20006, and offers excellent materials and assistance to any city interested in a kinship with a city in another country. It sponsors an annual meeting (the one in Rochester, New York, in August 1975 drew more than 500 delegates from 100 United States cities) and state workshops. It publishes a national directory of United States cities and their overseas affiliates.

All three national groups are given some financial assistance by the Bureau of Educational and Cultural Affairs, but all must rely on dues and contributions to stay solvent.

## A LOOK AT COMMUNITY ORGANIZATIONS TODAY

Community organizations providing services to internationals differ widely in structure and financial support. Some are expertly run by volunteers; others have professional staffs as well as a corps of volunteers.

In some cities the Council on World Affairs might house the International Service Committee; in others the chamber of commerce or a regional office of the Institute of International Education might do so; or the committee might be attached to a local campus. Some are not under the wing of another organization, but have their own offices and in some cases have fulltime paid staff. Many have incorporated.

Although all community groups are putting forth a sincere effort to bring in as participants a good mix of people of all races, religions, ages, economic levels, and political beliefs, this is not easy to achieve. It is even harder to involve lower income groups in these days of inflation than it was 20 years ago.

Commendably, however, these citizens' groups have upheld steadfastly their humanitarian purposes. Rarely, if ever, does one hear of a committee dominated by selfseekers, either social, political, or business. The committees are private (meaning nongovernment), non-profit, and extremely independent, with 100 percent citizen participation.

When organized along state and regional lines, such community groups represent a positive force for public participation in international affairs. A combination of hospitality committees in one state (Texas) successfully sponsored state legislation extending special tuition arrangements for international students attending state-supported institutions of higher education. Similar efforts supported by other hospitality committee combinations have endorsed legislative efforts in five other states (Colorado, Washington, Missouri, Kansas, and California).

## COMMUNITY/STUDENTS: THE TWO-WAY BENEFITS

Of all community programs for international students, probably the most universally offered is the host family program. It has endured and proved its worth. It is appreciated and enjoyed equally by student and host. The student does not live with the family, but is put in touch with the family at the beginning of the academic year. He sees them frequently, and often spends vacations and holidays with them. The family acts as his springboard into the activities of the city in which he temporarily lives and introduces him to people he would never meet, experiences he would never have if he remained on campus. Lasting relationships and enduring friendships grow out of host family relationships, as important to the family's growth as to the student's successful adjustment to a different culture.

What else can community groups do for international students? Another popular and growing program involves young United States career people, about the same age as graduate students and doctors. They plan monthly get-togethers with the students, discussing whatever interests them most. They sail, picnic, play bridge, dance, or just talk. Not intended to replace the host family program, this kind of activity supplements it and presents yet another facet of the community to the student.

The wives' committees serve a further purpose. More and more students are coming with spouses and small children. It helps immensely if foreign wives can come together with local women to discuss mutual interests and problems. Generally, there are monthly meetings, and many tools and aids are given to the newly arrived foreign brides — information on how to shop and how to get places, and sometimes directories are printed for their use. Babysitters are provided during meetings. Usually a United States wife acts as "big sister" to each foreign wife, and the visitor is encouraged to call her at any time.

Myriad other services are offered to international students: city tours and weekend trips, speakers' bureaus for those wishing to give talks about their countries, English classes, holiday programs, clothing and furniture banks, orientation, emergency loans, free tickets to cultural and sporting events, discussion groups, assistance with international

programs on campus, corresponding with the student before he arrives in the United States, meeting him at the airport. The activities expand as the needs arise. Not all communities offer all services, of course.

Mary Thompson, director of International Student Service, 291 Broadway, New York, recently observed new trends in hospitality and service programs. Mary travels throughout the country visiting community groups which receive international students through the ISS VISIT Program.[6]

She noted that foreign students are becoming involved in community service programs: "In Dallas, Norris Lineweaver has been working very closely with a large number of foreign students in what is termed the International Student Urban Services Corps. He had used students in a wide variety of community service operations, all on a volunteer basis. This same kind of thing has gone on in other communities, and it's increasing.

"In Phoenix, there was a project involving students in schools on the reservations near Phoenix. Students in the classroom, of course, is a program that has been going on for a long time, but again it is increasing.

"The architecture students at Columbia University who became involved with a block in East Harlem in terms of its being cleaned up and rejuvenated are another example," she stated.

### SHORT-TERM VISITORS

The United States government is unique in the manner in which it

6. The VISIT Program enables foreign students and participants to stay with families in each city when they tour the U.S. ISS coordinates these visits with organizations in communities where the students stop over.

programs its official guests. Private agencies in Washington, which are on contract to the United States government, first receive the visitor and outline his general program across the country. From that point on, the visitor is in the hands of the volunteer or professional staff of the receiving group in the city he visits. No financial support comes to these local groups from the federal government. The committees raise the money to carry on their activities in their respective cities.

However, some universities now charge for providing highly technical programs for government-sponsored visitors. As local budgets of receiving agencies become tighter and the number of visitors increase, a few cities are raising the question: should similar federal support be given to local groups? But the volunteer concept still remains strong, and there is little prospect for change.

The volunteer aspect of the program is an invaluable asset. There is freshness in the volunteer's enthusiasm for the visitor, knowledge of the local resources, expertise in programming in the particular community. The visitor knows he is not being given a showcase tour. The attitude of most programmers, either volunteer or professional, is that "you show the good with the bad," and a confidence exists that this country has enough going for it that the positive points will win out, without preplanning it that way.

Most foreign governments, by contrast, bear all of the expenses of a sponsored visitor's trip and activity, from the time he arrives in the country until he leaves, and at all times have perfect control of the program. There are pros and cons to each method.

Ruth H. Frank, assistant director of COSERV, says, "Over the past 10 or 15 years, the greatest changes in community services provided by volunteers and paid staff to international visitors have been evidenced in the degree of professionalism with which these services have been arranged. No longer is it a matter of hit or miss in arranging appointments and meetings suitable to the visitor's special interests. Experienced programmers have learned to know who's who in their communities as well as what's what and why. Through contacts which they have established over the years, they can now zero in on the visitor's needs and arrange programs that cut through the layers of irrelevance and quickly get to the heart of the question the visitor has come to the United States to study.

"Years of experience have also given community workers a keener perception and understanding of visitors' personal problems and concerns—fatigue, confusion, worry about family back home, language barriers—these and many others now easily spotted by community hosts and dealt with in a calm and reasoned fashion that did not prevail when programs serving international visitors were begun many years ago."

If there are any disadvantages in not having close central control of foreigners' visits to the United States, they are more than offset, most people believe, by the advantages of the fresh approach at the community level, the up-to-date knowledge of local events, and the originality of citizen-planned and -executed programs.

On the other hand, a lady from Asia told me, when we were together recently on an official trip to Germany, that some of her experiences in the United States were frightening. Although she was a government-sponsored guest, in many cities she was not met and was left to make her way to the hotel on her own. She found the neighborhoods around some of the hotels disquieting to a woman alone. She was never sure how much confidence to place in the local receiving representative.

Perhaps the lesson here is that the central programming agency should give special attention to visitors whose cultures are very different from ours, and it might be worth the investment for our State Department to furnish escorts for such visitors even if his or her English is perfect.

Obviously, an official visitor must have some degree of independence and flexibility to make the program work well for him in the United States. He is given a good briefing and told in Washington what he can expect in each city. He has the sponsors' names and addresses and a rough outline of his activities, but he does not receive his detailed schedule until his arrival in a city. If the local organization is good, his program reflects it. However, even the best of organizations can have slip-ups—when a volunteer becomes ill or a hotel has been changed or the person hosting a dinner cancels out at the last minute. In a metropolitan area, one cannot intimately know each volunteer. Some may be crashing bores. The wife might like to entertain foreign visitors, but the husband is not enthusiastic. These are exceptions, however, rather than the rule. In the 30-odd years since the short-term visitor program began, there have been few complaints. The majority have had excellent experiences.

The following excerpt from a letter received by Mary Catherine Jennings, International Activity, Department of Health, Education, and Welfare, points this up. The writer is Gertrud Puckert of Munich.

Back in West Germany again I would like to thank you for your wonderful help and advice during my stay in the U.S.A. All these international visitors' organizations whose names and addresses you gave to me, have been so kind and helpful while I was visiting social institutions—I would also like to mention that I was deeply impressed, how many Americans are contributing time and services as "volunteers." The kindness, hospitality and willingness to give information that I've experienced during these 5 months were overwhelming. I wouldn't want to miss this time. I will start working with mentally retarded in a day-care facility (kindergarten, school and sheltered workshop) and hope to start programs gaining some volunteers for this institution.

## PROTOCOL SERVICES OUTSIDE WASHINGTON

So far, we have looked at the volunteer side of the coin—the community organizations devoted to receiving international students and visitors and the national coordinating agencies which help give this massive volunteer effort its cohesiveness.

It would be remiss not to mention the substantial investment in time and money which some municipal and state governments throughout the United States are making to see that high-ranking foreign visitors are received properly and with dignity.

Increasing numbers of city and state governments are using professional protocol services that complement and enhance the efforts of volunteers. A state visit, or the visit of one of ambassadorial rank or above, makes attention to protocol a necessity. And ambassadors, heads of state, and others of distinguished standing are coming more often than ever before to cities and towns across the United States.

Protocol, says the dictionary, is "a code prescribing strict adherence to correct etiquette and precedence." It might be further defined as the fine embroidery that holds together the intricate tapestry of international hospitality. At best, it is almost invisible, but unmistakably there, lending impeccable smoothness to the whole picture.

One regional conference has been held on the subject of protocol for international visitors,[7] and COSERV devoted a section of one of its conferences[8] to the subject.

Yet, protocol services deserve far more attention than they have received. Few resources are available. Etiquette books give some information on protocol, and the United States Protocol Office in Washington will willingly and graciously answer questions. And that is it. Few books or other aids exist to help the person responsible for protocol when a dignitary is visiting at the state or city level. (One book[9] on the subject has been written by a former programming officer in the Southwest).

Unfortunately, attention to protocol is uneven throughout the United States. Some states and cities do a splendid job of receiving VIP visitors, but others are careless in observing that "strict adherence" to the prescribed diplomatic courtesies.

Cities and states in which consular offices are located have a special obligation to make sure that courtesies which are extended to our diplomats abroad are returned in kind when their counterparts come to the United States.

There is growing awareness now of protocol requirements, and it is hoped that more of the city and state officials concerned will consult with the United States Protocol Office in Washington or with the protocol offices of cities like New York, Philadelphia, and Houston that have established these services.

## LOOKING AHEAD

As we enter the last quarter of the twentieth century, we can anticipate even greater numbers of foreign students and visitors coming to the United States. Every available resource should be utilized to make these visits productive and useful to the visitor and all those who are touched by the visit. In a recent speech[10] on this subject, Dr. Joe Neal, International Director of the University of Texas, said:

Today's visitors are more sophisticated, cosmopolitan, and informed persons than the post-war travellers of three decades ago. Coffees, receptions, and similar occasions—even courtesy office visits—no longer suffice for the current wave of visitors who seek professional contact and technical observation. There is often an interest in long-term relationships leading to continuing cultural and commercial exchange. International hospitality committees of the mid-seventies have a responsibility to inventory their community resources and mobilize them for utilization by international visitors. At the same time, they have an obligation also to project the best in human resources available in their communities. The "little old

---

7. Rice Hotel, Houston, Texas, March 1968.

8. National COSERV Conference, Washington, D.C., 26, 27 March 1972.

9. James E. Lott, *Practical Protocol, Guide to International Courtesies* (Houston, Texas: Gulf Publishing Company, 1973).

10. NAFSA Region III Conference, Fort Worth, Texas, 24 October 1973.

ladies in tennis shoes," "social climbers," or even groups representing only one community segment—be it religious, social, or professional—are no longer adequate representatives of today's modern cities in the receiving of international visitors. Hospitality groups operate on the "raw edge" of this country's foreign policy and world affairs. Their obligation becomes daily more significant and responsible.

Community organizations throughout the United States have admirably demonstrated their alertness to the changing relationships between nations and the diversity and complexities of world events which have made all of us interdependent. They do not believe that person-to-person contact will save the world nor bring about instant peace. They do believe that increased understanding and appreciation of others' values will create a better climate for mutual cooperation.

We are all better informed for having participated in the programs and for having experienced not just a handshake but friendships with individuals from other lands. As any volunteer will tell you, "We get back more than we give."

ANNALS, AAPSS, **424**, March 1976

# Results and Effects of Study Abroad

By MICHAEL J. FLACK

ABSTRACT: "Results" and "effects" of study abroad present major problems for research and assessment. Positing largely post-return criteria of "effect," a number of propositions seek to indicate some aspects of "results" and "impacts" relating to (1) the individual, (2) the host institution and society, (3) the home society, and (4) intersocietal and international relations. The footnote lists compilations and analyses of pertinent literature.

*Michael J. Flack is Professor of International and Intercultural Affairs at the Graduate School of Public and International Affairs, University of Pittsburgh. Educated at the State University of Iowa and the Fletcher School of Law and Diplomacy, he is the author of* Sources of Information on International Education Activities, The Role of Culture in International Operations, *co-author of* The World's Students in the United States, *and editor of the forthcoming* Transnational Social Science Flows—Cultural Imperialism or Cultural Emancipation? *He is the current President of the International Society for Educational, Cultural, and Scientific Interchanges (ISECSI).*

FEW concepts in the area of general discourse on social policy are more frequently used, yet more difficult to analyze, identify, and "prove" than "results," "effects," or "impacts." The "effects" of "education" and of "personal experiences" involve particularly vexing and complex problems. Few of us would be too confident about identifying too specifically the results or effects of our own education on our own lives and careers, or that of others. Yet, the propensity of recent years to think in cost-effective terms, the need to justify the initiation or continuation of sponsored programs for both United States and foreign students, and the often loose claims about the public welfare/foreign policy/international relations implications of education have led to a substantially increased emphasis on "evaluating" programs, probing for consequences, and seeking to identify results, effects, and impacts. Basically, this expanded new demand—also applied to foreign students—is salutary. Obviously, beyond the issues of efficiency, it is important to learn what are the conditions, effects, and co-results of intercultural experience and learning, if for no other reason than because, in a variety of forms and methods, they will represent a growing imperative in preparing persons everywhere for constructive functioning in an increasingly interdepending and necessarily cooperating world. Also, the emphasis on the evaluation of results may in time lead to a more deliberate and comprehensive articulation, research, and thus knowledge of the many interacting and parallel factors that enter into and affect the dynamics of intercultural learning, encounters, and transfers of experience, and of their role in the all-important area of "knowledge-in-action."

## PERSPECTIVE

As of now, however, analyses of results of study abroad confront serious problems. Among them, two appear to be central:

1. An inclination in many to assume results, however identified, to be specific outcomes, products, or effects originating in, owing to, or caused dominantly and directly by the particular educational and social experience of the individual while sojourning abroad.

In this perception, the focus is almost entirely on the sojourn, from entry to departure, on the presumed causal impact of the educational-social inputs, on the resulting skills and attitudes, with the psycho-cultural make-up of the sample group studied representing only a type of absorbing facilitator or obstacle—one that covertly, though not expressly, is viewed as generally passive. It is imperative to stress the simplistic and questionable nature of this model.

2. An inadequate differentiation and articulation of the concept of results itself: Results of what? on who? on what? due to which whats? in what sequence, combination, and "sensitivity areas"? as of when? over what duration? manifesting themselves in what? differentially in what situations, contexts, and environments? instigating, as behavior with consequences, what secondary spillover results?

Such an overall model, of course, would necessitate taking into account an exceedingly complex network of inputs, outputs, and multiple feedbacks, which, in turn, would themselves represent new inputs and outputs. To design and apply it in research would require a degree of ambition and of longer-term funding that, as yet, is not around the corner.

In any case, it needs emphasizing that, even in the limited field of international educational exchange, here further restricted to the results of study by foreign students in the United States, the questions by far outrun reliable answers and knowledge—in evidence, scope, validity, and pertinence. The research agenda is wide and open—and waiting for concert in action.

## INTENT

Nevertheless, here we are, confronted with the question: "What results attending foreign study in the United States can we identify, claim, point to, given present knowledge and conceptual perspectives?" We shall attempt to deal with it in four general sections: Effects on (1) the individual, (2) the host institution and society, (3) the home society, and (4) intersocietal and international relations.

In each section, we shall state in résumé fashion the thrust of relatively established "knowledge." The formulations will reflect the not too copious records of those studies that have focused, wholly or in part, on the question of effects and results. Given the brevity of allotted space, they must be selective.[1]

1. Given the necessary brevity of this essay, we eschew, with one exception, citing individual studies. They would occupy several pages. The interested reader is advised to look for them in the following analytical and/or annotated compilations of research.

U.S., Department of State, Bureau of Intelligence and Research, *Cross-Cultural Education: A Bibliography of Government-Sponsored and Private Research on Foreign*

For the purposes of this article, we shall use the following arbitrary working criterion: "results" and "effects" of study abroad will relate to the kinds of knowledge, skills, values, attitudes, behaviors which, when compared subsequent to the completion of the study-sojourn with those obtaining prior to its initiation, indicate an expanded synthesis in which part of the difference may be sought among factors inherent in the ex-student's exposure to events, circumstances, and learning while abroad.

This formulation thus excludes considerations of "attitude changes" *during* the sojourn, as well as other findings noted "in course." It does not devalue them. In fact, they re-

*Students and Trainees in the U.S. and in Other Countries. A Selective Bibliography, 1946–1964* (Washington, D.C.: U.S. Department of State, April 1965).

U.S., Department of State, Bureau of Educational and Cultural Affairs, *Summaries of Evaluation Studies of the Educational and Cultural Exchange Program* (Washington, D.C.: U.S. Department of State, June 1967).

Margaret L. Cormack, *An Evaluation of Research on Educational Exchange*, Prepared for the Bureau of Educational and Cultural Affairs, U.S. Department of State (Washington, D.C.: U.S. Department of State, August 1962).

Margaret T. Cussler, *Review of Selected Studies Affecting International Cultural Affairs*, Prepared for the U.S. Advisory Commission on International and Cultural Affairs (Washington, D.C.: November 1962).

Barbara J. Walton, *Foreign Student Exchange in Perspective*, Research on Foreign Students in the United States, Prepared for the Office of External Research, U.S. Department of State (Washington, D.C.: U.S. Department of State, September 1967).

Seth Spaulding, Michael J. Flack, et al., *The World's Students in the United States*, A Review and Evaluation of Research on Foreign Students, 1967–1974, Prepared for the Office of External Research, Bureau of Intelligence and Research, U.S. Department of State (Washington, D.C.: U.S. Department of State, July 1975). Published in January 1976 by Frederick Praeger, New York.

flect in large part the intermediate factors referred to in the criterion.

## EFFECTS ON THE INDIVIDUAL

A review of research, made in conjunction with Spaulding's and this author's recent overview on foreign students, 1967–1974, supplemented by some pertinent earlier studies, yields the following profile of functionally relevant findings:

1. Improvement in the competent use of the English language yields benefits in the personal and professional lives of former students in their home countries and elsewhere, especially where such skill is supportive of the activity in which they are engaged.

2. The achievement of a United States academic degree, undergraduate or advanced, tends to bestow in most countries, though with variation relating to field or institution, an enhanced status, and generally tends to facilitate employment or promotion at home, participation in United States-related projects or operations, informed access to work with international agencies or associations, and further advanced training or research.

3. The specialized competence acquired in the field of major study, while not guaranteeing employment in that field, often permits those who are active in it to make innovative contributions ranging from those that are merely incremental to those that appear basic. Generally, however, major influence on change tends to relate to the level of a person's status and authority, thus frequently permitting results to become visible only later, when senior status has been achieved. This does not preclude earlier effects and results in situations where persons trained abroad are appointed to influential political or administrative positions, whether in their specialty or in other fields.

4. The experience and awareness of alternate or additional models of social institutions, roles, behaviors, and values—whether deemed by the ex-student to be directly applicable or not—afford an expanded comparative vision and register of possible personal and professional choices, and thus permit the returnee, within the leeway of home circumstances, a greater resourcefulness in the realm of social diagnosis, innovation, or even invention.

5. The establishment during the sojourn of acquaintances and relationships with host-country persons (faculty, fellow students, community persons, friends) or organizations, where maintained, has been of assistance to the ex-student's further activities. In many instances, however, unless nurtured by deliberate policies on the part of United States institutions or persons, or renewed by professional cooperation or visits, such relationships tend to subside with time.

6. Familiarization during the sojourn with a wide range of sources of professional and general information, documentation, and literature, as well as with pertinent United States and international organizations and programs, tends to benefit the professional careers of former foreign students. This includes the knowledge of basic reference and statistical compilations, textbooks, journals, experts, equipment, associations, annual meetings, United States government exchange opportunities, and so forth, enabling the returnee to be potentially more effective in his own career and his organization in comparing and using research and data.

7. In the psycho-social realm, the sojourn and educational experience tends to engender a more sophisticated, differentiated, personalized, and concretized knowledge and perception of the host society, its achievements and problems, its peoples and policies, and of its "ways of life," as compared to "knowledge" and images held before. This usually reflects itself in a reduction in the monolithic character of previously held ethnocentric stereotypes, greater understanding—approving and/or disapproving—of the functioning of the host society and of its governmental system, and a heightened awareness of the diversity of groups and positions within the polity. The result is a soberer appraisal of some of its features, values, and practices and of their relevance to one's own role, one's field of activity, and one's own country. Apart from this specifically host society related capacity to differentiate and note complexity, this greater analytical sophistication may, to a degree, "spill over," occasioning the discovery of similar factors in one's own society, as well as the capacity to anticipate and notice it in other societies.

8. A heightened, varyingly continuing interest in events, developments, publications about, and, general news from or about the society of former residence and study, thus an effort to keep informed, to read host country publications, and a motivation to claim expertise in interpreting to colleagues and others developments in it. Also, unless the experience abroad had been strongly negative, or the political situation advises the contrary, a measure of generalized continuing solicitude toward the former host country remains. This emphatically does not imply automatic approval of its policies or of some aspects of its social practice.

## RESULTS IN THE HOME SOCIETY

Most societies, and particularly the newly independent countries of the developing world, appear to have significantly benefitted from the accelerated infusion of qualified trained professionals in fields where existing national institutions have not been able to educate the needed numbers, or where higher levels of specialization and expertise appeared to be required. This particularly relates to the fields of technology, management, education, library science, engineering, business, agriculture, nursing, and medicine. The proposition is tenable that the provision of such qualified personnel trained abroad, supplementing the cadres available at the time of independence in the new governments and societies for the management of modernization programs, may have in some instances made the difference between viability and possible failure.

The presence and continuing growth in numbers of foreign-educated professionals—in some instances leading to oversupply—constitutes an as yet inadequately understood infusion of a new technocratic and professional elite, largely located in urban centers; active in government, education, industry, research, and the media; claiming authority and status on the basis of social performance rather than inheritance; and asserting its own standards, interests, and aspirations in and for its society. Many current government and societal leaders have studied abroad. The full scope of the attendant impacts of such study, and of the presence of large numbers of cosmopolitanized influentials in these societies, can as yet only be surmised. As of now, we do not even have adequate statistics of returnees, by country, field, profession, and employment.

The extensive training abroad provided over many years now to foreign military personnel from many countries, while devoted largely to professional preparation, has provided an additional layer of internationally exposed younger officers, high in organizational competence and often successful in rapid rise through the ranks. What specific nonmilitary effect their training abroad, often repeated, has had with regard to attitudes, their perception of conditions in their home society, their image of their public role and responsibility, is, due to the sensitivity of the issue, unavailable in research evidence. But the frequent presence of foreign-trained military personnel in military governments, in groups that participate or lead coups, or that exercise pressure for reform, suggests a potential accompanying side effect—regardless of whether one assesses such developments positively or negatively.

In the realms of education, research, and the media, the return of highly trained specialists in fields related to American studies, whatever the discipline, has led varyingly to the evolvement of new courses; the infusion of American references, readings, or case studies into existing courses; more publications on United States-related subjects; and also, hopefully, somewhat more sophisticated and systematic information on United States developments. While the traditional inclination would mark this and similar increases in attention to, and competence about, the ex-host country as a result or gain for the latter, it might appropriately be also viewed, possibly even more so, as a result for the home society. The home society has filled a deficiency, *it* is becoming better informed, *it* may, as a result, relate in the future more intelligently, comprehendingly, and in multiplied ways, to the United States as a society, a polity, a factor in the world.

There is contradictory evidence on that aspect of effects of study abroad that are commonly labeled "the brain drain" or "the migration of talent." Such effects, where studied, seem to vary by field, level, country, and region. In many instances, the nonreturn of certain professionals alleviates the pressures of an overflow of existing employable talent in particular fields; in others, the nonreturn can, in significant respects, be viewed as an inhibitor in current and future plans for development and specialization. Yet, the criteria of needs and demand tend to be unclear and the statistics incomplete and unreliable. The nationalist model stresses presumed immediate losses to the society in question. The internationalist model stresses the longer-term benefits to the home society (remittances, representation, possible later return with higher level of expertise) as well as the need for these societies to refashion their social and economic order so as to make more productive use of their skilled manpower and attract it back. A major recent United Nations Institute for Training and Research (UNITAR) study has found that most foreign students ultimately intend to return to their societies, even though many wish for a period of practical experience to follow completion of their studies. To what extent the export of knowledge, science, techniques, and administration from the more developed to the developing countries countervails those effects of nonreturn that are deemed depriving—effects that pertain also in relations among developed countries—what are the short- or longer-term losses and gains, and what is their ratio within particular fields and time spans are issues that require extremely complex assessments for each particular country and region—assessments that so far have yielded diverse and discordant conclusions.

On the personal and micro-societal level, returnees from study abroad have tended to import with them some of the tastes for "higher" culture, for a more mobile way of life, for a more purposeful management of funds and effort, and often, as the Useems found, "a new frame of reference for thinking [and living] —not just a new set of beliefs about the Western world." To the extent that such personal and family styles and proclivities become shared and are found attractive by others in the host society—often mutually reinforced within the ex-foreign student community—they contribute to processes of social change, a deprovincialization and diversification of modes of living and functioning, and the quickening of modernization catalyzed by economic, political, professional, and other inputs.

## EFFECTS ON THE UNITED STATES

### On institutions of higher learning

The effects of successive generations of foreign students on United States institutions of higher learning appear to be diffuse, diverse, but generally rather modest. In some in-

stitutions and states, the foreign student component has contributed noteworthy funding in tuition, other expenditures, and enrollment to keep some programs that otherwise would have been terminated, alive. Recent studies in Indiana and New York State identify foreign students' financial "exports" to those states as respectively the sixteenth and eighteenth largest "industries," with ramifications for employment.[2]

There are few studies that assess in adequate scope and depth comprehensive effects on intercultural learning, on curricula, on the "milieu" of the institution, or on administrative policies. Most evidence agrees that they are scant. One effect is that most institutions now have some type of "Foreign Student Advisor," providing counseling, but having almost no role in academic programming. Some institutions have added special language and orientation programs for incoming and occasional re-orientation programs for departing students from abroad. A few—particularly in professional areas—have introduced special courses or supplementary seminars designed to provide "applicatory relevance" for students from abroad. Some universities have joined into consortia to strengthen and/or coordinate varied aspects of the "international" dimension in their operations. While occasionally there is news about a significant achievement in research or leadership by a foreign student on some campus, no systematic study provides generalizable knowledge. Nor do we basically know what general impact, if any, foreign students have

2. "Foreign Students: An Economic Approach," *Post-Secondary Education in New York State* (Albany, N.Y.: July-August, 1973), p. 3.

on the political and cultural attitudes of their American colleagues and professors on campus. Such findings as there are, are too scattered to be salient.

On the whole, thus, the effect on United States colleges and universities seems to be local and ad hoc, and, in the curricula and mutual learning realm, largely minimal. The above represents an overall portrayal which does not invalidate occasional exceptions. On most campuses, contacts between foreign and American students are intermittent and infrequent. The size, milieu, and leadership of the institution seem to be decisive factors.

Where internationalizing changes in curriculum have been introduced, there are no data about the extent to which foreign students, by action or mere presence, have played a role in bringing such changes about. The changes may have had origins outside the foreign student group on campus. Regularized contact between the academic and administrative/service segments in the universities regarding the problems and opportunities presented by the presence of foreign students is largely nonexistent.

The impact of government or business-sponsored special short-term training ventures for middle or high-level personnel from abroad on the regular academic offerings in United States institutions in general seems to be minimal. With some exceptions, they are separately administered and remain largely isolated from the institutions' programs and life. Evaluation studies have focused on "satisfaction with the program" and "perception of its relevance," not on results for or impacts on the host institution. While many of such short-term programs use innovative techniques and produce experimental materials, these seldom find their way into the regular curricula. Thus the impact is largely one in prestige abroad and in the possible co-financing of expanded teaching staffs.

Some United States institutions have gained in employing foreign students as research and graduate assistants and/or, upon completion of their studies, as faculty and researchers. Some have made notable contributions, deriving from their personal genius and/or their bi-cultural background. No systematic or reliable data are in existence.

There is evidence that the returnee will advise others in his society to seek to engage in study, do research, or visit in his former host society or some of its institutions, and the likelihood that he will help in their efforts to be admitted to such study or sojourns.

The desire to "repay" in small measure some of the benefits received and the wish to strengthen his former university's resources concerning the returnee's society and its achievements often lead to arrangements for university libraries to receive publications, documents, journals, and other materials from the ex-foreign students' home countries, with a view to improving their resources for learning and research.

### On host communities

There is little evidence that, other than in some individual relationships with host families, the effects of foreign students on members of the community, or the community as a whole, have been widespread or of significant or continuing depth. In most instances, the residential community of the foreign student is the campus. The community provides opportunities for extracurricular events or experiences, friendly interest on the part of families or organizations who, in most cases, tend to be already internationally predisposed, and occasional invitations by some civic associations to selected foreign students to address them. The results of such visits have not been well researched and in overall perspective seem to have been, with exceptions, modest. The residue in the foreign student seems to exceed the residue in the host family or community.

Little systematic use has been made of foreign students as information and teaching resources for schools and colleges in the area or region. One of the significant exceptions is the so-called "Ogontz Plan for Mutual International Education" of Philadelphia, now in its fifteenth year, administered by a voluntary committee, which, in cooperation with community organizations, arranges systematically planned visits by selected foreign students to elementary and secondary schools as a purposeful cooperative supplement to their teaching curricula. As one release notes: "A pupil maturing through 12 years of Ogontz Plan cooperation will have the opportunity to meet people from 50 to 60 different countries under conditions that supplement formal learning." The purpose has been to evolve constructive intercultural attitudes through the planned interaction of American pupils, teachers, community, and foreign students in classroom situations and environments. Available evaluations indicate considerable success in broadening and motivating the pupils and teachers involved. In recent years, attempts have been made to expand the program to other areas. What the longer-term effects have been is not known.

During their sojourn, some foreign students avail themselves of the privilege of writing letters to the editors of local, regional, or national newspapers, or publish articles, often related to foreign policy and/or problems of their home region. They thus insert additional perspectives into the general discourse, as well as test their own ability to participate as active agents in the discussion of policies, in the education of the public, and in the exercise of initiative. There is no research that has assessed the effect of such communications, in specific cases or in more cumulative terms.

## IMPACT ON INTERNATIONAL RELATIONS

The realm of international relations is probably the most difficult and most complex of the effect areas considered. Earlier studies, particularly those following the end of World War II, have tended to focus on, expect, and in instances find evidence of a growth in "international understanding," of knowledge about each other, of inter-individual friendships; and, not unnaturally, they have invested much faith and hope in their ramifications for international cooperation and peace. Seldom, however, was "international understanding" operationally defined and then tested and followed up in action.

The Cold War largely swerved this orientation toward a competitive "struggle for the minds of men," with the support and assessment of its effects and results becoming a major preoccupation of government as well as researchers. Major concern in impact studies centered on the extent and ramifications of positive attitudes toward the host country, presumably generated by the sojourn, endowing them with political significance, and using them as justifications for continued support of exchange and training programs by the international affairs agencies of the United States government. Yet, while the attitudes toward the sojourn and the educational experience were, on the whole, consistently appreciative and Americans as persons were "liked" and cherished, there obtained, in study after study, with some fluctuations, considerable criticism of specific United States foreign policies and of certain features of United States societal practice (discrimination, social welfare, level of cultural life, ignorance of other societies, and so forth).

The wave of political emancipations between 1958 and the present has redirected attention to the role of foreign study in manpower development, in open society institution-building, and in socioeconomic modernization. A considerable array of studies indicate that these training programs in overall perspective have been effective and that they have strengthened the viability and prospects for stability in many of the new nations. While the issue is much too large to be contained in any one statement, the frequent claim about the crucial role of training abroad, while never studied on a wider global, regional, or even comprehensive national depth level, appears defensible.

"Change of attitude" studies abound. It can be viewed as established that foreign students, as a result of their sojourn, "change." The evidence further indicates that they perceive themselves to have changed for "the better" in knowledge, personal and professional

competence, self-assuredness, and in a sense of enhanced resourcefulness, effectiveness, and ambition. These changes and their consequences in fields of their activities at home represent valued achievements.

As mentioned before, there is also convincing evidence that, at least in the realm of attitudes, ex-foreign students have acquired a more realistic perspective on their former host society, and with it a more analytical and differentiated capacity to view their own, as well as other societies in socio-historico-economic and not primarily in ideological or idealized terms. This, too, represents an input of potential consequence.

Largely neglected as an aspect of continuing impacts are the results of relationships among foreign students on the same campus or in the same city. While research is scarce, it seems that, other than where official hostility divides nations, contacts among foreign students across national lines, but particularly within regional and civilizational groupings, are much more extensive and intensive than with American students. There is informal evidence that these interchanges lead to considerable mutual learning, that they heighten the degree of politicization in many, and that, in many cases, they result in relationships of friendship and cooperation that continue long after the return of ex-foreign students to different countries within the common region. Memoirs of older nationalist leaders (Nkrumah, Azikiwe) indicate that it was during their studies abroad that they developed a perspective on, and a determination for, the emancipation of their countries and the common interests of their regions. It may be that the inadequate state of research on this aspect of study abroad conceals a potentially most important and crucial set of effects.

How do these relate to "international understanding," cooperation, and peace? We have studies on attitudes, stereotypes, links—but how these relate to action, public behavior, or the exercise of influence within the constraints of national and international circumstances has not been adequately researched, is difficult to probe, and has only unsystematically become part of knowledge or hypotheses.

The most fruitful approaches in this regard are those of Kelman—especially the concluding chapter in his *International Behavior*—of Robert Angell in his *Peace on the March*, of the Useems and their concept of "the Third Culture," and of Marshall Singer in one chapter of his *Weak States in a World of Powers*.

While in earlier analyses cooperation seemed to be a matter of option, this is no longer so in a rapidly ingrowing and interlinked world. The infusion into almost all societies of internationally trained modern professionals, technicians, teachers, analysts, managers, and public servants who speak one of the international languages makes it practicable for the first time in human history to engage on a worldwide scale in coordinate, rather than superior-inferior, cooperative ventures; to negotiate within frameworks of commensurate competencies and complementarily understood principles and logics; to subscribe to joint criteria of evidence and performance; and to make feasible the many bi-, multi-, and international programs by the growing availability of counterpart personnel and leaderships, from almost all nations in our radically transformed world.

If—beyond the personal and human growth of the ex-foreign students involved, the greater sophistication in their perceptions and attitudes, the as yet profoundly inadequate impact they have been able to exert on their host institutions and communities, the professional, intercultural, and modernist influences they have exercised and shall increasingly cumulatively exercise on their own developing and isolation-transcending societies—study abroad has facilitated the achievements sketched in the preceding paragraph, then it would seem to have justified in good part both the investment and the effort. Despite the absence of solid and conclusive macro-level research, it might yet justify the faith, too.

*Kindly mention* THE ANNALS *when writing to advertisers*

# Book Department

## INTERNATIONAL RELATIONS AND POLITICAL THOUGHT

NISSIM BAR-YAACOV. *The Handling of International Disputes by Means of Inquiry.* Pp. viii, 370. New York: Oxford University Press, 1974. $24.00.

MANUS I. MIDLARSKY. *On War: Political Violence in the International System.* Pp. ix, 229. New York: The Free Press, 1975. $14.95.

The two volumes reviewed here demonstrate the wide variety of inquiry that remains legitimate in international politics today. Bar-Yaacov, of the Hebrew University of Jerusalem, has written a "traditional" book that reviews one method employed in the settlement of international disputes: inquiry. Presenting a historical and theoretical analysis of the institution of international inquiry since its creation at the First Hague Peace Conference in 1899, the author compares and contrasts inquiry and other mechanisms for dealing with disputes, such as conciliation. The bulk of the book deals with detailed studies of specific instances of inquiry or conciliation in the twentieth century.

In contrast, Manus Midlarsky, of the University of Colorado at Boulder, has written a highly theoretical and provoca-tive essay about war and political violence in the international system. His inquiry is an investigation of the circumstances under which political violence—internationally, regionally, and domestically—is most probable as well as those factors which most influence the intensity and the duration of conflict. Employing empirical data drawn from the war experience of more than 100 nation-states between 1815 and 1945, Midlarsky's volume places him in the ranks of J. David Singer, James Rosenau, Raymond Tanter and others who explore highly theoretical and empirically based analyses of the causes of war and the conditions for peace in the international system.

Reminiscent of Kenneth Waltz' three levels of analysis approach in *Man, the State and War,* but very clearly rejecting the "image" of the individual, Midlarsky focuses on the international system, within the individual nation-state, and within the boundary of state and system. He defines power as the ability to effect a reduction of environmental uncertainty and poses a series of provocative and disturbing questions about political conflict at the international level. Do alliances encourage or deter war? Do differences in structural power relationships make a difference in promoting conflict or peace?

Exploring the diffusion of political instability across national borders and the inconsistency between internationally ascribed and internally achieved national status, the author speculates about the role of peacekeeping organizations and the impact of *coups d'etat* in neighboring states. He concludes that the concepts of power limitations and social disorganization in the international system, as well as the status inconsistency of nation-states, explain the frequency of war.

While not sanguine about the probability of avoiding war in the new multipolar international order, Midlarsky believes that boundary maintenance and eventual complete systemic development, rather than peace through national development, may yield more successful peace-making efforts.

The avoidance of political violence in the international system—not its origins—is the concern of the inquiry process. Bar-Yaacov is relatively hopeful that the potential of international inquiry —as separate from conciliation—is improving. The shortcomings of the United Nations, and a growing awareness of the impact of violence in the international system, make the inquiry method particularly appropriate "for disputes which, although creating tensions, are unlikely to lead to hostilities" (p. 327). While the author's optimism may be justified in the instance of the case studies considered in his volume, none of which can be classified as major threats to international peace, inquiry will remain a limited and relatively marginal procedure in the settlement of major political conflicts in the international system.

Midlarsky's book is a welcome and stimulating analysis of a central theme in the study of the international system. Bar-Yaacov's volume will provide a useful reference on a relatively secondary aspect of international relations that will continue to be appropriate in very specific circumstances. The limitations of the process of inquiry again reaffirm the importance of current research on the causes of war and the prospects for peace in the international system.

RIORDAN ROETT
The Johns Hopkins University
School of Advanced International
  Studies
Washington, D.C.

SIR GEORGE CATLIN. *Kissinger's Atlantic Charter.* Pp. 144. Totowa, N.J.: Rowman and Littlefield, 1975. $12.00.

J. ROBERT SCHAETZEL. *The Unhinged Alliance: America and the European Community.* Pp. v, 184. New York: Harper & Row, 1975. $8.95.

There is a certain superficial similarity between Catlin's and Schaetzel's goals. Both are attempting to find means of improving European-American relations as a result of an analysis of the crisis in those relations and of a probe into the historical origins of the crisis. Catlin's superficial ruminations, based apparently upon a generation of conversation on the fringes of power, are a disservice to the cause he wishes to further. Schaetzel's analysis, the result of six years as American Ambassador to the European Communities, is deeply informed, temperately argued, and constructive in its proposals.

The flavor of Catlin's book is evident in his summation of Watergate which, he claims, "turned on the traditional quarrel about Presidential power and privilege and on the ambitions of an incompetent Congress and of an arrogant and highly irresponsible Press (p. 84). . . . What is at fault is a complete lack of sense of proportion in holding a balance. There is a masochism about all things sad and deplorable—which is the typical American vice—catered for by the flagellations of the unspeakable." Such judgments are not only curious in themselves but especially so in a writer who wants to cement an Atlantic Community. Catlin puts forward three main arguments. Britain should not enter the European Community but seek to preserve its special relationship with the

Commonwealth. The form of European union envisaged by forward-looking thinkers like Robert Schuman has been sabotaged irretrievably by the French themselves, and especially by de Gaulle. A new effort should be made to create an Atlantic Community which would include Australasia as well as selected parts of the European continent. The British referendum on EEC membership has repudiated the denigrators' claim to speak for the majority of the British public. French pressure for such common policies as agriculture and Third World relations is universally recognized to have been significant in forcing the Community members into closer economic integration. Hope for an Atlantic Community that would draw the United States into fresh commitments on the far sides of both the Atlantic and Pacific oceans is dead in the aftermath of the war in Vietnam.

Schaetzel argues convincingly that American interest lies in aiding the development of the European Community through specific, modest steps. In the larger sense, he explains the erosion of American understanding of the European Community as due to the inability of people in the United States, officials and public alike, to handle economic and political questions simultaneously. Political perceptions have warped economic, and vice versa. "After twenty years this problem of communication between the political and economic cultures remains largely unresolved." In the immediate sense, he finds the Nixon administration guilty of exacerbating European-American relations by omission and commission. After four years of ignoring Europe, the renewed approach was abrasive and overbearing. Connally and Stans in particular exemplified the inability of Nixon appointees to avoid creating antagonism among European negotiators (pp. 56, 119). But the preference of both Nixon and Kissinger for bilateralism made it difficult for them to deal effectively with the Community rather than with its individual members. Under Rodgers, the State Department "drifted on its own odyssey to irrelevance."

To remedy this situation, Schaetzel makes some concrete proposals. In economics, he argues that the United States should avoid the role of spoiler as EEC develops a common industrial policy. It should encourage, for example, the establishment of Community standards by collaborating with expert working parties in Brussels. Common action should be considered regarding multinational corporations. Trade relations might be bettered by a series of small package deals on specific products. Political relations, Schaetzel suggests, require the establishment of an informal cabinet level committee, including the American Secretary of State, the president of the European Commission, and the president of the Community Council of Ministers. There is hope for the American-European relationship, he concludes; but the work of restoring it to health will be long and very hard.

F. ROY WILLIS
University of California
Davis

ROBIN EDMONDS. *Soviet Foreign Policy, 1962–1973: The Paradox of Super Power.* Pp. xiv, 197. New York: Oxford University Press, 1975. $12.50.

This short book provides a useful summary of Soviet foreign policy from the Cuban Missile Crisis until the signing of the Soviet-American Agreement on the Prevention of Nuclear War in June, 1973. Edmonds (former Minister at the British Embassy in Moscow and now Assistant Under-Secretary of State, Foreign and Commonwealth Office) sees these two limiting events of his study as particularly significant, the first as the apex of the cold war, when the two superpowers almost stumbled into hot war, and the second as evidence of the fact that "the cold war was over."

The task that the author sets for himself is to determine what exactly has changed in the Soviet-American relationship over this period and why. Have both Soviet and American foreign policies been altered? Or is it only American foreign policy that has changed, with the predatory, expansionist Soviet foreign policy basically unaltered behind a facade of peaceful coexistence? Edmonds comes in the end to reject the latter view, arguing that not only are Brezhnev and others committed to a basic change in foreign policy but that their successors for some time to come will be bound by détente policy too.

But if this is a reasonable conclusion to reach, and Edmonds persuasively states this viewpoint in the final section, "The Future of Soviet Foreign Policy," it is not at all clear that he has supported his conclusion in the dozen or so chapters that form the central part of the book. The reason for this is not so much the ground the author has covered: as stated, his review of Soviet foreign policy during the period is basically sound. But the structure of the central portion of the book allows the reader (and the author?) easily to lose sight of the basic themes being examined. The basic approach of the book is a chronological review of events; in the heart of the book this degenerates into a series of short chapters, each dealing with a single year. Thus, rather than getting a single over-all analysis of Soviet-European relations for the crucial years 1970–1973 one gets yearly treatments of the subject, each averaging three-and-one-half pages, in four separate chapters. And in each of these chapters Soviet relations with other parts of the world, Asia, the Middle East, China, are also covered. This segmented approach to analysis requires the reader to provide whatever continuity he can for the review of events. To some extent this same problem mars the whole book: the author has eighteen chapters and about 180 pages of text and notes. This hardly facilitates easy arrival at answers to some of the basic questions he poses.

The author demonstrates good knowledge of the writings of Lenin, and is obviously at home in Soviet history and foreign policy. He appears to be on less sure ground in economics and internal politics, and his chapters dealing with these subjects suffer by comparison. But they do at least demonstrate the vital link between internal and external politics, a matter which many treatises on Soviet foreign policy tend to ignore. Edmonds is at his best at the end of the book where he departs from the chronological approach. Here he strongly supports the view that national interests, not ideology, determine Soviet foreign policy. The latter, he says, "is at most only slightly distorted by the lens of Marxism-Leninism." More important, he comes very close to predicting that the new generation of Soviet leaders, free from the taint of Stalinism, will be more liberal. Lacking any guilt of the Stalin period, they "may feel able to allow some fresh air, and with it some new ideas, into the Soviet Union." Sheer speculation, of course, but interesting; and not inconsistent with his view about the long-term Soviet commitment to détente.

DONALD D. BARRY
Lehigh University
Bethlehem
Pennsylvania

GALVIN KENNEDY. *The Economics of Defense.* Pp. 251. Totowa, N.J.: Rowman and Littlefield, 1975. $17.50.

This book considers world defense spending, national defense planning, the impact of military spending, disarmament, and many other controversial issues. Although the book studies global defense issues, it concentrates on Great Britain and the United States. It is the first study of defense written by a British economist in some years.

Several chapters deal with defense planning and budgeting utilizing the tools of economic analysis. However, the more interesting discussion in the book revolves around the need or justification for defense spending in the world. Conflicting viewpoints on defense expenditures in economic thought from Adam Smith through Keynes are traced in an early chapter. Kennedy admits that his work concentrates on Smith's view that defense is a necessity and should be done efficiently. He contends that the level of defense spending seems to be a function of the perception of the nature and extent of threats to a country. Military aid to countries such as those of the Middle East is not necessarily responsible for the international conflict. Kennedy maintains that it is not the access to weapons that promotes tension; the accumulation of weapons is a consequence of that tension, not the cause.

Kennedy specifically attacks the Marxian theory of capitalist crisis (Mandel, Kidron) which alleges dependence upon armament production for economic survival. The book statistically discloses that defense expenditures for typical capitalist nations have actually been a declining portion of public expenditure programs since 1956. Kennedy finds it incredulous to believe that stability could only be maintained by high levels of "unproductive" defense expenditures since the defense budget is only a small proportion of GNP in many capitalist countries (that is, the British defense budget represents 4.6 percent of GNP). Furthermore, if a deduction of wages and allowances is made for military personnel (whose incomes are no different from other social servants), the economic impact of defense budgets would be cut approximately in half.

The author finds the concept of a military-industrial complex to be an exaggeration. He presents data indicating that only a minority of corporations (mainly aerospace) are dependent on defense work to any degree. In fact, 33 of the largest 50 corporations in the U.S. have less than 5 percent of their sales in defense contracts. In the long run, he believes the balance of power lies with the government rather than with the defense contractors.

Kennedy defends sales to the Third World by suggesting that the donor country has little diversion of resource inputs since the armaments were probably produced in previous periods, and that military aid may be the only way the recipient nation would have access to advanced technology.

The views in the last chapter on dis-

armament may be predicted by the reader in relation to the context of the previous arguments. Kennedy sees general and complete disarmament with the experience of history as utopian; however, he is less pessimistic about partial disarmament. On the economic side, if defense expenditures were abolished, he asserts there would be more than enough alternative spending programs to replace defense expenditures. Kennedy submits, "There is no economic reason why aggregate demand should be composed of one set of activities as opposed to another in industrial economies." Defense expenditures are a political necessity, not an economic requirement.

The book is a useful addition to a continuing controversy in economic and political theory. Kennedy has utilized extensive references and documentation which add credibility to his arguments. However, the book may lend itself to criticism because of the author's attempt to defend almost every aspect of present defense programs and expenditures. In my opinion, he has expended too much time defending existing defense spending and has not given enough consideration to the possible benefits to society from a redirection of economic resources. Kennedy's views on several issues seem to be as onesided as his characterization of the Marxian view. Overall, it is a serious work worthy of careful consideration by those with divergent opinions on defense spending.

RUSSELL P. BELLICO
Westfield State College
Massachusetts

LEONARD KRIEGER. *An Essay on the Theory of Enlightened Despotism.* Pp. xi, 115. Chicago, Ill.: The University of Chicago Press, 1975. $9.25.

This short work attempts to clarify the idea of "enlightened despotism" as historically articulated in the eighteenth century. Whatever claims the concept of enlightened despotism has to be a political theory, were put forward in the main by French Physiocrats and certain Austrian and German Cameralists. Enlightened despotism, as Professor Krieger points out, was not only a logically defective theory, it was something more. Namely, it was the ad hoc rhetoric of central and eastern European monarchs responding to political exigency and, exclaiming their own idiosyncratic self-justifications—echoes of which were heard in America not too long ago.

One wonders, however, about the status of enlightened despotism as a theory. It was flawed as theory, the author suggests, because it embraced the contradictions of the human situation, although it is not explained why such contradictions necessarily make theory implausible. The impression is left that enlightened despotism is not really a theory, not simply because it was the handiwork of essentially minor league thinkers, but because Professor Krieger does not adequately identify it as a genus of rule. This may be allowable form for the purposes of intellectual history, but does not suffice for a political theory concerned with the structure and substance of ideas.

Nevertheless, this is a work of considerable but contestable subtlety. The most provocative thesis is that the thinking which gave rise to the idea of enlightened despotism was the same which subsequently helped reconcile absolutism and constitutionalism. This mentality manifested itself when it was duly recognized that the individual good was a distinguishable factor in the common good, but given the traditional tensions of politics, made a definition of the common good which could accommodate multiple individual interests, politically impossible. Yet, whether absolutism was actually reconciled with constitutionalism, is more easily asserted than proved. No doubt constitutionalism has at times facilitated the tyrannical exercise of power. But to view modern constitutionalism as a successor form of enlightened despotism, appears to be the fault of dealing too casually with categories of rule.

Still Professor Krieger does well in showing how a concern with the structure of government could be converted by monarchs claiming both power and knowledge, into governmental authority at odds with the impetus and rationale of constitutionalism.

A thoughtful book probing the critical antimonies of political life is always to be welcomed. If only the text of this one did not read as if it were untranslated from the German, that welcome in this instance could be more wholehearted.

PAUL L. ROSEN
Carleton University
Ottawa
Canada

STOCKHOLM INTERNATIONAL PEACE RESEARCH INSTITUTE. *Nuclear Proliferation Problems.* Pp. 312. Cambridge, Mass.: MIT Press, 1974. No price.

STOCKHOLM INTERNATIONAL PEACE RESEARCH INSTITUTE. *Safeguards against Nuclear Proliferation.* Pp. 114. Cambridge, Mass.: MIT Press, 1974. No price.

STOCKHOLM INTERNATIONAL PEACE RESEARCH INSTITUTE. *Tactical and Strategic Antisubmarine Warfare.* Pp. 148. Cambridge, Mass.: MIT Press, 1974. No price.

The study of arms control has become fashionable, but too little of the product has demonstrated the technical mastery of the subject shown in these three books under review. Indeed the Stockholm International Peace Research Institute (SIPRI) sets something of an international standard in this respect, issuing under its imprimature serious compilations of data and usually restrained essays derived from them. One scarcely needs reminders these days of the dangers inherent in the proliferation of nuclear weapons. Newspapers and public statements, at least in the West, are replete with the horrors in store if safeguards in the dispersal of nuclear material prove insufficient, if more regional powers attain nuclear status, and so on. Usually lacking, however, is any attempt to disaggregate the problem into its components, before which no serious consideration can be given to alternative remedies. Decrying a problem does not solve it, nor does it create the political will even for trying. The first step is some technical knowledge of the issues, and this is something undertaken in these three books.

*Tactical and Strategic Antisubmarine Warfare* is a short and much needed exposition on antisubmarine warfare, for the most part comprehensible to the lay audience. "SLBM forces remain the most stable component of deterrence in the foreseeable future," as is noted (p. 46); given which the dearth of material available is surprising.

*Safeguards against Nuclear Proliferation* makes the important point that all International Atomic Energy Agency safeguards "are as much measures to prevent or deter the proliferation of nuclear weapons as are the safeguards applied pursuant to the Treaty on the Non-Proliferation of Nuclear Weapons (NPT)" (p. 2). The volume makes little attempt to hide the principal problem: the "enforceability" of control measures "is open to some doubt" (p. 9).

By far the longest volume is *Nuclear Proliferation Problems*, a compilation of essays ranging in subject from nuclear fuel fabrication to nongovernmental nuclear weapon proliferation. The approach is in most cases analytical. In discussing terrorist threats, for example, Mason Willrich makes an important distinction between the international safeguards needed to detect "governmentally authorized diversion" and the national safeguards to prevent "unlawful" diversion (p. 168), and organizes the discussion accordingly.

One exception to the serious tone of the volume should be noted. A. N. Kaliadin's essay on the security of non-nuclear states and non-proliferation is a polemic, causing one to regret anew that most of the serious discussions of nuclear matters with a view of arms control take place, very unsymmetrically, in the West. "The NPT, despite its limitations, has inhibited the proliferation of nuclear weapons, while pressure for nuclear-weapon use has lessened due to factors such as the realization (in Vietnam) of the futility of imperialism. . . . The non-nuclear nations have demonstrated that they are in a position to uphold successfully their

national rights . . . and to counter effectively any imperialist military encroachments" (pp. 228–31).

A series of case studies on the "almost nuclear" powers (and one that has since "gone nuclear," India) underline the point that the critical perspective from which proliferation must be seen is not the interests of "greater humanity" but of those nation-states that must decide whether their security interests require an atomic arsenal. With possession of the bomb for better or worse a prerequisite of great-power status, and with ethnic conflict and resource-competition rising, it is small wonder (if regrettable) that the nuclear option is taken seriously. Indeed the painful conclusion from reading these pages is that the only countries with a serious interest in non-proliferation are those already armed with nuclear weapons, and those with no chance of ever so doing.

W. SCOTT THOMPSON
The Fletcher School of Law and
  Diplomacy
Tufts University
Medford
Massachusetts

THOMAS GEORGE WEISS. *International Bureaucracy.* Pp. vii, 187. Lexington, Mass.: Lexington Books, 1975. $14.00.

Though the topic of Weiss's book (problems of international bureaucracies, especially United Nations Secretariats) is both timely and very relevant, this study is riddled with contradictions and confusion. Weiss has succeeded in reflecting rather than dissecting the monstrous maze of political and organizational difficulties confronting practitioners and observers of international administration.

The major aim set forth by Weiss is to examine the "working hypothesis" that, ". . . the unwieldy administrative structures of functional secretariats are counterproductive to the idealistic goals that they have been created to pursue. International institutions fail to achieve their stated welfare goals and to further global interests . . . primarily because of the process by which resources are allocated." This statement actually turns out to be an assertion doggedly supported by a broad spectrum of evidence with little regard for validity. His information ranges from statements by important officials and a few basic documented statistics to a highly tenuous use of crude budgetary data, quotes from impromptu hallway conversations with unnamed officials whose views may or may not be representative of anyone, and thirdhand guesstimates of the efficiency of international organizations from the *New York Times*. Moreover, assertions are often made without supporting evidence.

After a brief review of international functionalist and new-functionalist theory, Weiss dismisses both primarily because they do not, in his view, espouse the global welfare goals necessary for a more "equal" distribution of the world's resources. Weiss goes on to examine the "conventional paradigm" as compared with the "reality" of the international civil service and identifies several already well-known problems, some of which are neither "structural" nor "internal" to an international secretariat. Then, after briefly presenting case material, especially on the ILO and UNICEF, several unwarranted comparative conclusions are drawn and a number of administrative reforms are suggested. For instance, Weiss notes UNICEF is smaller and more decentralized than the ILO. With sparse evidence, in twelve pages Weiss is able to conclude that the differences in size and decentralization explain why UNICEF is more flexible and therefore able to respond to global functional needs better than the ILO. However, this relationship is greatly obscured when Weiss introduces other factors such as: (1) the inherent universal nature of UNICEF's predominantly humanitarian goals, (2) an existing consensus among nation-states regarding those goals, and (3) the perceptions and attitudes of secretariat leadership. It is not clear whether greater achievement of global welfare is due to structural characteristics of a secretariat, any one of the three factors mentioned above, or some combination. Thus, the suggestion that smaller and more decentralized secre-

tariats are better suited for the achievement of global welfare goals is not supported by the analysis. Furthermore, Weiss makes no attempt to reconcile this suggested reform with his support for task expansion which may be directly correlated with increases in organizational size.

Two classic weaknesses apparently account for most of the confusion. The first is the inability of the author to separate descriptive analysis from what seems to be a deeply ingrained prescriptive framework. For example, when neo-functionalism is considered simultaneously as a descriptive theory and a prescriptive formula for action, sound objective analysis suffers. While neo-functionalists find support for the proposition that the external political climate constrains functional secretariats, Weiss rejects this factor not on the basis of careful analysis but because such an explanation is ". . . a fatalistic response that vitiates incentives to reform through immediate action." Thus, because his a priori action framework focuses only on internal structural reform, other factors which may be of equal or greater importance are rejected because of a prescriptive bias.

The second major source of confusion is the old problem of shifting levels of analysis. Though Weiss starts by committing himself to a structural analysis of international secretariats as analytical units, he ends up examining the external political context, small groups within secretariats, and individual perceptions and attitudes of secretariat leadership. Thus, he is able to lump suggested changes in the perceptions and attitudes of individual leaders with other "structural" reforms. A more comprehensive conceptual framework free of these restrictive normative assumptions seems imperative in order to avoid such confusion.

Yet perhaps this book should be carefully read. By providing a convenient and concentrated collection of the problems and confusion which is typical of the study of international administration, Weiss may inadvertently stimulate a more constructive approach. If so, then

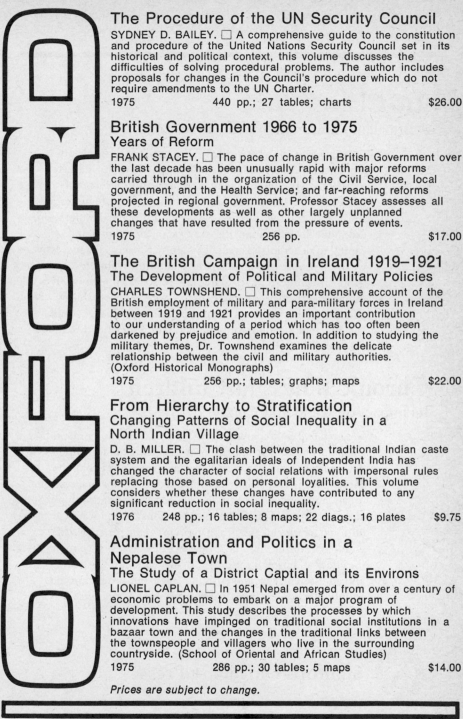

# The Procedure of the UN Security Council

SYDNEY D. BAILEY. ☐ A comprehensive guide to the constitution and procedure of the United Nations Security Council set in its historical and political context, this volume discusses the difficulties of solving procedural problems. The author includes proposals for changes in the Council's procedure which do not require amendments to the UN Charter.

1975        440 pp.; 27 tables; charts        $26.00

# British Government 1966 to 1975
## Years of Reform

FRANK STACEY. ☐ The pace of change in British Government over the last decade has been unusually rapid with major reforms carried through in the organization of the Civil Service, local government, and the Health Service; and far-reaching reforms projected in regional government. Professor Stacey assesses all these developments as well as other largely unplanned changes that have resulted from the pressure of events.

1975        256 pp.        $17.00

# The British Campaign in Ireland 1919–1921
## The Development of Political and Military Policies

CHARLES TOWNSHEND. ☐ This comprehensive account of the British employment of military and para-military forces in Ireland between 1919 and 1921 provides an important contribution to our understanding of a period which has too often been darkened by prejudice and emotion. In addition to studying the military themes, Dr. Townshend examines the delicate relationship between the civil and military authorities. (Oxford Historical Monographs)

1975        256 pp.; tables; graphs; maps        $22.00

# From Hierarchy to Stratification
## Changing Patterns of Social Inequality in a North Indian Village

D. B. MILLER. ☐ The clash between the traditional Indian caste system and the egalitarian ideals of Independent India has changed the character of social relations with impersonal rules replacing those based on personal loyalties. This volume considers whether these changes have contributed to any significant reduction in social inequality.

1976    248 pp.; 16 tables; 8 maps; 22 diags.; 16 plates    $9.75

# Administration and Politics in a Nepalese Town
## The Study of a District Captial and its Environs

LIONEL CAPLAN. ☐ In 1951 Nepal emerged from over a century of economic problems to embark on a major program of development. This study describes the processes by which innovations have impinged on traditional social institutions in a bazaar town and the changes in the traditional links between the townspeople and villagers who live in the surrounding countryside. (School of Oriental and African Studies)

1975        286 pp.; 30 tables; 5 maps        $14.00

*Prices are subject to change.*

 OXFORD UNIVERSITY PRESS
200 MADISON AVENUE
NEW YORK, N.Y. 10016

*Kindly mention* THE ANNALS *when writing to advertisers*

# Rio Claro
## A Brazilian Plantation System, 1820-1920

*Warren Dean.* Nowhere were the economic and social consequences of Brazil's dominance in the world coffee market more intensely contested than in the agricultural center of Rio Claro: land expropriation and the founding of huge estates, slave labor and the abolition of slavery, European immigration, economic diversification, the steady transfer of labor and capital to richer inland areas. This study concerns the successive waves of people who made up the plantation's labor force, from African-born slaves to free laborers and immigrants. It illuminates the basic character of the system—profitability, efficiency, labor relations, local and national influence—and has direct implications for other plantation societies throughout the world. $11.50

# Chronic Illness in Children
## Its Impact on Child and Family

*Georgia Travis.* Prepared expressly for students and practitioners in the human services, this comprehensive guide examines the medical realities and psychosocial impact of 13 common chronic disorders (such as leukemia, sickle cell anemia, cystic fibrosis, and congenital heart disease) on family relationships and on the mental life of the child. Sections on symptoms, outlook, treatment, and problems in pregnancy were written with medical consultation. Other sections discuss such topics as the effects of hospitalization, the dying child, family stress and adjustment, care and crisis management, foster care and adoption, schooling, personality development and socialization, finances, and public services. $19.50

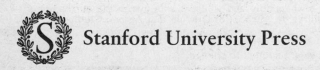 **Stanford University Press**

this book may contribute as a sort of negative catalyst.

MICHAEL E. AKINS
University of Pennsylvania
Philadelphia

## AFRICA, ASIA AND LATIN AMERICA

GARY D. ALLINSON. *Japanese Urbanism: Industry and Politics in Kariya, 1872–1972.* Pp. xiii, 276. Berkeley: University of California Press, 1975. $16.75.

Twentieth century Japan has experienced a scale and pace of urbanization that is remarkable not only in Asia but also in the modern world. In the brief span of fifty years that separated the 1920s from the 1970s Japan was transformed from a society of rural agriculturalists, which comprised more than 80 percent of the Japanese population in 1920, to an urban industrial society in which more than 80 percent of her population now lives in cities.

This book represents the first systematic attempt to inquire into the nature and effects of the urbanization process in a small Japanese city, Kariya, over the century from 1872 to 1972. The results include some important new insights into the relationship of industrial expansion to Japanese urban growth and the peculiar manner in which Japanese cultural and political forces attempted to deal with the rapidly changing urban environment.

The author traces the development of Kariya from a small, rustic feudal castletown in the early Meiji period to a dynamic, industrial city of ninety thousand which now serves as a center for several major firms in the Toyota complex. The historical focus concentrates on three periods: the years from the 1870s to the 1920s during which the city remained largely a commercial settlement in an agrarian countryside; the period from 1920 to 1945 during which the city underwent rapid industrial expansion; and the period from 1946 to 1972 during which the city moved from initial postwar stagnation to extensive new economic growth as part of Japan's vigorous industrial recovery.

The history of Kariya, as the author makes amply clear, is intricately related to the history of the Toyota firm. It was Toyota's decision in 1922 to locate its new textile plant in Kariya that brought "industrialism" to what had been a small urban community desperately trying to integrate itself into the national economy that emerged with the Meiji Restoration. It was Toyota's transformation in the 1940s and 1950s from a minor textiles manufacturer to a heavy industrial complex concentrating on the automotive sector that brought the second industrial revolution to Kariya.

Although this book tells us a good deal about the development of the Toyota enterprises and contains much useful information about one of Japan's leading industrial houses, the author's chief purpose is to use Toyota and Kariya in order to analyze the broader social and political consequences of industrialization in the Japanese city. Professor Allinson is consequently interested in patterns of leadership, the community and company power structure, changes in political organization, and the nature of local social values. All of these are explored in considerable detail.

The author's findings in reference to such questions confirm the high degree of Japanese social cohesion that has served to cushion the shocks of rapid and potentially disruptive economic change. He demonstrates that Kariya's "heritage of social values"—as he likes to refer to them in distinction to "traditional values"—served the community well by permitting gradual and orderly change.

This work is an important contribution and deserves attention from those interested in a comparative approach to urban and political development.

F. G. NOTEHELFER
University of California
Los Angeles

LEWIS AUSTIN. *Saints and Samurai: The Political Culture of the American and Japanese Elites.* Pp. vii, 197. New Haven, Conn.: Yale University Press, 1975. $12.50.

This is probably the Ph.D. thesis work of Professor Austin, who contrasts the social attitudes of Japanese and American government and business leaders—the 42 Japanese filled out their questionnaires in 1969 and the 42 Americans in a Yale alumni reunion meeting in 1972. Austin admits in the appendix containing the questionnaire and pictorial tests that the samples are too small to be representative of the elites and not randomly chosen but the contrasts between the individually-oriented Americans who always stress achievement and individual advancement and the Japanese who stress congenial social behavior are enough to show how different the two societies are.

Austin stresses first the hierarchical relationships in the two elites, with many comparative questions on, for example, "What is a good leader?" and "How should a leader treat his subordinates?" in which the two samples differ largely in terms of the achievement versus personality congeniality patterns mentioned above. Dozens of tables give the comparative results to sets of questions on leader treatment of followers; peer relationships; how to handle misunderstandings or insults; how to regard the job compared with life itself or family relationships; and Austin concludes with a brilliant final chapter summing up how these psychological tests and social perceptions relate to the broader issues of American-Japanese relations.

Americans tend to be individually-oriented, anxious for personal success and willing to compete aggressively for advancement, whereas Japanese value social cohesion and consensus and the need to avoid conflict as much as possible. Again, one cannot generalize too much because in a Japanese society of 110 million and an American society almost twice as large and much more diverse, many exceptions to the generalizations made here will be found. Also, the age and elite status of the informants do not include any generational contrasts which are very notable in both societies, although more so in the United States. The work ethic, which Austin correctly stresses as exemplified in his sample's identification of a job with life itself—unity of career and leisure, whereas Americans tend to separate the two—is far more retained by youthful Japanese than by their American counterparts.

The chapters 2 through 6 give all the results of the written questionnaire, and chapter 7 ("The Persistence of Tradition") notes the broader social and international significance of the cultural differences. For example, Japan was very shocked by the failure of the Nixon Administration to consult it before the 1971 approach to Peking, and also by the temporary suspension of soybean sales to Japan. Japanese expect partners or allies to consult before making decisions that affect the other, as they do as individuals, and Austin properly advises any ally of Japan to keep in closer touch and listen to her reactions or criticisms. Japanese avoid confrontation at an elite level, but they do expect peer consultation and also superior-subordinate consultation as is seen in replies to several questions on how peers and men in a hierarchy should settle disagreements over policy.

In this sense, the Austin book despite its data limits provides a good insight into the ways in which Americans and Japanese often misunderstand each other at the elite, business, or governmental levels. Further studies are needed to elaborate and expand on this one, and to extend the analysis to different age groups and social levels within the two cultures. But Austin has given us a challenging set of hypotheses that fit in with other types of studies of the two cultures and life-styles, and others should apply them to different kinds of people.

DOUGLAS H. MENDEL, JR.
University of Wisconsin
Milwaukee

RALPH N. CLOUGH, A. DOAK BARNETT, MORTON H. HALPERIN and JEROME H. KAHAN. *The United States, China, and Arms Control.* Pp. 153. Washington, D.C.: The Brookings Institution, 1975. $8.95. Paperbound, $2.95.

The Shanghai Communiqué, negotiated by Chou En-lai and Richard Nixon during the former president's much-publicized visit to China in February 1972, formally brought to an end two decades of mutual Sino-American hostility, and laid the foundation for a normalization of governmental relations by identifying guidelines for cooperation rather than conflict or confrontation in the relationship between the two countries. For both countries, the Shanghai Communiqué represented a virtual 180-degree turn in official policy. Détente with China required a fundamental reformulation of basic American attitudes toward the People's Republic. Having so long viewed China as threatening enemy, Americans were invited to consider the unfamiliar notion of China as friend—and even China as potential ally. Policy analysts were presented with a special challenge: how could the United States best cooperate with China? Given the opportunity finally to talk with the Chinese about prospective policies of mutual benefit, what might some constructive proposals be?

*The United States, China, and Arms Control* is one of the first concrete answers to that challenge. A joint effort by four Brookings Institution analysts (with the assistance of two others, Alton Quanbeck and Barry Blechman, who contributed an appendix on China's nuclear capability), this study focuses on arms control policy but frames its analyses and conclusions within the broader perspective of the entire bilateral relationship between the United States and China. Contained in this slim volume are an impressive number of separate interpretations and policy prescriptions, all based on a common set of assumptions and argued in terms of an integrated logic.

After spelling out their basic premises in the first several pages of the book, the authors distinguish between what they see to be "the tactical view" as opposed to "the strategic view" in Chinese foreign policy formulation. Arguing that the tactical perspective determines current Chinese policy, they observe that Peking's tactical posture is basically defensive—not aggressive or expansionist. Throughout their exposition, the authors

consistently take pains to relate their proposals regarding Sino-American relations to two assumed, paramount objectives in US policy: maintaining a close ally relationship with a non-nuclear-armed Japan; and being sure not to destabilize the American détente with the Soviet Union.

The Brookings analysts suggest that the United States initiate arms control discussions with China at a bilateral level in combination with negotiations focused on potentially mutual interests (for example, the neutralization of Southeast Asia) as a means of beginning a process which would culminate in Chinese participation in multilateral arms control negotiations. Their basic assumption is that the People's Republic of China is not interested in arms control agreements which would tend to freeze the present strategic situation in which China's weapons capabilities are vastly inferior to those of either the United States or the Soviet Union.

The study's main policy prescriptions are organized into four "packages," each of which is designed to develop a common Sino-American policy objective. Among these proposals are included: technical measures to prevent the accidental or unauthorized launching of nuclear weapons; an American no-first-use of nuclear weapons pledge; nuclear-free zones in East Asia; and procedures for involving China in existing multilateral arms control agreements. An important theme that runs through virtually all of the study's conclusions is that the United States must not become increasingly dependent upon nuclear weapons in its own defense posture. The authors' basic principle seems to be that, contrary to the old policy of "containing" China, security arrangements in East Asia today should be based on cooperating with the People's Republic in terms of common interests and mutual benefit.

I suspect that the Chinese Communists will be less than enthusiastic about many of these ideas since all of the book's proposals seem designed to stabilize the status quo in East Asia, often calling for a renunciation of the use of force on the Communist side in return for only modest concessions on the part of the United States. Yet for the Chinese, regional political stability may presently constitute a more important priority than revolutionary social change, especially when faced with Soviet efforts to expand its power into countries on the periphery of China under the guise of "collective security in Asia." Presumably, the Chinese reaction to the kind of American policy initiatives suggested by the Brookings study would provide something of an empirical test of which priorities were actually most important for China.

One major obstacle to Sino-American cooperation on arms control or virtually any other significant issue, which this study does not address, is the failure of the American government to take the final step in normalizing relations with China by granting the People's Republic full, formal recognition as the government of China. It is difficult to understand how the United States can hope to achieve greater cooperation in the Sino-American relationship if we persist in officially recognizing the exiled Kuomintang regime in Taiwan as the rightful government of China.

In sum, *The United States, China, and Arms Control* is a thoughtful, cogently argued description of possible first steps toward a more substantial and productive cooperation with China. It deserves careful consideration by policy-makers and citizens alike.

PETER VAN NESS

University of Denver
Colorado

ROBERT L. GALLUCCI. *Neither Peace nor Honor: The Politics of American Military Policy in Vietnam.* Pp. 187. Baltimore, Md.: The Johns Hopkins University Press, 1975. $10.00. Paperbound, $2.95.

PETER D. TROOBOFF, ed. *Law and Responsibility in Warfare: The Vietnam Experience.* Pp. 280. Chapel Hill: The University of North Carolina Press, 1975. $13.95.

In the scholarly study of American involvement in Vietnam, the two volumes

reviewed here should earn acceptance as valuable if not "definitive" works. Both books are pertinent to more than just understanding the case of Vietnam so long as the possibility exists of American intervention on the side of an incumbent government against revolutionary insurgents.

Gallucci takes exception to the prevailing images of American policymaking on Vietnam for failing adequately to explain why an unsuccessful policy could be maintained for so long. The "quagmire hypothesis" held that involvement was the result of incremental decisions made without adequate understanding of probable consequences. The *Pentagon Papers* provided ample evidence that decision-makers were much less ingenuous than the quagmire hypothesis suggested, and Leslie Gelb and Daniel Ellsberg offered the interpretation that American policy was stalemated by the need of successive administrations, for domestic political reasons, to do what was minimally necessary to avoid losing a war. Gallucci finds both of these images too simple and seeks a more complex interpretation through application of a bureaucratic process model. The applicability of this model to the Vietnam case has been indicated by Roger Hilsman and is here carried through with detail and skill. The Gelb-Ellsberg view is not contradicted, but rather significantly enlarged by evidence that the decision-making process was shaped not only by presidents concerned with the need to get elected but also by the bureaucratic-political apparatus which defined the situation and options within which presidents attempted to make policy. The result is a most depressing portrait of bureaucratic players subverting rational planning, deliberative choice, and the national interest. It is impossible to disagree with the conclusion that "the way we make and carry out our foreign policy appears to have a lot to do with the quality of the policy that is produced and the chances of its succeeding. Of the many lessons that might be learned from Vietnam, this ought to be among the least debatable." Unfortunately, Gallucci's own evidence suggests that "the way we make and carry out foreign policy" may not be susceptible to rectification by the organizational jiggering he evidently favors, especially if we would avoid Vietnam-type interventions altogether and not merely improve our ability to discontinue them once unwisely begun.

One of the consequences of decision-making in the manner Gallucci describes was the low incentive for bureaucratic actors to evaluate the effects of American actions inside Vietnam in any other terms than the value to their respective organizational interests. This fact as much as geographic distance, cultural and ideological estrangement or racism accounts for much of the behavior that has stirred a lively, often acrimonious debate on the legality of American intervention and conduct in the war. The volume edited by Peter Trooboff is a cross-section of this debate growing out of a symposium sponsored by the American Society of International Law. The principal issues raised are the legality of high-technology counterinsurgency against a low-technology insurgent, the legality of lachrymatories, napalm and herbicides in customary and conventional international law, and the responsibility of individuals in command. A striking aspect of the treatment given these issues by twenty-two contributors is the lack of consensus on the state of international law pertaining to such wars as that in Vietnam and disagreement over what actually happened in the war itself. The latter problem is vividly demonstrated by an acidulous exchange between Richard Falk and Robert Komer on both interpretation of events and reliability of sources. This and other exchanges involving individuals in government service, incidentally, rather neatly confirm Gallucci's point that perspective is a function of role, although it also is obvious there may be important exceptions to this rule. One problem in such debates with respect to international law is that there is a tendency to argue the merits of cases and content of law separately from the political conditions that encourage or inhibit violation of law and hence determine to a

large extent the "relevance" and even content of the law itself. A parallel reading of the Gallucci and Trooboff volumes compels one to question whether law can have much impact on state behavior during war when the distance and difference between the parties may make at least one party unable to conceive of circumstances in which the other could retaliate in kind or in which reconciliation and cooperation might be desirable in the future. The interrelated problems of making decision-makers both politically and legally responsible remain.

WILLIAM S. TURLEY
Southern Illinois University
Carbondale

PETER HARRIES-JONES. *Freedom and Labour: Mobilization and Political Control on the Zambian Copperbelt.* Pp. 256. New York: St. Martin's Press, 1975. $19.95.

RICHARD L. SKLAR. *Corporate Power in an African State: The Political Impact of Multinational Mining Companies in Zambia.* Pp. x, 245. Berkeley: University of California Press, 1975. $12.00.

Apparently, and perhaps surprisingly, Zambian copper mining is a subject for which the time has come. At least so one might conclude from the appearance in the same year of two books on divergent aspects of that topic.

Peter Harries-Jones, an associate professor at York University, Ontario, collected data in Northern Rhodesia from January 1963 to February 1965 for a study of urban sociology and anthropology in the Copperbelt, seven towns which comprise the largest urban concentration in what is now Zambia. The problem for analysis: mobilization and introduction into African party politics of semi-illiterate workers in a time of great and violent social transformation, the chaotic process disguised in scholarly literature under the bland name "modernization." As Harries-Jones relates it, the formation of the United National Independence Party and the party's drive to independence and nationhood under the slogan "Freedom and Labour" have considerable interest. The book opens with a translation of a text written by a woman organizer for the party, an extremely personal and powerful narration, then turns to analysis of interaction, tension, decision, and values within the evolving party. Harries-Jones comes to the challenging conclusion that the ideology of independence and self-rule developed well ahead of an ideology of Zambian nationhood, so that values of various party factions remained in conflict.

Richard L. Sklar, professor of political science at UCLA, focuses on the changing relation of Zambians to the mining industry which has dominated their country's economy for two generations, an industry which in turn requires study as a multinational corporation. The author's ambitious intention: "to demonstrate the efficacy of class analysis as an approach to the study of multinational corporate expansion." Sklar notes the importance of business adaptation to postcolonial conditions in Africa, the portent of multinational corporations as repositories of values and interests that transcend sovereignty and alter distant cultures and policies, then the proposition that "international capitalism" may in this context become analogous to "international communism." The study in its details concerns the adjustment of the mining companies to new operating conditions in the era of Zambian nationalism and nationalization. In all this, what Sklar means by class analysis is his attempt to ask and answer this central question: who will win the struggle between elitist and popular power in Zambian political and economic development, that is, between corporate and Zambian people's power?

It is difficult to assess two such books in a brief, joint review; but one must try. Harries-Jones and Sklar have both fallen somewhat short of their grander goals in the familiar problem in social science: generalization from one case. Both writers have prepared reasonably clear and interesting analyses, and both have overreached their analyses in making the philosophic and assertive statements

which editors and manuscript referees favor as theme or thesis. There is much infelicitous diction in Harries-Jones' volume, and some unsolved organization problems. Sklar has produced a work clear in structure, well-written, with all the marks of mature scholarship, so that one may not hold against him his confusing terminology in setting international capitalism against international communism in this unusual application of class analysis.

These books may be signs of the times in one important sense. It is obvious that westerners have entered a new and better-informed era of scholarship on Africa. Is it possible that the ideas of Nixon and Brezhnev—their disinclination to compete in Africa—will have provided Africans and western scholars some interval for work, development, and study without the trouble that flows from great power competition in such areas? Will scholar-observers continue to show sense enough in Africa to look, but not to touch?

Thomas H. Etzold
United States Naval War College
Newport, R.I.

Kung-chuan Hsiao. *A Modern China and a New World: K'ang Yu-wei, Reformer and Utopian, 1858–1927.* Pp. 669. Seattle: University of Washington Press, 1975. $25.00.

This volume, which is number 25 of the publications on Asia of the Institute for Comparative and Foreign Area Studies, continues earlier work on K'ang Yu-wei done at the University of Washington with the encouragement of Professor Franz Michael. Articles for journals published in Taiwan and three new chapters are now brought together to form 11 chapters under four sections: "The Family and the Man," "Philosophical Commitments," "Reform Proposals" and "Utopian Ideas." The result is not a tightly argued monograph but rather a compendium of often overlapping discussions through which certain themes are repeated.

Kung-chuan Hsiao is extraordinarily well qualified for this study of a Chinese intellectual who grappled with the traumatic changes of the late nineteenth and early twentieth centuries. To understand K'ang Yu-wei it is necessary to understand both imperial China and Republican China, Chinese civilization and the impact of Western civilization. Professor Hsiao has authored an authoritative history of Chinese political thought in Chinese and one of the most detailed and comprehensive studies of nineteenth century rural control published in English. His facility with English and Chinese, the breadth of his reading and his grasp of factual details are manifested throughout the heavy annotations of these essays. K'ang Yu-wei is viewed sympathetically, almost apologetically, in an effort to appreciate his accomplishments without in any way disguising his shortcomings.

K'ang Yu-wei, one of the leading Chinese thinkers in the generation preceding the emergence of Chinese nationalism, might be characterized as a cultural revivalist since he drew heavily on the Chinese tradition as a sanction for change. At the same time he looked beyond the nation state to a future universal order in which elements of a de-Sinified Confucianism would play a part. Trained as a youth in the Confucian classics he became dissatisfied by the 1880s with orthodox interpretations and explored alternatives both within the Chinese tradition—especially Buddhism—and in Western learning which was then becoming available in translation. K'ang was obsessed with the problem of China's weakness at the hands of the imperialist powers and pointed the finger of blame at the distortions of Confucian philosophy which had accreted over the ages. Taking advantage of existing disputes over the authenticity of various classical texts he developed a radical interpretation of Confucius whom K'ang now identified as a reformer. K'ang's new views bent the classical sanction to the breaking point, and were too far at odds with the conventional wisdom for most scholars to accept.

The peak of K'ang's career came in 1898 when he gained the confidence of the young Kuang-hsü emperor and at-tempted to modernize the Ch'ing government by decree. This was the only time K'ang ever exercised real influence. Although he was forced out by a conservative coup d'etat his continuing loyalty to the Manchu rulers on the Ch'ing throne was symptomatic of his preference for the universal institutions of the imperial state over the particularistic claims of the Chinese nation. Several years after the establishment of the Republic he earned general disapprobation for supporting the efforts of a warlord to restore Manchu rule in 1917.

Perhaps the most enduring of K'ang Yu-wei's achievements will prove to be his utopian vision. His ideas were most fully expressed in the *Ta T'ung Shu* (which has been translated by Laurence G. Thompson). Professor Hsiao discusses the evolution of K'ang's utopian thought and relates it both to possible sources and subsequent influence. Even where influence is not claimed he notes how ideas such as world government, social equality, communal property and equality of the sexes often anticipated later developments. K'ang is portrayed as a conceited and stubborn man, fond of physical pleasures, who despite his vision did not in his personal life depart very far from existing practice. His most striking ideas concerned the status of women and equality of the sexes. The family and with it the authority of age over youth would be abolished. So would marriage. Children would be cared for by the state. Women would receive educations and enjoy the same rights as men. Both sexes would wear the same style of clothing and persons interested in mating would negotiate intimacy contracts for periods from one month to a year on a basis of complete equality. Abortion would have to be outlawed since presumably most women would seek to avoid childbirth.

EDWARD L. FARMER
University of Minnesota
Minneapolis

E. J. KAHN, JR. *The China Hands: America's Foreign Service Officers and What Befell Them.* Pp. xi, 336. New York: Viking Press, 1975. $12.95.

This book is a chronicle of the careers of John Service, John Davies, John Carter Vincent, and other Foreign Service Officers (F.S.O.s) who reported from China in the early 1940s, and later were accused by Senator Joseph McCarthy and his ilk of being among those who had "lost China." It is an enthralling account of a crucial era in the shaping of American foreign policy and of the character of the United States Foreign Service.

E. J. Kahn, Jr., a *New Yorker* staff writer since 1937, has succeeded in setting the record straight about these Old China Hands in a way that, once one gets through the jumble of rather corny anecdotes in the first couple of chapters, has the gripping quality of high drama.

In China, Mao and Chou sit like monks in the caves of Yenan, angling with visiting F.S.O.s for an invitation to visit Washington. Chiang Kai-shek's government, centered in Chungking, becomes more viciously repressive as it comes apart at the seams. U.S. Ambassador Patrick Hurley, who later would accuse the Old China Hands of being agents of a foreign power, shows a number of their confidential reports to Chiang's brother-in-law, T. V. Soong.

Later, back in Washington, the McCarthyites bring forth their Kafkaesque clues and charges, and the China Hands rummage through their pasts to try to prove they *did not* do this or that. When the crunch comes the men at the top turn aside, and the Old China Hands go quietly offstage to private enterprise, retirement, or obscure Foreign Service postings.

Now, after Vietnam and Watergate, the exoneration of the Old China Hands falls under a harsher light than the rosy (not pink) glow which surrounded the concepts of loyalty in the 1950s. Kahn proves that these men were entirely loyal to United States policy as fixed by the Department of State, and that their undoing was the telling of the truth while serving in the Foreign Service. When their reports were repressed, distorted, and finally used to shunt them into obscurity, they by-and-large avoided "going public" with what they knew about the deliberate coverup of what was truly happening in China.

John Davies wrote in 1945, "Our foreign relations are in a fantastic state—wishful thinking, vacillation, secret skeletons, and pervasive confusion. For these reasons the Foreign Service is not an exhilirating business. To get out of it and be able to speak the truth would be a refreshing experience. On the other hand, somebody has to carry on with the the job. We can stay on hoping that things will be better, that our experience can be productive of some good."

Davies was fired in 1954, and went quietly into the furniture business. That was the year that the Ngo Dinh Diem government, loudly touted by the State Department as a democratic alternative to Asian communism, was set up in South Vietnam.

JOHN LEWALLEN

Oakland
California

CLAUDIO G. SEGRÈ. *Fourth Shore: The Italian Colonization of Libya.* Edited by Robin W. Winks. Pp. vii, 237. Chicago, Ill.: The University of Chicago Press, 1974. $15.00.

Italy was a late entry in the scramble for Africa. Several decades of indecision on colonial policy preceded Italy's claim to sovereignty over Libya in 1911; and political conflict over the colony's future marked the first decade of Italian rule. Subsequently, however, Libya became the keystone of Italy's plans for an African empire as Fascist governments combined a desire for hegemony in the Mediterranean with the need to resolve internal problems of unemployment and rural overpopulation. The plan was to transform northern Libya into a *quarta sponda,* or "fourth shore," by means of peasant agricultural colonization. Colonization programs of the 1920s and 1930s intended to develop a dense network of small, independent land owners on the best agricultural land in Libya. They culminated in the 1938 and 1939 mass migrations of peasant families to occupy the large-scale settlement projects which state supported colonization companies developed and managed. Authorities planned to expand colonization after the war. However, the story of colonization after the Axis defeat trails off into a long epilogue that ends with the expulsion of the remaining permanent Italian residents from Libya in the summer of 1970.

Claudio Segrè's monograph concentrates on agricultural colonization during the three decades of Italian rule in Libya. He carefully explains policy objectives, including conflicts over them, and then evaluates their impact in Libya. The conclusions demonstrate clearly that political considerations of Fascist governments governed colonization. For example, the assertion that colonization was necessary as an outlet for the rapidly growing population of unemployed, landless peasants of the South was a myth. The total number of colonists ever in Libya was small, and they came primarily from the industrial North rather than the agrarian South. Segrè also evaluates the continuing conflict between political directives and technical evaluations of the Libyan environment. The latter, he concludes, were generally discarded in favor of colonization policies based upon political expediency and propaganda effect. The Fascists expanded their imperial design to African soil in the late 1930s. But when the colonial era so abruptly ended, the Italian agricultural settlements were, in fact, threatened with serious economic, social and, indeed, even political problems.

European colonization in Africa combined imperial political ideologies with an ethnocentrism which led governments to develop racist policies toward indigenous peoples. Professor Segrè's contribution toward understanding the ideology and policies of Italian colonization in Libya is significant. He also provides a better analysis of Italy's policy toward Libyan peoples than other books. The fact is that Italian agricultural colonization was developed upon Libyan land with Libyan labor. Segrè considers these issues as well as the social and economic impact of Italian agricultural colonization upon Libyan people. This effort ultimately fails, however, because his sources are exclusively Italian (or European) and primarily from people who were in, or closely associated with, the national and colonial governments. As he notes in the bibliographic essay, the Libyan history of Italian colonialism in Libya remains to be told. It cannot depend upon Italian sources.

GARY L. FOWLER
University of Illinois
Chicago

TARLOK SINGH. *India's Development Experience.* Pp. vii, 458. New York: St. Martin's Press, 1975. $25.00.

In *India's Development Experience,* Singh contributes, in effect, an impressive in-depth country case of rationale—and operational criteria—for a new national/international economic (and social) order. As a member of India's Planning Commission from 1950–67, a major contributor to the first four 5-Year Plans, and a student of later planning, he builds his case upon comprehensive factual synthesis of policies, data, numerous major studies, and India's general experience. He concludes that India has the potential to "abolish the extremes of poverty . . . in the present decade." Gunnar Myrdal aptly observes, in a foreword, that "every economist interested in planning in under-developed countries will have strongest reasons to study carefully this book before venturing further."

Singh sees no alternative to a "total national plan for economic and social change"—aimed toward equality, and broadening of the economic base. This includes shifting from past emphasis on capital investment toward development of economic organization and human resources. Basic to the plan, generally, is an increase in productivity of land and labor. Other basics include reversing the decline in savings, and correcting price policies and economic controls.

In chapters on sectors, Singh treats: *population* as a critical factor in *inequity;*

the need to capitalize on India's vast human resource—with *"jobs for all"*; the "rural economy as the most critical issue in development," and key to a next priority, *hunger*—to be approached through a "mutual cooperative system"; and *broadened social services*. A chapter on industry advocates gearing *industry* to serving society as a whole, with new emphasis to the smaller consumer-type sector producing for community needs and agricultural development. Additional chapters take up *transportation* as the "heart of development"; analyze relationships between the *public* and *private* *sectors*; criticize undue reliance on material incentives to foster lagging *exports*; propose ceiling on *income* and *land* holdings; discuss reform of the *tax* *system* as a prime target of social discontent.

Always stressing integrated development, Singh addresses linkages of the organized and relatively weakened unorganized sectors to help transform the latter. He regards balanced regional development as a primary instrument for integration.

Concluding that India now has the potential to be largely self-reliant economically, Singh assesses pros and cons of foreign aid to India which he thinks may be useful to countries still heavily dependent on external help.

Singh highlights certain political requisites for development such as citizen participation, better relationships between government and people, and reducing corruption. He also links economic development to India's political future. As he finished *India's Development Experience* in June, 1973, he noted that "development has slowed down," with "large sectors of the population" having suffered "from hardship and deprivation." Listing about a dozen priority reforms covered in the foregoing, he says that they are "overriding administrative and political imperatives for freedom and democracy," and continuation of "diverse political parties."

DANA D. REYNOLDS
International Center for Dynamics of
    Development
Arlington
Virginia

W. SCOTT THOMPSON. *Unequal Partners: Philippine and Thai Relations with the United States, 1965–75.* Pp. vii, 183. Lexington, Mass.: Lexington Books, 1975. $13.50.

Professor Thompson has set himself a dual task. First, to examine and assess the external, United States sources of the foreign policies of Thailand and the Philippines. The domestic sources of foreign policy are to be the subject of a subsequent work. Second, to test whether democracies or authoritarian regimes more effectively protect the state's interests through their foreign policies, other things being equal, or whether circumstances determine which is more efficacious. The specific cases he studies in detail are the Thai and Filipino responses to American pressures for involvement in the Indochina War, and their adaptation to American defeat and withdrawal in the face of communist victories.

I find much of *Unequal Partners* to be informative and enjoyable reading. But Professor Thompson has not, in my opinion, fulfilled his objectives. The Thai and Filipino decisions are examined in some depth for the decade prior to 1975. This is where the value of the book resides. He explores the sociocultural contexts of the respective politics, the decision-influencing and -making individuals, groups and bureaucratic entities; as well as the personal and group beneficiaries of both specific policy decisions and the American response to those decisions. In short, the *domestic* sources and beneficiaries of Thai and Filipino foreign policy decisions are well elucidated. And a judicious picture of the Ferdinand Marcos dictatorship is presented. On the other hand, the actual *American* input into the decision-making, other than that which accrues to varying degrees of rewarding largesse or parsimony, is more sketchily dealt with.

As to the circumstances under which democracies compared with autocracies can obtain more through and be more adaptive in foreign policy, the sample of two states during one decade simply cannot provide adequate evidence for even a tentative conclusion—leaving aside the question of the extent to which the Philippines was a true democracy prior to 1972 or Thailand after October 1973. We can reach a conclusion from common sense or from other evidence, but not from this book.

The question is raised, at times directly and often implicitly, as to official U.S. attitudes to democracies in the Third World. From the recent Thai and Filipino evidence (and ignoring the evidence of a string of countries from South Korea to Paraguay by way of Spain), American officialdom appears to prefer regimes that are anti-communist and "stable," which is often equated with the leadership of generals or military-backed civilian autocrats such as Marcos. If this is true, then democracies in general will make poor bargainers in their dealings with American officials.

Lastly, a criticism that is somewhat unjust: Thompson often discusses policies in terms of their beneficial or detrimental effect on "the state." He is amply aware that "the state" (or "Thailand" or "the Philippines") consists of many politically unequal and often self-serving elements. But the anthropomorphosis of "the state" keeps creeping in, which means that wittingly or not the "good" of "the state" is associated with the welfare of its privileged leaders. What is good for Marcos or even for 25 percent of Filipinos is not necessarily good for "the Philippines."

DONALD HINDLEY
Brandeis University
Waltham
Massachusetts

FRANKLIN TUGWELL. *The Politics of Oil in Venezuela.* Pp. 210. Stanford, Calif.: Stanford University Press, 1975. $8.95.

The recent history of Venezuela offers an opportunity to study the impact of a dominant major industry (90 percent of export earnings and two-thirds of government revenue) in a democratic nation's development. The Venezuelan government's treatment of the petroleum industry raises a number of interesting questions relating to conflicts between industry and government, internal politics, and the quality of social develop-

ment. An analysis of the situation should be useful not only in understanding Venezuela's past and future, but also in providing lessons for policymakers in other countries.

Based on research conducted between 1966 and 1974, Professor Tugwell addresses the variety of relationships between multinational corporations and Venezuelan political and economic development. Following introductory comments and a chapter on the policy setting, the book treats pre-1958 petroleum policy and then deals in individual chapters with the evolution of policy during the Betancourt Administration and the Leoni Administration, and in two chapters, with the Caldera Administration. The final chapter draws conclusions from these descriptions of the development of petroleum policies. The book is well written and provides a great deal of information on the role of petroleum in the economy while tracing the increasingly assertive posture of the state.

Among the more interesting insights is that the role of experimentation in developing a position with respect to foreign corporations is critical, given the frequent lack of information and domestic managerial expertise. Flexibility and luck have evidently played important roles in policy evolution. Also, it was interesting to note that because of the large contribution of oil revenues to the state, much economic development has taken place without the necessity of sacrifice by the elite groups. Despite the uncertainties in the world petroleum market, a prosperous future is anticipated for Venezuela as the nation prepares to nationalize foreign oil holdings.

While readers interested in Venezuela should enjoy *The Politics of Oil in Venezuela*, as one with less knowledge of that particular country and a broader interest in development problems, I would have appreciated more analysis and conclusions on topics concerning strategies for less developed countries to employ in bargaining with multinational corporations, and more emphasis on lessons to be learned from the Venezuelan experience. Also, a more detailed development of some of the themes such as the role of the elite, the quality of social development, and the future of Venezuela with respect to the United States and to OPEC would have been valuable, although there is a limit to what can be included in 175 pages of text.

FRED MILLER
Department of Transportation
Salem
Oregon

FRANZ A. VON SAUER. *The Alienated "Loyal" Opposition.* Pp. vii, 197. Albuquerque: University of New Mexico Press, 1974. $12.00.

EVELYN P. STEVENS. *Protest and Response in Mexico.* Pp. 372. Lawrence, Mass.: MIT Press, 1974. $17.95.

Senator Fulbright is alleged to have once told a group of Latin Americans that what their countries needed to overcome political instability was to imitate Mexico. He is said to have been nonplussed when it was pointed out that the stability of Mexico had been achieved at the terrible cost of the tenth part of its population.

The senator clearly had no idea of the savagery of the Mexican scene, much less realized that Mexico, to those who had not been misled by the official propaganda, was the "sociedad de la gran mentira," the society of the great lie.

Sauer and Stevens were not blinded by the material advances or the unruffled surfaces. They were aware of the economic growth of the country and knew that some economic development had accompanied it. But they were also aware of the ruthlessness of the regime and its ability to create structures for the control of popular participation in decision-making. It was no secret to them that the government had manipulated the political process in such a way that there were few channels "through which to express noncomformity with existing policies or to exert pressures toward adopting alternative policies."

The books under review are especially timely in these days of change because they deal with vital aspects of Mexican incomformity, Sauer with noncomformity on the Right, Stevens on the Left. The methodology is not the same and neither are the basic assumptions, but the books complement each other nonetheless and together reveal very well the dark side of Mexico's political life. If they had been available to Senator Fulbright, he might have spared himself the embarrassment of his naiveté.

In her superb investigative report of the railroad strikes of 1958–1959, the physicians' strikes of 1964–1965, and the bloody student strike of 1968 (the latter the most dangerous protest movement in Mexico since 1910), Stevens admirably points up the rigidity of the system, its unwillingness to brook opposition, its inability to "dialogue," and how much it has veered in effect from the democratic principles of an open society first advocated by Francisco I. Madero. What the protesters wanted, ultimately, was a reallocation of national resources and a review of national priorities, but the "endemic obstacles to expanding pluralism" and "the regime's methods of discouraging participation in the political process" crushed them mercilessly.

Sauer traces the history, not of a series of happenings, but of the Partido Acción Nacional (PAN), "the first permanent counter-ideological movement" of a Right that found itself alienated from the Revolution. He speaks of its antecedents, of its founding in 1939, its ideological growth, its essential loyalty to Madero's principles of democracy, and the contributions of this minority party (so badly understood by American political scientists) to the political life of Mexico.

Stevens will forgive me for finding fault with her methodology. My tastes are less social science than hers, and I would have preferred a more humanistic approach. Sauer handled the subject more to my liking, along somewhat traditional lines. I could quietly recognize the actors on his stage and easily understand their postures.

Sauer occasionally refers to the gullibility of American students of the Mexican politics for having accepted at face value the official revolutionary bunkum. He does not look upon PAN (as Frank Brandenburg does) as a form of traditional conservatism but rather as a new revolutionary conservatism. PAN is ready, as he believes, to give Mexicans, within the existing constitutional system, an alternative to the regime.

Stevens' massively researched book is proof enough of the unfulfilled hopes of the Mexican Revolution and of the foolhardiness of the government in resurrecting the philosophy of economic growth that led to the overthrow of Porfirio Díaz in 1910. Because of her autopsy of the three protest movements, and also because of Sauer's telling account of the frustrations of PAN, the observer of the Mexican political scene will now have grounds for saying what he has suspected all along, that Mexico is far from the model democracy that Fulbright imagined it to be.

MANOEL CARDOZO
The Catholic University of America
Washington, D.C.

## EUROPE

DANIEL R. BROWER. *Training the Nihilists: Education and Radicalism in Tsarist Russia.* Pp. 248. Ithaca, N.Y.: Cornell University Press, 1975. $12.50.

The title of this solid informative study accurately suggests its contents. Concentrating on the social dimensions of the period from the 1840s to the mid-1870s, this work examines the evolution of the relationship between education and radical youth.

What motivated so many Russian students to join the radical movement and what were the institutional characteristics of this process of recruitment? These questions make up his central theme. They are explored in chapters describing the social environment in which these radicals are raised, and follows them from their familial setting into the education system. The book examines the process by which formal education prepared and promoted young Russians into the upper occupational levels of society. It studies the development of the student

community, the "key to radical recruitment," according to the author. Brower asserts that within this student community "were generated the special institutions, ideals, and models of behavior that functioned as a 'school of dissent' capable of disrupting the orderly process of education." In this sense, this book studies the recruitment and training of the nihilists, largely from among the scions of the privileged classes then being trained in the educational system to become autocratic Russia's future elite.

Brower deliberately avoids the use of the word "intelligentsia" as being too vague and misunderstood by various groups of scholars. Instead he substitutes the word "radical" as identifying the political outlook of these alienated youth as that of extreme opposition to the prevailing system of Russia, excluding those individuals whose views were "reformist liberal." He adopts the politically neutral term "subculture" rather than "counterculture" to describe and identify the common patterns of deviant outlook among the radical youth. This reviewer finds no great objection to Brower's attempt to solve the terminological problem by using the simplest labels for groups defined by easily identifiable traits.

Brower does well in cautioning the reader about his conclusions drawn from biographical data about some 405 radicals active over the period 1840–1875 largely in St. Petersburg, most of whose educational levels and social origins could be ascertained. Drawing largely on memoirs and police files, he is attempting to draw a collective portrait of the young radicals and relies on considerable generalization. More than three-fourths of these radicals had attended a university or professional school, the highest rung of the Russian educational ladder. Brower's conclusion drawn from the material on social origins is that "the radical youth were probably no different in class composition than the student group from which they came."

Would similar studies of radicals active in Moscow or Kiev during the same period yield similar conclusions?

An intriguing question but one that must await further study. Likewise his provocative assertion that this "school of dissent" or process of recruitment of radical youth developed during this 35-year-period "was probably more influential in sustaining the movement in later decades than the ideological systems so passionately debated by the writers."

Generally well-written, amply documented, with a select bibliography and index, the book is enhanced by its collection of brief biographical sketches about the more obscure radical figures. There are a number of intriguing insights in every chapter, several of them at odds with prevailing views on the subject. Brower has judiciously supported his assertions by assiduously assembled evidence. This book will be of interest to all social scientists studying 19th century Russia and those seeking historical parallels to the "New Left" movement in the 1960s. In all, *Training the Nihilists* is an important, surely a seminal study of the school of dissent. This book must be reckoned with by all future students of the subject.

DAVID H. KITTERMAN
Northern Arizona University
Flagstaff

JOSEPH FRANKEL. *British Foreign Policy, 1945–73.* Pp. vi, 356. New York: Oxford University Press, 1975. $22.50.

Between 1945 and 1973 Britain lost much of her power. Her difficulties in this period, the author argues with great conviction, were very much augmented by her failure to realize how her status had diminished. (As late as 1959, 72 percent of the British élite thought she was the third most powerful nation.) She wallowed in unreality because she was unable to relinquish certain fallacies such as the existence of a "special relationship" with the U.S.A., or the compensating value for loss of Empire in being at the center of the Commonwealth, or the possession of a world role with oceanic implications precluding any integration with Europe.

The result of these misconceptions, mirrored by similar failings in domestic policy, was that the pragmatic, case-to-case British approach to foreign policy was inappropriate. Reflective, long-sighted re-appraisals were needed; but the unaccustomed speed of the changes and the compulsions of the situation, as well as the prevalent intellectual tradition, prevented them from taking place. The author believes that more recently there has been an increasing tendency to see Britain's position in truer perspective. The entry into Europe will even more restrict freedom of action, a situation in which British pragmatism may again be of benefit.

Professor Frankel asserts that British foreign policy still remains élitist, though no "single integrated power élite exists in post-war Britain." Furthermore, the élite consists of people in top positions "within the political, diplomatic, bureaucratic and military hierarchies," as well as ginger groups among M.P.s, television commentators, journalists in the "quality press" and the Crown and its advisers. Public opinion is obviously a factor, but the public plays a relatively minor role in debate. Surveys have shown that foreign policy is an issue of "diminishing salience" in British politics. The political leaders have made little attempt to correct this decline.

It would, perhaps, be carping to complain that this sociological analysis of British foreign policy-makers is unsupported by hard evidence. Professor Frankel agrees that it is impressionistic. Nevertheless it does raise the question of whether the actual process of formation of foreign policy has changed with the fragmentation of the élite. But this is not criticism of the book which will be widely regarded as a standard work on the content and orientation of British foreign policy in the post-war years.

FRANK BEALEY
University of Aberdeen
Scotland

RICHARD S. LEVY. *The Downfall of the Anti-Semitic Political Parties in Imperial Germany.* Pp. vii, 335. New Haven, Conn.: Yale University Press, 1975. $18.50.

Anti-Semitism has a long bibliography but it remains an inexhaustible subject. Among all the approaches to its mysteries a careful, well-researched account like Mr. Levy's of the rise and fall of political anti-Semitism in one country, makes a substantial contribution to discovering why and how anti-Semitism has operated in that place and under those circumstances. Mr. Levy concentrates on a period of some 30 years following the unification of Germany after the Franco-Prussian War up to World War I, a period that many writers have considered a continuation of past German malefactions against the Jews and a prelude to the rise of Nazism that intended to put an end to the need for any kind of anti-Semitism as far as it found itself in a position to solve the problem. What these political anti-Semites aimed to do was in effect to repeal the Emancipation Laws, to stop Jewish immigration from the East, and to drive Jews out of government and teaching positions in the *Volkschulen*. Some impressive German figures were to be found in the movement, among them Heinrich von Treitschke, who coined the phrase the Nazis would later make their own: "The Jews are our misfortune." But on the whole the anti-Semite spokesmen were distinguished mainly by sound and fury as they repeated their accusations against what they saw as the foreign bodies in their midst.

Levy demonstrates how the *Mittelstand*, the amorphous group of non-proletarian, mainly small businessmen who felt themselves threatened by the growth of organized capital and by Socialism, were the core of the anti-Semitic movement. Their enemies, aside from the Jews, were moving targets, sometimes the Junkers, even Wilhelm II, who had a few Jewish friends, but mainly the Social Democrats who they believed were dominated by the Jews. Parties other than the Social Democrats, Conservatives and Centrists for example, had anti-Semitic interludes and factions but they were not dependable allies of the movement.

The anti-Semitic parties had a brief flowering. From 16 seats in 1893, they went to 12 in 1898, to 11 in 1903, up again to 17 in 1907 but by 1912 they had only 6 deputies in the Reichstag, 5 of whom were absorbed in the Conservative Party. After 30 years of campaigning, only 130,000 German voters supported anti-Semitic candidates. It was a poor harvest but a more revolutionary generation was on its way to work.

EUGENE DAVIDSON
Conference on European Problems
Chicago
Illinois

PETER H. MERKL. *Political Violence under the Swastika: 581 Early Nazis.* Pp. xiv, 735. Princeton, N.J.: Princeton University Press, 1975. $30.00. Paperbound, $10.75.

It is exceedingly difficult to plow new ground in a crowded field such as Nazism but this excellent book has done precisely that. Merkl concentrates on the Party's middle echelons or "little Nazis" rather than its well-known leaders, on its inner dynamics rather than external achievements, on motives rather than ideology, and applies social science methods rather than historical narrative or literary approach. As a result the reader gleans insights not only into Nazism but also extremist movements in general.

The study is based on the personal biographies submitted by 581 early Nazi Party members to Columbia sociologist Theodore Abel for an essay contest in 1933. Merkl candidly acknowledges the material's weaknesses but argues convincingly that it is probably the best available source. While stringently applying statistical analysis, he displays a reassuring caution in seeking patterns and a humanistic sensitivity toward the individuals involved. His conclusion reinforces Arendt's view that evil can be banal: "The lives of these early Nazis were commonplace and understandable indeed. There is very little to be found in them that seems sinister or ominous. And yet the consequences of their common foibles, errors, and delusions cost an estimated fifty million human lives and untold destruction and misery" (p. ix).

Merkl investigates three general areas of motivation for early Nazis to join the Party. One was social dynamics: class impulses were highly differentiated and have "few common denominators except for frustrated upward mobility and an in-between or misfit status between the two powerful camps of the liberal bourgeoisie and the organized working class" (p. 668); childhood experiences such as the lack of a father, poverty, physical beating and/or excessive discipline were apparently further factors. Another general area of motivation is the formative experiences of war, revolution and counter-revolution of which war was the most important but which vary according to generation. The third major impulse was what Merkl calls "the Weimar youth revolt" which produced the violent Nazi cohorts of the late twenties and gave the initially war-motivated movement the staying power to triumph in 1933; he examines the process of their politicization and mili-tarization, and then proposes a theory of extremist deviancy and identity to ex-plain it.

Merkl then turns to the movement itself. He first examines the escalation of political violence through distinguish-able stages (pre-political, militarization, politicization and membership) which vary according to individual, geography, religion and, above all, generation. He then considers the role of ideology and finds that the usual presentation of Nazism as a logically consistent system or outgrowth of German intellectual traditions is misleading; most early Nazis had random beliefs which varied con-siderably but included the well-known elements of anti-semitism, anti-Marxism and chauvinism compounded with para-noia. In a final section Merkl focuses on life within the Party including the time and circumstances for joining, the role of the most violent members (storm troopers and the so-called "day-and-night" fighters), and the eventual careers in the Third Reich of pre-1933 Party office holders.

Merkl's study does not diminish the importance of more traditional studies but adds an illuminating dimension. While the genius of Hitler should not be denied, this study shows not only how current and thus unoriginal his ideas were but also how receptive at least some Germans were.

L. L. FARRAR, JR.
Boston College
Chestnut Hill
Massachusetts

MARSHALL LEE MILLER. *Bulgaria During the Second World War.* Pp. viii, 290. Stanford, Calif.: Stanford University Press, 1975. $10.95.

ANTONY POLONSKY. *The Little Dictators: The History of Eastern Europe Since 1918.* Pp. xi, 212. Boston, Mass.: Routledge & Kegan Paul, 1975. $16.50.

When during the Munich crisis, Prime Minister Chamberlain balked at the prospect of Britain going to war over the rights of peoples about whom neither he nor the British people knew very much, it in part was because the history and affairs of Eastern Europe had largely been ignored by the scholars of the western nations. This ignorance was to exact a very high price when the war did begin in 1939, and it had its origins in part in the unresolved national and territorial conflicts among peoples whose historical memories were set against ethnic diversity and fragmentation. Only in the postwar world have English speaking scholars begun to inquire in a systematic way into the complex past and present of the region, stimulated in part by the emergence of the Soviet Union as the dominant power in the area. The two volumes reviewed here are among the latest additions to a growing literature in the English language, and both are representative to some extent of the state of the art.

The more important work of the two is Marshall Lee Miller's study of Bulgaria during the Second World War. While an attorney by profession, his book demon-strates that he is a serious student of Bulgarian history, although the work does possess some minor technical flaws. His research includes an impressive array of archives and libraries, including several repositories in Bulgaria, as well as a number of personal interviews with surviving participants in the events he describes. The author, however, was not always able to handle his material in a systematic and coherent way, with the result that the narrative falls somewhere between a chronological and a topical approach, and forces the reader to labor a bit more than necessary. Occasionally there is a serious lapse that does damage to the work itself. For example, after carefully describing the background that led to Bulgaria's casting her lot with Germany, the author informs the reader that Bulgaria yielded to German pressure and signed the Tripartite Pact on March 1, 1941. We are not told how this yielding came about. Was it a decision of the king? Did the cabinet discuss the matter, and, if so, what prompted them to act at that particular time?

Political and diplomatic themes constitute the basic thrust of the work, although economic and social factors are introduced when they are needed to explain either the general or immediate background of the behavior of the Bulgarian government. Central to understanding Bulgarian behavior (and most particularly that of King Boris) is Bulgarian nationalism. This theme is implicit throughout the work, and is present in the territorial questions, in the reluctance of Bulgaria to do more than the minimum required by her German ally, and in her difficulty in disengaging from her participation in the war after the tide had turned and Bulgaria itself was subject to attack. Whatever may have been appearances to the contrary, Bulgaria pursued a Bulgarian course; the King particularly was opportunistic, flexible, and pragmatic, but he was firmly resolved to gain for Bulgaria those territories lost at the Congress of Berlin, to participate actively in the war as little as possible, and to avoid antagonizing powerful neighbors such as Turkey and the Soviet Union. In the course of making any accommodation, the government, whether "pro-German" or not, would only go as far as it felt it had to. Out of this attitude came the contradictory maintenance of diplomatic ties with the Soviet Union while allied with Germany. On the other hand, Bulgaria felt free to declare war against the United States; it seemed a very cheap way to please her German allies and America was very far away. It was a decision that Bulgaria was very much to regret when the American air forces brought the war to Sofia a short two years later. And, as the war turned in favor of the allies, Bulgaria found that her policy of pragmatism and flexibility became more difficult to manage. Her desire to reach an accord with the allies conflicted with her wish to retain those territories she had gained and with her fear of a German occupation. This dilemma, and poor leadership following the death of the king, was reflected in a policy of delay and procrastination that in the end led to a declaration of war by the Soviet Union and occupation by Soviet forces.

The author addresses other controversial questions that are of more than passing interest. Perhaps the most important of these is his examination of the suspicious circumstances surrounding the death of King Boris. After a careful review of all the known facts and of the heated rhetoric generated by proponents of one or another assassination theory, he sensibly concludes that the king probably died of natural causes rather than as the victim of one or another plot.

The work by Professor Polonsky reads as if it may have been a set of lectures designed for undergraduates. In between a short introduction and an epilogue are six short chapters, each of which is concerned with a single country (Poland, Austria, Rumania, Yugoslavia, Hungary, and Czechoslovakia) while Greece, Finland, Bulgaria, and the Baltic states are each disposed of in a paragraph or two. The author's approach falls between stools; the story he tells is already known to specialists in the field, while the extreme sketchiness of the narrative and the oblique references that characterize so concentrated a work, presume too much prior knowledge on the part of the reader to make this volume useful for non-specialists. There is some redemption in the fact that a statistical appendix, constituting a full quarter of the book, provides a handy reference to demographic data for the interwar period. As a work of serious scholarship, however, it does not compare with Marshall Miller's study, which, despite its imperfections, represents a solid contribution to our increasing understanding of this complex and fascinating region.

FORRESTT A. MILLER
Vanderbilt University
Nashville
Tennessee

STEVEN E. OZMENT. *The Reformation in the Cities: The Appeal of Protestantism to Sixteenth-Century Germany and Switzerland.* Pp. vii, 237. New Haven, Conn.: Yale University Press, 1975. $12.50.

Professor Ozment of Yale University has written a most extraordinary work of scholarship. His monograph is rich in scholarship and critical detail, and yet it is a work of great value for the non-specialist. It is a work filled with astute assessments of trends in the historical research on the Protestant Reformation, and yet it is a book which focuses on fundamental issues in a manner intelligible to the general reader. Based on assiduous research in both Catholic and Protestant popular religious literature of the period—catechisms, dramas, tracts, and confessional manuals—Ozment's work presents a very favorable overview of the Reformation's role in modern history. To Ozment the fundamental role of the Reformation in European history was one of liberation and freedom, liberation from the traditional religious superstition and tyranny and an evangelical freedom which contributed much to the development of a rational and moral approach to religion.

Ozment's monograph is a synthesis of two major methodologies in Reformation studies. The one is the historiographical tradition which analyzes the ideas of the Reformation in terms of late medieval philosophy, theology, and religious dissent. The other—far more recent— seeks to place the Reformation in a contemporary urban perspective. The one has, microcosmically in most cases, labored over the intellectual origins and religious antecedents of the Reformation in the late medieval period, while the other often just as narrowly focuses on the social history of cities and regions during the Reformation. Ozment very masterfully combines the history of ideas and social history in a work of exacting scholarship and persuasive argumentation. It will no doubt become a seminal work in its field.

JOHN S. WOZNIAK
Fredonia
New York

GEORGE DANIEL RAMSAY. *The City of London in International Politics at the Accession of Elizabeth Tudor.* Pp. x, 310. Totowa, N.J.: Rowman and Littlefield, 1975. $21.50.

Throughout England's history the city of London has dominated various aspects of the country's life in a fashion which perhaps transcends that of any of Europe's other great cities. Certainly it is true that in the Tudor era London was so much the greatest English city in commercial and political matters that the influence of other cities is virtually negligible by comparison. This carefully researched work focuses on a neglected but important aspect of London's history during that era: the interaction between the affluent leaders of the Company of Merchants Adventurers and those who were responsible for the formulation of Britain's foreign policy in the early years of Queen Elizabeth's reign.

Drawing on an impressive array of original sources, most notable of which are English state papers and contemporary financial and administrative records, Dr. Ramsay traces the economic and related problems which were an outgrowth of deteriorating Anglo-Dutch relations in the late 1550s and early 1560s. Following two useful opening chapters which delineate the corporate characters of Antwerp (a "Metropolis at its Zenith") and London ("A Satellite City"), the developments which culminated in virtual English exclusion from Antwerp's international commodity market are analyzed in detail. The activities of the leaders of the Merchants Adventurers loom large in this account. Demonstrably this energetic, "pushy" group of men wielded considerable political influence, and this they brought to bear on England's leaders to the fullest possible extent. However, showing the aggressiveness and adaptability which were so characteristic of the Elizabethan commercial scene, they also made doubly sure their interests were protected by seeking alternative outlets for their trade in Emden and other markets. In the end both efforts enjoyed some success. By early 1565, Antwerp had once more been opened to the Merchants Adventurers, and as a result of the commercial hiatus the Emden mart had achieved new prominence.

This is a solid, if rather narrow, piece of combined economic and political history. The author writes well on a subject that too frequently lends itself to pedestrian prose, and his work serves the dual purpose of elucidating one segment of the history of Elizabeth's reign and demonstrating the manner in which studies of this type can cast light on both local and national affairs. The work will be required reading for all serious students of Elizabethan diplomacy and commercial enterprise.

JAMES A. CASADA
Winthrop College
Rock Hill, S.C.

A. J. SHERMAN. *Island Refuge: Britain and Refugees from the Third Reich, 1933–1939.* Pp. 291. Berkeley: University of California Press, 1974. $11.50.

This is the latest addition to a vast and still-growing literature on the subject of the western democracies' attitude and behavior vis-à-vis the Jews trapped in Hitler's Germany. The general feeling has been that these countries did not do their utmost to enable the victims to escape before their fate was sealed. As ruler of a global empire which contained huge unpopulated territories and especially as keeper of the League of Nations mandate over Palestine, Great Britain was considered to have been in a particularly favorable position to provide assistance—and didn't. For this reason, Britain has been singled out for harsh criticism. In *Island Refuge,* A. J. Sherman has undertaken to document in detail British behavior toward the refugees and, in the process, to defend the erstwhile empire's record by showing that under the circumstances the British did their best; that their record is as good as, if not better than, the other western powers, including the United States.

His scholarly task of documenting British behavior, Sherman performs admirably. He demonstrates an ability for organizing a huge, enormously complex variety of documents and for arranging their essential contents into readable prose. The result is a book that no reader who has a serious interest in the fateful pre-World War II years will want to miss.

Ironically, it is his very craftsmanship as a scholar, his scrupulous quest for full impartial documentation that prevents Sherman from successfully executing his non-scholarly task of defending the British record. Contrary to the author's avowed intention, the picture that emerges from the pages of *Island Refuge* is one of callous obstructionism on the part of British bureaucrats and diplomats, coupled with hypocritic double-talk often intermingled with outright scorn for refugees in general and for the Jews in particular. Yes, Britain is eager to help the victims, but with many Britons out of work, how can they possibly provide a haven for Germans? Besides, admission of refugees might intensify anti-Jewish sentiments in Britain. (When pursuing this line, the British managed to recognize the "Germans" for what they were—Jews.) Financial contribution toward solving the refugee problem? They would love to, except that the British do not wish to depart from the "principle" that the Jews ought to foot the bill. After all, the British Jewish community initially agreed to this. That the burden has become unbearable is not ground enough for Britain to become unprincipled. Intervention with the German government? God forbid! It might irritate the gentlemen; it might prevent them from returning to the League of Nations and thus deny the world the pleasure of their company. Overseas territories? Of course! Except that the respective administrators are unwilling to cooperate. (The peak of hypocrisy was reached in the case of Britain's fake offer in Guiana —see pp. 207–209, but especially pp. 230–234.) Palestine? Naturally Britain wants to fulfill its obligation under the mandate, but after all, she has to be fair to the Arabs.

It is interesting, often painful, to observe how Sherman's otherwise sound scholarly sense deserts him when he attempts to force his apologia. From the beginning of the book, Sherman builds up in the reader an expectation that during the last few months before the outbreak of the war, a radical change occurred in Britain's negative attitude. The promise remains unfulfilled. The only bit of evidence Sherman produces actually demonstrates the opposite of what he wishes to prove. When Czechoslovakia crumbled under the German boot, some genuine concern was afoot in Britain for threatened social democrats. The contrast between this and the lack of similar concern for the Jewish victims (especially on the part of the Labourites who consistently objected to an influx of refugees on the ground that Britain has a high unemployment rate— see Chapter 6, especially pp. 143–148) stares one in the face. Yet Sherman does not notice the problem. On the contrary, the contrast is blurred by treating both categories as "refugees," thus creating the impression that Britain has had a change of heart on the subject and is now seriously doing something about the problem. The author's carelessness is, mildly speaking, disappointing.

Similarly, Sherman's customary craftsmanship is just not to be found in his treatment of the Palestine question, which, by his own admission (p. 16) is central to the problem at hand. His scattered statements on the subject repeat the official British line, without any trace of documentary support. For example, Sherman states matter-of-factly that Britain was helpless in the face of the 1936–1939 "Arab revolt." This assertion goes undocumented, which is especially unfortunate in view of the controversial nature of the subject. Even his mention of the fact that the Arab terror suddenly ceased at the outbreak of the war is not accompanied by an explanation. Is it possible that the whole "revolt" of the Arabs was "made in Britain"? that, therefore, as the war rendered it inconvenient for them, the British made a quick end to it? It is, of course, not certain that this was actually the case. However, a scholar does have an obligation to explore possible explanations, to choose between alternatives, and to defend one's choice. Our author does nothing of the kind, leaving the reader puzzled and, again, disappointed.

It is unfortunate that an obviously competent scholar of Sherman's caliber has not resisted the lure into the treacherous waters of political-historical polemics. Had he resisted the temptation, this otherwise fine book might have been a truly excellent one.

ISRAEL RUBIN
Cleveland State University
Ohio

GRAHAM WOOTON. *Pressure Groups in Britain, 1720–1970.* Pp. 375. Hamden, Conn.: Shoe String Press, 1975. $20.00.

It is not clear whether this book, described by the author as an "essay," is intended as an exercise in taxonomy or explanation. If the former it is incomplete and if the latter incomprehensible. In either case its value is seriously reduced by the absence of an index. In a brief general introduction the author makes a not very successful attempt to squeeze a definition of the title into a sociological framework. There follow eighty-five inelegantly written pages of hurried social, economic and political history in which a vast number of nongovernmental organizations ranging from chartered companies to the Abortion Law Reform Association are briefly mentioned and then twelve pages of "interpretation." It is not clear on whom the pressure groups are presumed to operate: on government or Members of Parliament; in some of the organizations quoted they operated on neither, but on employers or as groups within political

## Governing Science and Technology

W. HENRY LAMBRIGHT, The Maxwell School, Syracuse University. □ "For anyone who asks why a country that can land a man on the moon cannot solve its domestic social problems *Governing Science and Technology* should be prescribed reading. This is a perceptive and stimulating analysis of the major range of problems involved in the relation of politics to big technology—a relation which scholars have too often ignored under the delusion that technology and science are the same thing."—Don K. Price, Harvard University. (Public Administration and Democracy Series)

1976            224 pp.            cloth $9.00     paper $4.00

## Party Dynamics
### The Democratic Coalition and the Politics of Change

RICHARD L. RUBIN, Columbia University. □ A penetrating analysis of the weakening of past relationships within the Democratic party, this book also provides insights into the dynamics of the American party system. Professor Rubin examines the coalition of groups that has traditionally made up the party, the elite groups which have now come into prominence, and attempts to reconcile these two divergent socio-political forces, as well as the changes and instability which have been brought about by their interaction.

June 1976            224 pp.            cloth $9.95     paper $4.00

## Politics, Position, and Power
### The Dynamics of Federal Organization
### Second Edition

HAROLD SEIDMAN, University of Connecticut. □ Statistics and references have been revised and fresh material added to bring the second edition of this book up to date. In addition, former President Nixon's attempt to achieve a "new American revolution" through executive branch reorganization is fully documented. "A good, readable contemporary study of the realities of federal government organization and its impact on current affairs."—Kenneth L. Knotts, Northwestern State University. "An informed and sophisticated account of the failure of traditional public administration solutions for federal malaise."—Sam Postbrief, University of Maryland

1975            370 pp.            paper $4.00

## The City Boss in America
### An Interpretive Reader

Edited by ALEXANDER B. CALLOW, JR., University of California, Santa Barbara. □ This anthology brings together interpretive essays by historians, political scientists, journalists, sociologists, politicians and a novelist that explore the critical features of machine politics. "This book is most helpful in that it provides a balanced, interdisciplinary approach—drawing on a rich array of literature from a variety of perspectives. It should be of interest to an audience well beyond the confines of American history."—Michael H. Ebner, Lake Forest College

1976            350 pp.            paper $6.00

*Prices and publication dates are subject to change.*

*Kindly mention* THE ANNALS *when writing to advertisers*

# New Yale Paperbounds

## Coups and Army Rule in Africa
*Studies in Military Style*

Samuel Decalo

Samuel Decalo presents detailed evidence from Dahomey, Togo, Congo/Brazzaville, and Uganda that African military coups are engineered by coteries of cliques composed of ambitious officers seeking self-advancement. He successfully refutes prevailing theories that military rule has fostered socioeconomic or political development or stability.   c. $17.50   p. $4.95

## Essential Works of Socialism
Edited by Irving Howe

The authoritative one-volume anthology of major socialist writings, is now once more available. Offering a historical perspective of democratic socialism from Marx to contemporary writers, it is the essential resource for understanding socialist thought.   c. $20.00   p. $8.95

## Authoritarian Brazil
*Origins, Policies, and Future*

Edited by Alfred Stepan

"The focus is on: the origins of the authoritarian regime; the political economy of authoritarian Brazil; the political future of authoritarian Brazil. . . . For their insights, understanding, analysis, explanation, and useful interpretation, these essays are essential reading for student and scholar alike."—*Journal of Politics*
c. $11.50   p. $3.95

## The Shaping of Southern Politics
*Suffrage Restriction and the Establishment of the One-Party South, 1880–1910*

J. Morgan Kousser

"A meticulous and heavily documented research production. . . . The chief merit of the Kousser volume is its state by state analysis of the means and devices employed in the South to prevent political control by Negroes and illiterate whites and its refined estimates of the impact of these restrictive measures upon the electorate."—*The Annals*   c. $16.50   p. $4.95

## Modern Social Politics in Britain and Sweden
*From Relief to Income Maintenance*

Hugh Heclo

"This book is an important and significant contribution to our understanding of the politics of income maintenance policies on a cross-national basis, and it provides a fascinating study of the impact of political culture on the policy-making process. . . . A valuable contribution to all students of European politics and to students of comparative public policy."—*Perspective*

Winner of the 1975 Woodrow Wilson Foundation Book Award   c. $17.50   p. $4.95

## The Politics of Electoral College Reform   Second Edition
Lawrence D. Longley and Alan G. Braun
Foreword by Senator Birch Bayh

"Provides considerable insight into the legislative process as well as the outside forces which impinge on legislative decision-making."
—*The Annals*   c. $11.50   p. $3.45

## Selling the People's Cadillac
*The Edsel and Corporate Responsibility*

Jan G. Deutsch

This extraordinary book shows that corporate social responsibility should be treated as a legal rather than as an economic problem. Reconstructing the history of the Edsel—one of corporate America's greatest debacles—Jan Deutsch places it in its cultural, economic, and psychological setting.   c. $20.00   p. $8.95

Yale University Press   New Haven and London

parties or as charities. One who has been on the parliamentary receiving end would feel that there were some powerful omissions from recent times: The Navy League, the Aircraft Industry, the British Road Federation, Amnesty and the various bodies such as the British Science Guild, the Association of Scientific Workers and the Parliamentary and Scientific Committee which have formed an active lobby for science and technology. If those which operated within political parties are to be included where is the Tribune group? Perhaps the most active pressure groups are some foreign embassies, and their methods and effectiveness would have been worth assessing. A strange omission is the powerful Zionist movement which only gets an indirect reference in five lines devoted to the "Arab cause" and "the fate of Soviet Jewry."

The rest of the book consists of a hundred and one quotations from documents, the choice of which appears to be random. Some of the quotations are a few lines from the minutes or from a history of the organization, some are rules or statutes, some press cuttings. Inevitably they present a very incomplete picture and little attempt is made to distinguish the successful from the unsuccessful or the reasons for the difference. In a mention of one of the most successful recent pressure group campaigns, that for commercial television, there is no reference to the detailed study made by the late Professor Hugh Wilson.

The author has a theme: that the groups helped to weaken and break the oligarchic structure of British political life and encourage democratic values and the movement towards equality as society adapted itself to the rapid changes of the nineteenth century. While many of the activities of the pressure groups were taken over by the mass parties (for instance, secular education and temperance by the Liberals, tariff reform by the Conservatives, socialism by the Labour Party), powerful groups such as professional associations, the Trade Unions and commercial and industrial organizations have become institutionalized

parts of the decision making process of government and new ones, dealing with matters of individual social policy, with amenity or with the problems of immigrants, have arisen.

This is a large subject and it would be worthwhile testing and developing the theme against an extended study of the material available.

AUSTEN ALBU

Sussex
England

## UNITED STATES

THOMAS M. COFFEY. *The Long Thirst: Prohibition in America, 1920–1933.* Pp. xii, 346. New York: W. W. Norton, 1975. $9.95.

This is not serious history. Apart from selected research into contemporary press accounts, certain oral history interviews, and government documents, Thomas Coffey has relied principally on secondary sources. Even then, he has consulted works published for the most part during the 1920s and 1930s and is not conversant with contemporary scholarship on the 1920s. The result is a highly impressionistic and not always reliable study, often prone to sweeping unsupportable generalizations, and displaying a simplistic understanding of the politics and values of the 1920s. The reader might well conclude that prohibition was the single most important issue of the 1920s. Further, Coffey makes no attempt to understand prohibition's relationship to those other forces shaping American society during the New Era—namely, immigration restriction, the rise and respectability of the Ku Klux Klan, attitudes toward labor unions, and the dominant conceptions of intelligent governmental policy.

*The Long Thirst*, however, is not without merit and offers revealing insights into the personalities, and hence the dominant values, of this decade. This is solid narrative history intended to "tell the story of prohibition in human terms, through the lives of a number of real people, some famous, some obscure, some funny, some tragic, some honest, some crooked" (p. xii). A good read, *The Long Thirst* consists of a series of inside stories of the lives of a diverse number of people ranging from governors and bishops to prohibition agents and rum runners. Throughout, Coffey sustains the reader's attention. For the knowledgeable student of the period, this personal dimension might be highly rewarding.

Yet, *The Long Thirst* is no more than a complex of character sketches detailing how particular individuals shaped and were shaped by the national attempt to enforce prohibition during the 1920s. These sketches are deficient because Coffey fails to capture the complexity of these individuals' lives, to attempt even to understand their more general political and social philosophies, and to relate their lives to the dominant currents of the broader society. Anecdotal history has definite limits, particularly if its purpose is to inform us about a society at a particular period of time.

On the whole, the book cannot be recommended because it is far too impressionistic and simplistic. We should expect good biographical and narrative history to be accurate and sophisticated, and to demonstrate a mastery of the politics and priorities of the period under study. A good history of prohibition, thus, remains to be written. Until then, the reader might better consult Andrew Sinclair's *Prohibition: The Era of Excess*.

ATHAN G. THEOHARIS

Marquette University
Milwaukee
Wisconsin

JOHN PATRICK FINNEGAN. *Against the Specter of a Dragon: The Campaign for American Military Preparedness, 1914–1917*. Contributions in Military History, no. 7. Pp. ix, 253. Westport, Conn.: Greenwood Press, 1975. $12.95.

This excellent study provides considerable insight into the 1914–1917 preparedness movement, and it is a valuable addition to the growing number of monographs examining the development of the modern military and its relationship to American society and civil authority. Finnegan's research is thorough, his writing is lucid, and his narrative is interpretive.

The book's principal thesis, which is convincingly demonstrated, is that the preparedness movement was unrelated either to American foreign policy or to the specific threats to national interests and security arising from the war in Europe and instead expressed the army's desire for peace-time expansion and the progressive concern with social peace and unity. Especially successful is Finnegan's explication of how, why, and to what extent the movement was nurtured by the General Staff, civilian advocates, Congressional spokesmen, and the Wilson Administration. Originating in the efforts of military reformers and civilian administrators to overcome serious deficiencies in the strength and readiness of the armed forces, preparedness was fueled after 1914 by war-bred anxieties about national security, by the progressive commitment to national efficiency, individual duty, and social order, and by the electoral advantage-seeking of Wilson and his opponents. As the movement gathered momentum, the army reformers and civilian advocates of preparedness demanded ever larger regular and reserve forces and finally sought universal military training.

Finnegan also identifies the principal opponents of preparedness—farmers, organized labor, German-Americans, and socialists—and carefully examines their attitudes and arguments, but he fails to explore the reform commitments of some of these groups and thus misses the opportunity to clarify the relationship of preparedness to progressivism. One is left to wonder too about the response of women, workers (as opposed to those who claimed to speak for them), and the middle classes of the towns and smaller cities to the preparedness cause.

There are also some questionable conclusions. The assertion that the preparedness movement was essential to the effectiveness of the American war effort after April, 1917 rests upon inferences rather than evidence, and the accusation that Wilson failed to consider the relation of national military capacity to his foreign policy objectives seems unwarranted in view of the anti-imperialist and anti-militarist nature of those objectives. Wilson's goals may have been unrealistic, but they hardly called for the creation of a "creditable deterrent."

The most striking quality of the military and civilian proponents of preparedness —although Finnegan refuses to label it —was their unabashed militarism. Professional officers sought to apply Prussian ideals to American military organization and expansion. Civilian reformers hoped to bridge class antagonisms and to compensate for social dislocation through universally shared martial discipline and values. Their goal, universal military training, contradicted long-standing American concepts of freedom. If attained, it would have revised even the processes of maturation in American society. National security requirements might have justified such impositions; but as Finnegan demonstrates, universal service was unnecessary for national defense or for attaining any conceivable American foreign policy objective. The genuineness of the convictions of preparedness advocates cannot be gainsaid, but that does not mean that their aspirations were legitimate ones for a free society. Professor Finnegan should have said so more explicitly than he has done.

Despite its limitations, this is an impressive book. At the very least, it is a definitive treatment of the aims, organization, and activities of the champions of preparedness.

THOMAS M. HILL
Miami University
Oxford
Ohio

ALTON FRYE. A *Responsible Congress: The Politics of National Security.* Pp. xii, 238. New York: McGraw-Hill, 1975. $10.00.

Since the Founding Fathers created a separation of powers system when they wrote the Constitution, the relationship between the legislative and executive branches of the national government has always been a matter of very great concern, and it has had its ups and downs. It changes with the times; it reflects the character of the people who are in seats of power; it responds to the problems which confront the nation.

The general thesis of this fine book is that while over a long period of time Congress deferred to the Executive branch in the fields of foreign affairs and national security, this deference led to the creation of what has been called the "imperial presidency," and in recent years to a reaction now moving in the other direction.

Mr. Frye brings to this book a remarkable grasp of the facts in this area of American government. He is a Senior Fellow and Director of Special Projects for the Council on Foreign Relations, and is also Director of the Institute for Congress Project, supported by the Carnegie Endowment for International Peace. In addition, he serves as a consultant to the Subcommittee on National Security Decision-Making of the Committee for Economic Development. He has also been a consultant, particularly for Senator Edward W. Brooke of Massachusetts, on national security and foreign policy. He has taught at UCLA and Harvard, and was for a time a member of the RAND Corporation.

Mr. Frye argues that Congress began to get itself involved actively and significantly in the debate over atomic weapons. In particular, he believes that Congress began to assert itself in the complex, heated and lengthy debate over the concept of an anti-ballistic missile system. Since then, he argues, there has been more and more congressional involvement in national security and foreign affairs matters, resulting eventually in the new Congressional Budget Act, the Impoundment Act, and the War Powers Act. Thus the resurgence of Congress has come a long distance since the opening round of debate over ABM.

Finally, he develops the interesting thesis that this resurgence of Congress is good for the country, and indeed, good for the presidency. He argues that our constitutional system "must be insulated from the perils of an over-weaning Presidency" and that in addition, the President is in a much stronger bargaining position in dealing with the foreign countries if he has behind him the support of Congress.

Specific points stand out in this discussion. It is clear, although this is well known, that the staffs of the members of Congress, and of the committees, are very influential in the development of public policy. He also makes the familiar point that the committee staffs are not as helpful as they might be because they do not include enough expertise. He also makes the point that individual Senators may count a great deal. For example, Senator Brooke took the lead and persistently argued the case involving the desirability of the MIRV missile system. He also points up the tremendous influence of Senator John Stennis, Chairman of the Armed Services Committee. That determined and well-informed individuals make a difference is not an original discovery, but it is a point well worth making in view of the collegial character of the two Houses of the Congress.

Thus, while Congress got into the act late, it has come a long way, according to Mr. Frye, and now exerts tremendous influence in such delicate areas as the control and reduction of armaments, the foreign aid program, and international economic policy. This book is full of detailed and reliable information on a subject of surpassing importance to contemporary America.

DAVID FELLMAN
University of Wisconsin
Madison

EDWARD F. HAAS. *DeLesseps S. Morrison and the Image of Reform: New Orleans Politics, 1946–1961.* Pp. xii, 368. Baton Rouge: Louisiana State University Press, 1974. $12.95.

During his fifteen years as mayor of New Orleans, DeLesseps S. Morrison enjoyed a national reputation as a dynamic, progressive, urban reform leader. The Women's Research Guild cited him for restoring integrity to public office, he received the LaGuardia Award for his contributions to municipal government, and New Orleans was named an "All American City" by the National Municipal League. Alas, as this book makes clear, Morrison's achievements were more a testament to the effectiveness of his public relations than his accomplishments while in office. The Morrison era, Professor Haas points out, was a time of "public waste, police corruption, arbitrary rule, spoils politics, and racial discrimination."

Mayor Morrison possessed abundant political talents. Following his unexpected victory in 1946, Morrison employed the traditional techniques of alliances and patronage to put together a powerful political machine. He dominated New Orleans during his lengthy term of office, and he successfully fought off Governor Earl Long's attempts to subject the city to state control. Despite considerable talk about reform, however, Morrison lacked a commitment to good government. "Repeatedly," Haas emphasizes, "the mayor chose personal ambition and political expediency over the welfare of the city."

Professor Haas has written an incisive reportorial account of Morrison's public career but not a substantive work of history. The mayor emerges as a one-dimensional figure. This may simply indicate Morrison's unreflective nature; or, more likely, it is the result of limited material. Also, the author's focus is excessively narrow; he makes little effort to place Morrison's career in a broad interpretive framework. Although this book does make a contribution to our knowledge of postwar southern politics, the contribution is slight.

WILLIAM M. LEARY, JR.
University of Georgia
Athens

COY HILTON JAMES. *Silas Deane—Patriot or Traitor?* Pp. viii, 152. East Lansing: Michigan State University Press, 1975. $8.50.

This book was written by a specialist in modern European and in American colonial history. Until his recent untimely death, he served for many years as Chairman of the Department of History at Albion College. Unfortunately, he died shortly before his book appeared.

The chief character is, of course, Silas Deane. Since historians have had little or nothing to say about him, before trying to master this scholarly work, most readers should glance at the brief account of Deane's life and contributions in volume 7 of the 1966 edition of the *Encyclopaedia Britannica*. Moreover, after reading Professor James' little book, it might also be well to examine the volume entitled: *Papers in Relation to the Case of Silas Deane*—which was published in Philadelphia in 1855 for the Seventy-Six Society. Suffice it to say that the above was "published from the original manuscripts."

Who then was Deane? He was nothing less than a member of that first generation of geniuses who laid the foundations of this our American Commonwealth. Although he does not rank with giants such as Washington, Jefferson, and Franklin, nevertheless, he made certain contributions that helped to assure the success of that great venture. For, after serving as a secret agent in France not more than a year, he succeeded in obtaining not less than eight cargoes of arms—arms which played a large part in the defeat and surrender of General Burgoyne at Saratoga on October 17, 1777. It is also certain that, while on this mission in France, he put the cause of freedom first even to the point of sacrificing personal interests.

In spite of the above, Deane's life became tragic because a certain group of American politicians, under the leadership of Arthur Lee, accused him not only of profiting at the expense of Congress, but also of actually turning traitor. Interestingly enough, even today there are those who believe this. Thus on page 149 of his book, *The Federal Union: A History of the United States to 1965*, John D. Hicks tells us that Deane "ultimately went over to the British." At any rate, one reason why James' book is important is the fact that, while admitting that Deane was indiscreet, it shows he was

neither dishonest nor disloyal. James builds his case on the following facts: (1) the sacrifices that Deane made for the cause; (2) besides his strong affirmations of innocence, the fact that many others continued to stand with him; (3) in spite of his many letters asking for a fair trial, the persistent refusal of Congress to grant his request; and (4) the decision of the Senate Committee on Revolutionary Claims as well as that of the House in 1841 that he had been treated unjustly and awarding his heirs $37,000.

Although James' book is a bit brief and ends rather abruptly, besides proving his case, there is another reason why it is very important. This is the fact that, in this investigation of a much neglected revolutionary figure, the author throws light on the gigantic problems which the Founding Fathers faced. After all, part of the time at least, no one less than Franklin worked with him in Paris. Suffice it to say that, in terms of an addition to the historical record of the critical Revolutionary Era, this book serves as good reading during the Bicentennial Year of 1976.

ARTHUR W. MUNK

Albion College
Michigan

BERNARD KNOLLENBERG. *Growth of the American Revolution, 1766–1775.* Pp. v, 551. New York: Free Press, 1975. $15.00.

Bernard Knollenberg, in the introduction to his first book, *Origin of the American Revolution: 1759–1766* (1960), wrote: "Had the imperial relationship not been disturbed by the many new and vexing British measures introduced from 1759 to 1765 and afterward continued or renewed, it might I think have endured . . . for many generations, perhaps even to this day." Having established his research problem—the "vexing" issues that created dissension—Knollenberg, with considerable documentation, began a discussion which brought the colonies to the brink of rebellion in 1766. His current volume completes the investigation as to why the first British Empire commenced to unravel in 1775. Prior to the study's conclusion, Bernard Knollenberg died, but his widow and Professor John R. Alden saw the "virtually complete" manuscript through publication.

Considered in relation to his earlier study, this volume shares identical strengths and weaknesses. As its predecessor, the focus is largely on the legislative and constitutional dimensions of the issues that agitated the Empire— the Townshend Acts, *Liberty* Riot, *Gaspee* Affair, Intolerable Acts, and the First Continental Congress. The treatment of these matters and of their related operation within the English political community is detailed and professional. The book consists of 196 textual pages, 171 of appendices and 264 of notes and bibliography. Knollenberg singles out for special emphasis the Massachusetts Regulating Act which not only abolished the colony's governing pattern but, more importantly, confirmed the wisdom of radical whig prophecy and the Continental Congress' adoption of the Continental Association, the organization which ultimately provided the critical transition mechanism for organized resistance. The essential outlines of the subjects covered are well known. Knollenberg's virtue—and it is one that requires the reader to dig—is his examination of the extended juridical implications of these developments. These contingencies are extrapolated in literal fashion from the documents, and may or may not have been clear to the era's protagonists.

Conversely the juridical qualities of the book that historians will find of greatest value also underline the study's major failure—its narrow conceptual framework—a limitation that is particularly troublesome in a chronicle which purports to set down the basic story of the revolution's coming. The author, quite legitimately, chose to concentrate on a constitutional and legal theme but other forces, totally excluded from serious consideration, also affected the revolution's growth: the troubled economic health of the Empire, the dislocative social tensions present within the colonies—some contiguous to the imperial crises, others wholly separate— the fractionalized character of the various assemblies, and overlying all of this, the attendant and often very divergent ideological perspectives that existed both in an inter-colonial and intra-colonial fashion. All of these elements shaped the dimensions of the imperial confrontation into thirteen very different configurations. Equally fundamental, most of the material in this volume—with the exception of certain legal explications and some of the discussion involving Parliamentary maneuvers—is familiar. Unlike the years of Knollenberg's previous volume, 1759–1766, a period in which only a few able historians had ventured and where his research method contributed important additions, the content substance of the period 1766–1775 has been worked over by many scholars, several of whom have created more comprehensive syntheses.

RONALD HOFFMAN
University of Maryland
College Park

STEPHEN C. SCHLESINGER. *The New Reformers: Forces for Change in American Politics.* Pp. vii, 238. Boston, Mass.: Houghton Mifflin, 1975. $7.95.

The timeliness of *The New Reformers* relates to the upcoming presidential sweepstakes primarily. However, these catalytic groups may fail to organize coercive forces within the major parties, and the real value of this book may be its guide lines of "how to do it and how *not* to do it." This handbook for pressure people should, therefore, be read by inspired reformers who venture into the crossfire of big-time politics.

It is a bit of a shock to find the author indulging in the first person singular throughout his narrative of ideological battles, but this is his story and he has a right to spice it with his own eyewitness evidence. Please recall that St. Luke wrote his Gospel and then added *The Acts of the Apostles* which included his own acts. Stephen Schlesinger was founder and promoter of *The New Democrat*; he has been a believing reformer and apostle of political change.

The author's biases are unhidden. He expresses his values in selection of foci of reform: unequal distribution of wealth, corporation control, abuse of civil rights, inflation, poverty, unemployment, defense spending, and the like. Some other writer might choose right wing causes for reform movements.

Schlesinger produces interesting and profitable data on six reform groups: contemporary women's rights, Black power, labor unions, middle class liberals, Congressional reformers, and selected minorities.

These are some of the imperatives taught by analysis of case histories which reformers should observe: Be flexible in making alliances to win elections; don't make isolated deals at the expense of the reform coalition; don't waste resources on irrelevant internal disputes; show white blue-collar workers their common cause with Blacks and others; separate basic causes from symptoms and rhetoric; build a majority coalition for long range wars; exploit party regulations to get delegates to conventions; develop tactics to pressure the power merchants of Congress; protect reforms from "scuttling tactics" by rightists; use constitutional and legal protective sanctions; raise the sights of grass roots supporters; employ emotional appeals to stimulate hunger for power; don't wait for gifts of political power—you have to take it; realize that ideological foundations surpass personalities; admit the existence of "demons" in race reforms; and recognize that national fear is a fact.

Wistfully Schlesinger suggests that new reformers might produce a candidate for a political constituency which could take over the federal government in 1976. This proves that reformers like him feed on dreams.

D. LINCOLN HARTER
The College of Insurance
New York, N.Y.

JON C. TEAFORD. *The Municipal Revolution in America: Origins of Modern Urban Government, 1650–1825.* Pp. 152. Chicago, Ill.: The University of Chicago Press, 1975. $9.75.

This study covers the period 1650–1825 in the evolution of American urban government, and fills in depth the literature on the subject as it relates to such cities as Boston, New York, Philadelphia and Charleston. It relies mainly upon source materials not readily available before, and develops a closely-knit, proficient legal-historical text.

It starts with the English municipal background of the 17th century with its close corporation based upon trade and occupation. Growing stronger as the English kings from the Normans through the Stuarts granted charters of incorporation, it became virtually independent of the Crown by the beginning of the American colonization.

The early American municipal corporation following the English pattern also became a focus of trade and industry. It fixed prices, regulated weights and measures, and administered markets. The majority of aldermen and councillors were merchants and artisans. The freemen had the monopoly of the commercial activities of the community.

In New England, however, things were different. Here the town and the town meeting based upon religious membership fought for a more democratic system. Health and general welfare were desired, rather than trade. Revenues came from property—not from the commercial establishment. Liberty rather than monopoly guided the domestic policy. Later on, other colonies followed the Yankee example.

After 1720, the pattern gradually changed in all colonies. Exclusive trading rights were eliminated; the new governmental structure included separate agencies for fire protection, public safety, streets, health, poor relief and even planning. Price fixing, monopolies and commercial regulations declined. Adult males obtained voting rights. Taxation on property and persons became the basis of municipal finance. The old corporate bodies became lethargic, so life terms for their officers gave way to frequent elections.

New charters issued by the state legislature gave citizens the right of suffrage. Often they appealed to the legislature for

# 154 THE ANNALS OF THE AMERICAN ACADEMY

redress from actual or fancied wrongs and neglect, and the state politicians were happy to oblige (being generally against the old aristocracies of the corporations). Local separation of powers established independent judicial, administrative and legislative bodies.

Thus came the American urban revolution. It set the style for the development of American city government in the 19th and well into the 20th centuries. It laid the foundation for state control and democratic local institutions.

Professor Teaford deserves praise for a fine, solid job of scholarship. There are helpful notes and a good bibliography.

HAROLD F. ALDERFER
The Pennyslvania State University
University Park

HANS L. TREFOUSSE. *Impeachment of a President: Andrew Johnson, the Blacks, and Reconstruction.* Pp. xii, 252. Knoxville: University of Tennessee Press, 1975. $10.95.

Hans Trefousse, who is professor of history at Brooklyn College and author of several works on the personalities and politics of the 1860s, strengthens our understanding of Andrew Johnson and his presidency appreciably in this well-knit, argumentative book.

It is his thesis that Johnson's behavior toward Congress was governed by deep, unwavering racist convictions rather than by dedication to constitutional principle or a wish for the reconciliation of North and South, as many hold. His overriding purpose was to maintain the principle of white supremacy in the South. His strategy was cunning and guile.

If Johnson was widely misunderstood in his own day, it was for lack of candor, says Trefousse, not irresolution. He acted within the logic of his values, which he believed to be those of a majority of his countrymen, North and South, obstructing the radicals and their program of racial equality at every turn before and after his trial. He was vindicated by acquittal, Trefousse concludes, and ultimately by the failure of radical reconstruction.

It is intriguing to put Trefousse's Johnson next to, say, Eric McKitrick's (*Andrew Johnson and Reconstruction,* University of Chicago Press, 1960), the latter a complex, compassionate man with an honest belief in equal rights. McKitrick does not regard Johnson as a racist, given the popular sentiments and social problems of the day. He does not quarrel with Johnson's program for the introduction of only highly qualified blacks into the electorate.

But far from clever and undaunted, McKitrick's Johnson was a beaten man by the time of his impeachment, having dissipated his power as president and party leader and widened the division of North and South.

How can careful scholars differ so? First, they bring different values to their work—uncompromising egalitarianism *versus* gradualism, roughly. One man's racism is another's prudence. Johnson's reputation has fluctuated more than any other president's, according to sides taken on questions of civil rights, the presidency, and most recently the impeachment of a president.

Second, Trefousse and McKitrick marshal evidence differently. Trefousse favors the unguarded language of private correspondence, a kind of precursor of the White House tapes, which in the case of Johnson and his intimates includes racial slurs, while McKitrick prefers to build on a broad base of secondary sources. The two volumes are most informative together.

Recommended, in tandem.

ROBERT J. SICKELS
University of New Mexico
Albuquerque

## SOCIOLOGY

GEOFF DENCH. *Maltese in London: A Case-Study of the Erosion of Ethnic Consciousness.* Pp. 302. Boston, Mass.: Routledge & Kegan Paul, 1975. $21.00.

A certain number of Maltese in Britain were associated with "an international

vice empire," and their unsavory reputation was partly transferred to the whole of this small minority. This slight work, largely about how assimilation supposedly takes place under such peculiar circumstances, would at best be of slight importance. And "at best" applies to nothing in this book.

The level of scholarship is indicated by the population figures. The author rejects the official data as inadequate and offers a radically different set as the demographic base of his analysis, informing the reader, however, that "this is not the place for a full exposition of the demographic sources drawn on for this analysis, nor of the procedures adopted and computations made; in fact I hope to publish this material separately at a later date." All the inferences, thus, drawn from the imputed sizes of the migration, the return migration, the fertility, the settlement pattern, and so on must be accepted on faith—but faith in Dr. Dench is the last characteristic a critical reader is likely to develop.

Much of the discussion is based on a questionnaire administered to some Maltese in London. Which Maltese would be a crucial matter, and the sample design, as the author sums up his exposition, was "very much a compromise." The questions posed in the survey range from matter-of-fact to preposterously naive. As Paul Lazarsfeld pointed out several decades ago in a paper since become a classic, one cannot ask a question like "Why did you leave Malta?" and hope to get usable responses. As a completely different example, if a marketing firm seeking guidance for the next season's styles asked respondents, "Why are you wearing a red dress?" it might receive replies ranging from "Because my green suit is at the cleaner's" to "Because I left the nudist movement six months ago." In the course in survey analysis that Lazarsfeld used to give at Columbia, such questionnaires as the one Dr. Dench put together were used to teach students what not to do.

As the campaign against white slave traffic developed, the English public generally associated pimping with Maltese ethnicity. In the chapter he devotes

to the issue, Dr. Dench is never able to resolve it. From his political predilections he was inclined to believe that the sense of grievance of the ordinary Maltese at this "most undeserved defamation" was indeed "understandable and legitimate." However, Maltese were arrested and deported in far higher proportion than any other group, and this record was not merely the response of police antipathy. Maltese vice offenders were "unlikely to have just been innocent victims of a vice squad frustrated by failure to trap the Messina Brothers." In sum, those who condemned the Maltese were wrong, though the substance of their condemnation was correct: "there does seem to be a leaning among Maltese in London towards the sex trade."

In the concluding chapter, the author spells out the ideological biases implicit in the rest of the book. He is opposed to the liberal principle by which each individual, alien as well as citizen, is responsible for his own acts, for this "creates the problem of racialism." To denote this as simplistic is the kindest word that one can use to characterize such sophomoric philosophizing.

WILLIAM PETERSEN
Ohio State University
Columbus

ROGER HOOD, ed. *Crime, Criminology and Public Policy: Essays in Honour of Sir Leon Radzinowicz.* Pp. xxii, 650. New York: The Free Press, 1975. $29.95.

The subtitle of this book suggests that an objective review of *Crime, Criminology and Public Policy* might be somewhat difficult. Can the reviewer pretend not to be interested in the fact that this collection of essays was assembled as a tribute to one of the most eminent criminologists of our time? My own answer to this question has to be an honest "no." Likewise, I suspect that this volume will be more readily read and received among students of criminology because of Radzinowicz's name than might otherwise have been the case.

Hood has set out to cover the many

facets of Leon Radzinowicz's lengthy career by bringing together twenty-nine original essays written by former colleagues and students, as well as prominent scholars and others in government and public life who were associated with him during his years at the Cambridge Institute of Criminology. The subjects of the various selections in the volume each deal with a theme which reflects an interest or concern of Radzinowicz including such important topics as: the social history of criminal law, the administration of criminal justice, penal reform, public attitudes toward crime and criminals, the proper scope of individual rights in the criminal process, police accountability, and law reform. In addition, several selections summarize empirical research findings on selected problems in criminology such as Wolfgang's "Crime in a Birth Cohort" and Christiansen's "Seriousness of Criminality and Concordance among Danish Twins."

A common flaw of most edited works that could be expected to be all the more true in this case is the lack of consistently sound contributions on the topics covered. As independent contributions to the field of criminology, some of these selections would not survive editorial review. The selections included are indeed quite variable. Some are not interesting; they do not stimulate the imagination. Others are not informative. Some papers are not relevant to the interests of United States students of criminology. Many are excellent studies in criminology however. In particular we might note the chapters by Walker ("Lost Causes in Criminology"), Sellin ("Slavery and the Punishment of Crime"), Cressey ("Law, Order and the Motorist"), Ancel ("The Relationship Between Criminology and 'Politique Criminelle' "), and Wechsler ("The Model Penal Code and the Codification of American Criminal Law"). Also, of some note is an annotated bibliography on the writings of Radzinowicz by Hawkins. In terms of an overall assessment, it can be stated, however, that reading this collection was deemed well worth the time investment. One not only gains a perspective on the tremen-

dous diversity of Radzinowicz's scholarship but one also develops an appreciation of the widespread influence of his work for the development of criminological knowledge. Moreover, a reading of this volume conveys a sense of the import that Radzinowicz placed on the interaction between criminology, criminal law and penal policy. Although the volume only modestly claims to provide a vehicle for the colleagues and friends of Radzinowicz to pay tribute to his scholarship, if a common theme unifies these papers it is a sense of the importance that Radzinowicz placed on the interplay between criminological evidence and public policy.

In sum, this is a unique and rather specialized book for those interested in a personal tribute to the work of a most productive and important criminologist. Finally, although I'm not sure this will remain a valid point for long in our changing economy, the price of this volume strikes me as excessive. Many interested readers might indeed find better buys considering the amount of material presented.

DAVID M. PETERSEN
Georgia State University
Atlanta

J. HOWARD KAUFFMAN and LELAND HARDER. *Anabaptists Four Centuries Later: A Profile of Five Mennonite and Brethren in Christ Denominations.* Pp. 399. Scottsdale, Pa.: Herald Press, 1975. $9.95.

The original Anabaptists, stalwarts of the radical Christian movement in sixteenth-century Europe, emphasized the need to separate the church from state affairs, taught love and nonresistance, opposed military service, taught that membership in the church should be a voluntary decision symbolized by adult baptism, and exemplified rigorous personal morality. In this study J. Howard Kauffman and Leland Harder, established Mennonite scholars, attempt to learn just how closely modern Anabaptists maintain the standards of their sixteenth-century forbears. To accomplish this they administered a carefully-constructed questionnaire to nearly 3,600 of the 200,000 members that make up the five major Mennonite and Brethren in Christ denominations in the United States and Canada.

Their precise sociological profile reveals that for the most part modern Anabaptists adhere rather closely to the vision and beliefs of the original Anabaptists. They are a very conservative group in comparison with other churches —"more orthodox than all other major denominations that have been studied, both Protestant and Catholic, with the notable exception of the Southern Baptists." They have a strong *in-groupness* as evidenced by the fact that three-fourths choose spouses from the same denomination. Traditional views on women's roles prevail among both men and women. They are strongly committed to traditional moral attitudes, including pacifism. They remain a rural people isolated from many of the changes that have rocked other denominations. They are leery of political power and tend to withdraw from the political process.

Social ethics is the one area in which modern Anabaptists seem to fall short of traditional ideals. They do not share the early Anabaptists' concern for the poor and there is evidence of opposition to racial minorities and prejudice toward Catholics and Jews. The authors suggest that the modern Anabaptists may have been affected by their association with the fundamentalism movement which has been militaristic and nationalistic and threatens their original ideals. They conclude that in the years ahead Anabaptists must strive to build cooperatively with other denominations and work to overcome their lack of concern for minority groups and the needy.

Unfortunately they are much more effective in identifying Anabaptist traits and attitudes than they are at explaining why these characteristics prevail. Their findings become more understandable, however, when placed in a proper historical context such as that furnished by Walter Klaassen's *Anabaptism: Neither Catholic nor Protestant* (1973) and Frank Epp's *Mennonites in Canada*

(1974). The authors obviously respect Anabaptism—Kauffman is a sociologist at Goshen College and past president of the Mennonite Historical Society and Harder is an ordained Mennonite minister and theology professor at the Mennonite Biblical Seminary. But to their credit they refrain from the filial piety that scars many church studies.

Despite their relatively small numbers the Anabaptists have received extensive attention from scholars. Much of the work has been of high quality, including this well-crafted volume which will serve as a model for the study of other denominations.

ROBERT DETWEILER
San Diego State University
California

EUGENE LITWAK and HENRY J. MEYER. *School, Family, and Neighborhood: The Theory and Practice of School-Community Relations.* Pp. xi, 300. New York: Columbia University Press, 1974. $11.00.

This book is different from other books treating school-community relationships. It is "must" reading for school administrators and community members who are concerned with influencing school policy and practice.

The first four chapters establish a theoretical framework. The authors take the position that in some situations the distance between the school and its families, neighborhoods, and community should be decreased, but in other situations it should be increased. They say that the performance of some tasks in education require experts but that others can be handled by non-experts. Eight mechanisms that can be employed to link the school and external groups are described and rated in terms of initiative, intensity, expertise, scope, and usefulness in creating or closing social distance. Administrative styles are categorized and rated as to their organizational structure, compatibility with organizational tasks, and relationship to the various linking mechanisms. In a similar manner, family types and neighborhood types are described and rated.

Contrary to the views of some other sociologists who hold that neighborhoods are no longer viable in the United States, Litwak and Meyer hold that the neighborhood has important social functions to perform and possesses means for their performance.

The last eight chapters are devoted to the eight linking mechanisms: descriptions, dimensions, uses, forms of influence, techniques of operation, limitations, and costs. In the main, these chapters are addressed to the use of the mechanisms by the school as it seeks to influence external groups, but they include discussions of the use of the mechanisms by external groups that seek to influence the school.

The volume is based in large part on research carried out over a considerable period of time in Detroit. This research involved many sociologists as well as school administrators, teachers, and children. It employed systematic surveys of children, mothers, school neighborhood residents, and teachers in eighteen elementary schools. The authors are well-known for earlier research that they have done, both cooperatively and individually, on several aspects of schooling and relationships among social groups. The reader may regret the omission of a bibliography, yet he will value the few dozen footnotes that point to further published research relevant to many of the issues and positions set forth.

The book does not provide ready-made solutions to the multifarious problems involved in school-community relationships. But it offers a useful theory of those relationships and a fresh approach to dealing with them. The classifications of the elements involved and the discussions of the meshing of those elements are valuable contributions to both theory and practice.

WILLIAM H. CARTWRIGHT
Duke University
Durham
North Carolina

CHARLES R. PERRY et al. *The Impact of Government Manpower Programs: In General, and on Minorities and Women.* Pp. 511. Philadelphia: University of Pennsylvania Press, 1975. $18.50.

This book represents an ambitious attempt to summarize over 252 evaluation studies of manpower programs under MDTA (1962) and EOA (1964). As such it reviews a decade of direct federal involvement in manpower policy. About one-third of the book is devoted to an overview of the manpower programs and their overall impact. The remaining two-thirds consists of separate chapters devoted to the analysis of the following individual programs: Manpower Development and Training Act (MDTA); Job Opportunities in the Business Sector (JOBS); Public Service Careers and New Careers (PSC); Apprenticeship Outreach Program (AOP); Public Employment Program (PEP); Opportunities Industrialization Centers (OIC); Concentrated Employment Program (CEP); Work Incentive Program (WIN); Job Corps; Neighborhood Youth Corps (NYC); and Operation Mainstream.

The first part of the book is an attempt by the authors to summarize the overall evidence for the various manpower programs. They group the programs into those focusing upon skill training (MDTA), those focusing upon job development (PEP, PSC, JOBS, AOP), those focusing upon employability development (OIC, WIN, CEP, Job Corps) and those focusing upon work experience (NYC and Operation Mainstream). As might be expected, they find that the economic benefit, as indicated by post training jobs, declines as the program focus moves away from skill training. Furthermore, minorities and women tend to be concentrated in those programs where skill training is least. The exception to the above is AOP, in which minority males predominate and economic benefits are high. For women, both black and white, economic benefits are most likely to result from skill training in the clerical or health-service fields. Nevertheless the benefits are mainly in terms of stable employment due to high demand rather than any increase in wages.

The authors devote a part of their

analysis to the non-economic benefits in spite of the fact that there is little hard evidence available. Does the training provide important supportive services such as health care and child care? Apparently operating under a culture-of-poverty hypothesis, the authors are curious whether programs improve "personal attitudes" and remedy "incomplete societal acculturation." Nothing is said about the possible negative non-economic benefits such as heightened discouragement and lowered self esteem when, after having completed the training program, the individual is still unable to obtain a good job.

In doing the study, the authors are forced to deal with the existing data. These data, as the authors note, are either inadequate, especially in terms of good control groups, or virtually non-existent, as in the case of non-economic impact. A good analysis of the problems with the existing data is presented and the authors make some good suggestions for future program evaluation.

Although the study represents an admirable synthesis of an overwhelming amount of data collected in disparate ways, it does not deal with many broader implications, especially those raised by the shift to decentralize manpower programs in the Comprehensive Employment and Training Act of 1973 (CETA). Now that local communities have greater control, what will happen to the manpower mix? The *New York Times* (September 26, 1975) reported that aid is being directed away from the disadvantaged. However, even before the CETA, the most disadvantaged workers, the blacks and the women, were more likely to enter programs such as WIN with less economic pay-off. Furthermore, the fact that successful programs—that is, MDTA-OJT and AOP—focused on training for which jobs were more likely to be available, indicates that a critical variable has been overlooked. Of what relevance is a manpower policy aimed at training during periods of high employment, except, to perhaps reorder those individuals in the job queue.

SALLY BOULD-VAN TIL
University of Delaware
Newark

PAUL RABINOW. *Symbolic Domination: Cultural Form and Historical Change in Morocco*. Pp. xv, 107. Chicago, Ill.: The University of Chicago Press, 1975. $8.95.

Many American anthropologists have moved away from the global notion of culture as all learned behavior or as the theme or pattern that encompasses all custom. Rather, they have limited culture to institutionalized symbol systems, and differentiated it from social systems, which are seen as patterns of interaction, and personality systems. One advantage to this approach is that no assumptions need be made about the relationship(s) between culture—that is, beliefs and values—on the one hand, and relationship patterns, personality, material artifacts, and the like, on the other hand; the conceptual distinction of culture as symbol systems from these other phenomena encourages empirical investigation of the interconnections. Causal efficacy can remain an open question; indeed, many anthropologists reject the general materialist and idealist positions and argue for a loose systemic model in which culture may be the influential factor in some cases, material conditions in others, interaction patterns in yet others, and in which the determination of causal efficacy is an empirical issue that must be settled by case analysis of historical instances.

It is in this spirit that Paul Rabinow approaches his account of Morocco. He is concerned especially with the relationship between religious and political ideas and beliefs, and power and authority structures. This is because "meaning is not found on the cultural level alone but in the partial and imperfect relation of symbols to the particular historical conditions in which they are situated" (p. 99). Thus the framework of Rabinow's account is a temporal, historical one, in which he places the life of the saint Sidi Lahcen Lyussi and the lives of the saint's descendants within the contexts of the pre-protectorate, protectorate, and post-protectorate periods. However, the substance of the discussion is not a reported sequence of events characteristic of the chronicle, but rather an exploration of Moroccan concepts and ideas as they exist within, influence, and are influenced by the social and political context: the hereditary-genealogical claims of the *shurfa* (descendants of the Prophet) versus the charismatic-miraculous claims of the saints; *haqq*, especial closeness to the divine; *baraka*, divine grace; *bled*, domain; *bled l-makhzen and bled s-siba*, the realms of government and dissidence; *qbila*, social reference category; *sellah*, mediation; *shih* and *ayyan*, strength and weakness.

The ultimate ethnographic point of reference in the discussion is the group of Sidi Lahcen villagers who claim descent from the saint Sidi Lahcen Lyussi. Part of the symbolic analysis is of their legend of the saint's life, which Rabinow characterizes as "a claim of legitimate domination," and of the ceremonies that commemorate the saint's birthday and death, the *museum*. These discussions are supplemented with historical vignettes of *zawiya*, saint's lodges, and short biographical sketches of Sidi Lahcen Lyussi and a few of his living descendants. What Rabinow finds is that the ideology of the saint's descendants, which is a reflection of the conflict between the charismatic and hereditary principles in previous historical times and which was an adaptation to those times, has become outmoded in present historical circumstances. These *wlad* Sidi Lahcen Lyussi, in successfully maintaining their claims for specialness in traditional terms, have unintentionally cut themselves off from the economic and political benefits of the current period with its quite different bases of power and authority. Thus "they are acutely aware of the great power of the saint and deterioration of their own" (p. 96), with a resulting tension, anxiety, and growing alienation from their own framework of meaning and identity.

This well written and sensitive account is more an essay in cultural interpretation than a detailed history or ethnography. Most of the description is on a fairly general level, and must be taken on faith. For example, the anxiety and alienation of the *wlad* Sidi Lahcen Lyussi is asserted but not documented; even quoted statements of informants are few. And for such a wide ranging discussion, there is precious little bibliographic reference. It was a source of surprise to this reviewer that the work of Gellner on saints and of Burke on the concepts of *bled l-makhzen and bled s-siba* should not be cited. Finally, one might have hoped that the University of Chicago Press would have done better with such a small, expensive book than gluing it as if it were a paperback.

PHILIP CARL SALZMAN
McGill University
Montreal, Quebec
Canada

## ECONOMICS

HENRY J. AARON. *Who Pays the Property Tax?: A New View.* Pp. ix, 110. Washington, D.C.: The Brookings Institution, 1975. $5.95. Paperbound, $2.50.

Although the property tax has been the major means of financing local government since Colonial times, probably no other fiscal device has been as vigorously and continually criticized. As one economist put it back in 1931, "If any tax could have been eliminated by adverse criticism, the general property tax should have been eliminated long ago. One searches in vain for one of its friends to defend it intelligently." Though not necessarily a friend or advocate of this tax, Henry J. AAron, a senior fellow at the Brookings Institution, has written an excellent analysis of the property tax that reflects the revised thinking of many other economists and suggests the real potential of property taxation for achieving a more equitable tax structure.

Traditionally, property taxation has been reviled for its regressive incidence (forcing those who have less to pay a disproportionate share) and for its inequitable administration by local authorities which results in unequal burdens on households in otherwise similar circumstances. AAron challenges both of these arguments and concludes that, on balance, the tax is neither regressive in its incidence nor is it incapable of fair, efficient administration.

For years the prevailing view held that the property tax was regressive because it functioned as a kind of excise tax on the consumers of goods and services produced by taxable real property. For example, renters had to bear the property tax levied on their residences and auto buyers indirectly bore the burden of taxes on the factories that produced their cars and the materials from which they were made. The burden of tax was borne in proportion to the consumption of commodities. Following this logic, the tax was regressive because consumption (especially of housing in whose price the property tax is a very large element) is much greater in the budgets of lower income families than in higher income groups.

AAron, however, argues that this view is erroneous because it only considers the distributional effects of property taxation within a given locale. If the nation as a whole is the frame of reference, the property tax is not an excise on consumers, but a tax on capital. As such, the burdens of the tax are shared by all owners (even those not directly subject to the tax) through adjustments in the rate of return on capital. Since ownership of capital is progressively distributed, the property tax is, on balance, progressive. The importance of this revisionist analysis of property taxation for the debate over tax reform is clearly enormous. As AAron recognizes, "Advocates of greater progressivity in our system should recognize that the property tax advances rather than obstructs achievement of egalitarian objectives." Indeed, wider understanding and acceptance of AAron's new view of property taxation could alter the whole tax reform debate and, perhaps, put local government in the forefront of reform rather than in its backwaters.

By the same token, AAron argues that inept and fragmented administration of the property tax is by no means an inherent failing of the tax itself. The author shows that many remedies are now at hand. He calls for such things as the elimination of very small assessing jurisdictions, more frequent and accurate revaluation of property, providing more information on assessment methods to taxpayers and a speedier appeals process.

This book is written with the purpose of improving public debate by making the layman aware of recent advances in the economic analysis of property taxation. Although this goal is only partially achieved—it is doubtful that many individuals without economic training could understand the author's discussion of property tax incidence—this is still a nicely written work that conveys its essential points well. *Who Pays the Property Tax?* is an important contribution which should be of major interest to those concerned with tax reform and the future of local government.

PAUL KANTOR
Fordham University
Bronx, N.Y.

GEORGE F. BREAK and JOSEPH A. PECHMAN. *Federal Tax Reform: The Impossible Dream?* Pp. ix, 142. Washington, D.C.: The Brookings Institution, 1975. $6.95. Paperbound, $2.95.

If there is to be any significant, meaningful tax reform in the near future for the United States, this text will undoubtedly serve as the basic guide. Since a national election year is approaching, the probability of a change in the tax laws appears imminent; however, a change need not be a positive reform. This text expertly provides a comprehensive analysis of the economic effect of various proposed changes in tax policy. The authors conclude that tax reform is not an impossible dream; however, it is an elusive target if attempted on a piecemeal basis rather than as a comprehensive program.

The objective of any tax reform is to transfer control of resources from one group in society to another without interfering with other macroeconomic or microeconomic goals of society. The fact that taxation serves dual masters—the stabilization function and the general revenue function—complicates the role of tax policy, and the special pleadings of interest groups often make for a political struggle rather than a rational policy decision; however, tax reform can be a positive sum game if the merits of reform can be conveyed to the public and the political authority. This book provides the analysis and data from which such a policy can evolve. The authors evaluate tax policy in terms of achieving the principal goals of equity and economic efficiency. Although vertical equity or progressivity cannot be determined by any positive method, the authors offer proposals that would improve the tax incidence based on the accepted canon of ability to pay. They also offer numerous proposals to enhance horizontal equity to place equal burdens on equals. Each reform proposal is also evaluated in terms of the possible distortion effect on private action and public goals—especially on the probable impact on incentives to work or to save.

The basis for tax reform in the United States must solve three basic current weaknesses: (1) the regressivity of payroll taxes, (2) the horizontal inequity in the middle and upper income classes, and (3) a need for diversification of federal revenue sources. The authors evaluate and quantify the costs and benefits of different options for two-earner incomes, municipal bond interest, investment tax credit, depreciation rates, capital gains rates, consumption taxes, inheritance and estate taxes, minimum taxes, and most every other significant exemption or deduction. These various reform measures are then classified into four separate packages or reform strategies. The change in the effective rates for various income classes and the change in tax revenue are then estimated from the data on the 1972 tax file of the Brookings Institution. Each proposal is evaluated in terms of the consequences on the economic goals of society as well as the impact on equity and efficiency goals of tax policy. These estimates of the incidence of the existing tax structure and "tax expenditures" provide a data base to make more objective and rational decisions concerning tax reform.

The summary chapter provides the specification and estimation of the four packages of reform proposals that range from modest to ambitious reform that would result in a more progressive, equitable, and diverse system of taxation than the existing tax system. This book is the latest in a series of studies by the Brookings Institution that provide a strong empirical and theoretical justification for a more optimal tax policy. This is a balanced, readable book for both the professional economist and hopefully for all legislators; a most valuable contribution to the area of public finance and public policy.

WILLIAM E. SPELLMAN
Coe College
Cedar Rapids
Iowa

MARY O. FURNER. Advocacy and Objectivity: A Crisis in the Professionalization of American Social Science, 1865–1905. Pp. xv, 357. Lexington: The University Press of Kentucky, 1975. $17.50.

Professor Furner's subject is more specific than her title suggests. She traces the professional activities of a group of scholars who pioneered the development of economics as an academic discipline during the general transformation of American universities in the late nineteenth century. In 1865 economics or political economy was taught in an elementary fashion, from a rigidly laissez-faire perspective, as part of moral philosophy. Students of economics joined with doctors, lawyers, humanitarians and politicians in the recently established American Social Science Association, which worked to provide a broad scientific basis for social reform. By the eighteen-eighties, with the formation of the American Economic Association, the older Social Science Association declined as an important forum for economists. Wider opportunities for postgraduate training, especially in Germany, had provided Americans with skills which were increasingly valuable in the universities and bureaucracy of rapidly industrializing society. The interests and ambitions of economists both widened and narrowed. The majority became less rigidly committed to laissez-faire and had developed expertise in new areas or technical aspects of their subject. They were beginning to write in language which was less immediately intelligible to laymen. Economics was firmly dissociated from socialism and other general critiques of American society. Economists who continued to see their subject as providing a basis for social reform movements declined in professional prestige. Economists were very reluctant to defend radical colleagues and were most active and successful after 1896, when American society was more secure after over a decade of political protest, and economists themselves felt that their subject was more firmly established. Those radicals like E. A. Ross, who were supported by their colleagues, rarely questioned fundamental American values. More radical scholars had their careers destroyed or retarded, frequently retreated into more specialized and less controversial areas of their subject, a process which strengthened the idea that economics was a technical subject designed to assist the smoother working of a capitalist economy.

Professor Furner's analysis of academic economists concludes with a brief and less convincing account of what she sees as similar developments among political scientists and sociologists by 1905. Although we already have masterly treatments of American economic ideas and studies of some of her principal participants it is useful to possess a coherent account of economists as a group, based largely on their personal papers. Unfortunately, as a study of professionalization the book has limitations. It provides no information about total numbers of professional economists, their pay or conditions of work. Although the majority were apparently university teachers, students, work loads and methods of teaching do not figure in her study. The question of academic freedom is examined in detail but there is surprisingly little information about routine relationships between economists and businessmen, politicians and university administrators on whose patronage social scientists ultimately depended. The

book also seems narrowly specific and culture-bound: the writer might have considered the quite different development of the social sciences in late nineteenth century Europe.

LOUIS BILLINGTON
University of Hull
Yorkshire
England

JOHN KENNETH GALBRAITH. *Money: Whence It Came, Where It Went.* Pp. 324. Boston, Mass.: Houghton Mifflin Company, 1975. $10.00.

Galbraith's purpose in this volume is to make monetary history, from the Kings of Lydia to the present time, teach us to be strict textbook Keynesians while, at the same time, accepting the inevitability of direct wage, price and foreign exchange controls. More specifically, monetary history teaches Galbraith that monetary policy is useless and that greater reliance must be placed on fiscal policy in combating domestic recession. This, of course, is the strict (at least pre-1960s) textbook view of Keynes. Further, returning to the theme of his earlier works, he learns that both monetary and fiscal policy will be largely useless in combating inflation, except in those sectors of the economy which are still ruled by the market. Where there is market power (that is, administered prices and wages), direct wage and price controls will be necessary. By extension to the international economy, direct controls on large blocs of mobile currencies will be required to prevent disruptive speculative attacks on weak currencies.

Galbraith is at his best in the first two-thirds of this volume, tracing the history of money, monetary policy and monetary ideas from ancient times to the end of World War II. He makes available to the general reader much of the existing highly-specialized research in the area of monetary history. His highly readable and entertaining history is largely anecdotal. A recurring lesson is that any enduring association with money is "capable of inducing not alone bizarre but ripely perverse behaviour." He delights, both himself and the reader, in chronicling how history's monetary geniuses and financial wizards have often passed not only into obscurity but into penury, jail and worse. Of particular note, for those interested in the history of ideas, is his discussion of the process and persons through which the "new" Keynesian Economics found its way from Cambridge, England to Cambridge, Massachusetts and, thereby, to Washington in the late 1930s and early 1940s. Galbraith was himself an actor, albeit minor, in this process.

Galbraith fails in the last, critical, third of the volume with his critique of what he calls "modern" economic theory and in the theory (or non-theory) which he brings to bear on interpreting recent monetary events. It is, of course, from the recent past that Galbraith derives his major lessons. A minor irritant, to the professional economist reading this book, is Galbraith's contention that current economic theory does not provide an explanation of current events. It is unlikely, however, that a majority of economists, Keynesian or Monetarist, hold the naive views which Galbraith attributes to them. (This discussion contains only one reference to any serious academic theorizing in this area in the past 15 years.) The recent literature is, in fact, ripe with theoretical explanations of "stagflation." It may well be true that recent theory does not provide *the* explanation of current economic events and it is certainly true that Galbraith's view of "modern economics" provides no explanation.

But the major fault is that Galbraith's interpretation of recent history does not support many of his major findings. A critical example is his view that monetary policy is useless. This view comes from his observation that monetary policy caused the worsening of stagflation in the late 1960s and early 1970s. Monetary tightness in this period, so his argument goes, suppressed economic activity and employment, while the market power of unions and corporations could keep prices rising as before. Thus, the giant

leap to the view that monetary policy is useless in combating stagflation. However, Galbraith's argument suggests that monetary policy was quite effective, but was applied in the wrong direction. It takes little thought to turn the argument around: had monetary policy been easy, rather than tight, employment and economic activity would have expanded while the rate of inflation would have been no worse, being determined by corporate and union power, which is unhindered by the discipline of the market. Even in Galbraith's world, then, there may be a strong role for monetary policy in combating the stagnation side of stagflation and/or the inflation side in the market sector of the economy. Further, there is no doubt that corporations and unions have market power. However, a critical question to which Galbraith never addresses himself is whether or not there will be an inducement to exercise such power in a period of falling general demand as a result, say, of a tight money policy. Moreover, even were corporate prices rising while demand, market prices and employment are falling, one suspects that the concomitant fall in output in all sectors would lead to a declining rate of inflation, *properly measured*. Finally, he advocates exchange controls on international currency movements with very little supporting argument. He has little to say about the possible role of monetary policy in offsetting speculative attacks on weak currencies or in strengthening currencies. The implication is that, in this area too, monetary policy is useless.

Leaving monetary policy, this last third of the volume also provides a good summary of the recent experience with fiscal policy, especially with respect to its inflexibility. He puts forward several useful arguments and proposals for increasing the flexibility of fiscal policy along lines originally proposed by Professor Tobin.

This will be a useful volume for the general reader interested in a survey of monetary history and some of the recent issues in the use of fiscal policy.

It will be much less useful for those interested in the current state of monetary theory.

JON HARKNESS
McMaster University
Hamilton, Ontario
Canada

IRVING B. KRAVIS et al. *A System of International Comparisons of Gross Product and Purchasing Power*. Pp. xi, 294. Baltimore, Md.: The Johns Hopkins University Press, 1975. $20.00. Paperbound, $7.50.

National income accounting has been used by many countries domestically with considerable success. On the national level, it facilitates planning, research and policymaking. However, a worldwide system of reliable and mutually consistent comparisons of product, income and expenditures along with purchasing power has not yet been developed. This volume represents the first stage of the project which is being carried out by the concerted efforts of the Statistical Office of the U.N., the World Bank and the International Comparison Unit of the University of Pennsylvania.

This study serves two main purposes: (1) to develop methods for a system of international comparisons and (2) to produce such comparisons for a selected group of countries differing in income levels, economic organization and location. It contains the binary and multilateral comparisons of national products, income and expenditures of six countries —Hungary, India, Japan, Kenya, England and the United States—in 1967 and of ten countries—with Colombia, France, Italy and West Germany added —in 1970. In addition, methods are developed for extending the study to other countries. Comparisons are given for the gross domestic products—its three major parts: consumption, capital formation and government expenditures—as well as for over thirty subaggregates. Appendixes contain even more detailed data to enable users to make their own aggregations.

International comparisons of national income figures are indispensable for the study of economic growth and development. Over the past two decades, statistical methodology underlying such comparisons has greatly improved. Yet, a major limitation to comparability has been the inadequacy of official exchange rates for converting national incomes expressed in national currencies to a common basis of valuation.

Price comparability is improved by the use of "hedonic regression" methods of price comparisons which permit holding different quality variables constant across countries. Moreover, conventional binary comparisons are complemented by simultaneous methods which are employed to obtain transitive base-invariant indexes. The authors also describe alternative methods, expecially a Monte Carlo experiment to establish the degree of precision in comparing gross domestic products and in establishing purchasing power parity.

The volume represents a significant contribution to the standardization and systematization of national income accounting with the purpose of developing a more meaningful cross-sectional analysis of economic systems needed for a better understanding of the phenomena of economic growth and development, for facilitating national and international economic planning and for providing a more adequate basis for economic policies on both the national and international levels.

OLEG ZINAM
University of Cincinnati
Ohio

PETER D. MCCLELLAND. *Causal Explanation and Model Building in History, Economics, and the New Economic History*. Pp. 290. Ithaca, N.Y.: Cornell University Press, 1975. $12.50.

My feelings about methodological discussions are akin to those about death— reckoned with once, they are best forgotten for they are issues which can never be entirely resolved. Peter McClelland, on the other hand, is a bit more optimistic on the benefits of methodological theorizing. He believes his book not only clarifies this complex subject but also solves some longstanding issues. Although he must be commended for investigating a subject I wouldn't touch with a ten-foot pole, he gives me about as much new guidance on these issues as does Billy Graham on those others.

The book is divided into five sections: (I) "On Models, Theories, and Causal Explanations," (II) "Causal Explanation in History," (III) "Causal Explanation and Model Building in Economics," (IV) "Counterfactual Speculation in History, Economics, and the New Economic History," and (V) "Causal Explanation and Model Building in the New Economic History." The first develops the seminal notion that ". . . the unity of method in causal explanations of all disciplines . . . turns upon two assertions." The first is that causal explanation consists of subsuming specific facts under generalizations of the form

If $(C_1, \ldots, C_n)$, then E.

The second is that because knowledge is uncertain, all causal generalizations must be prefaced with the word probably (p. 63). This is McClelland's central finding, and the remainder of the book explores its relevance to economic and historical research. In applying this concept to section II, McClelland does not add much, and the next section, that on economics, concludes pessimistically that although economists approach causation correctly they have nonetheless failed. Their discipline has enabled them to discover the direction of "likely tendencies linking causes and effects" but has yielded them nothing on precise magnitudes (p. 143). His conclusions on counterfactual explanation seem flawed to me. Although McClelland states that "there is an *enormous* difference between (a) attempting to identify some of the causal factors that actually contributed to an observed effect, and (b) attempting to specify what the world

would have been like minus one of the causes that actually did occur" (p. 163), do we not implicitly answer (b) in accomplishing (a)? (Counterfactuals are always embedded in causal reasoning.) In his final chapter on the new economic history McClelland again raises his initial point that "causal explanations cannot be deductive in form, that is with all generalizations prefaced with the word probably, they can never be characterized as explanations derived by deductive inference from universal causal generalizations known to be universal" (p. 171). He then reviews some of the assumptions employed by new economic historians, such as Cobb-Douglas production functions and linear demand schedules but does not assess their impact on our understanding of historical events. Thus, the book can be conveniently described as 290 pages of "Probably, if $(C_1, \ldots, C_n)$, then E," and boredom sets in early. But one cannot be too harsh, because McClelland has nicely summarized an impressive body of methodological literature and (probably) has added something new.

A major problem with this book is that McClelland is writing within the confines of defining quantitative history as economic history and economists as its only "competent" (p. 243) practitioners. However, many so-called cliometricians are not content with historical data and models narrowly defined as economic but are instead widening their horizons to encompass the demographic, political, and social aspects of history. The methodology of this new field, properly called quantitative history, is no different from that of, say, econometrics, but the scope of its questions is different. It is the definition of this field which is the relevant issue; not the meaning of causation. The topics which then might have been discussed are partial versus general equilibrium analysis, general versus specific historical paradigms, and problems of formulating models of political activity, to mention a few. These are the new and interesting issues in methodology.

Peter McClelland's book has rehashed a debate which can probably be discussed ad nauseam with little progress. The book is too long and too tedious. However, I am somewhat pleased with this volume, for I now have a reference for my students who, being less agnostic than I, would like to pursue methodology.

CLAUDIA D. GOLDIN
Princeton University
Princeton, N.J.

MIRIAM OSTOW and ANNA B. DUTKA. *Work and Welfare in New York City.* Pp. v, 93. Baltimore, Md.: Johns Hopkins University Press, 1975. $7.95.

This is a brief book. It seeks to ascertain some things about the nature of the recipients of public welfare—who they are (age, ethnicity, family status, education, origin, family size), why they are on public welfare and the length of their welfare dependency. It also seeks to throw light on the relationship between welfare dependency and employability —to what extent welfare recipients are customarily employed, how intermittently their gainful employment occurs, why (and how frequently) they return to welfare, and what specific steps might be taken to reduce a rising incidence of welfare dependency through a general strengthening of employment opportunities in the private sector. Data upon which answers to these queries could be based emerge from a sample of 1698 welfare-receiving families in New York City. Families comprising the sample were recipients of one or another of three kinds of welfare—home relief, aid to families with dependent children and aid to families with dependent children where the head of the household was unemployed. The families were randomly selected and then interviewed in depth; a large sample, initially envisioned, had to be trimmed because of difficulties in obtaining sufficient or usable responses. Interviews were undertaken intermittently between 1971 and 1973. The authors acknowledge that worsening economic conditions in this period might conceivably have distorted the sample somewhat. And some sub-groups in the sample possibly are over-represented,

the authors acknowledge, relative to their employment potential. Notwithstanding some flaws, none really major, the study has merit.

The sample disclosed a preponderance of ethnic minorities (Negroes and Puerto Ricans) on the welfare rolls, in contrast to their lesser occurrence among the general adult population. (Caucasians comprised approximately 70 percent of the city's population, but only about one-fifth of each welfare sample.) Households headed by females ranged between one-third and one-half of each sample, depending upon the relief category. Only one-fifth of the males heading welfare households, and one-fourth of the females so designated, were high school graduates, whereas for the city's total adult population the percentage has commonly exceeded fifty for both sexes. Eighty percent of the welfare-receiving families headed by females had one dependent child, and 54 percent had two or more. In a large number of female-headed families, moreover, the age of the head (usually with no dependent children) was beyond forty years of age. Two-thirds of female-headed households represented broken marriages, but only one-fifth of male-headed households. Chronic illnesses loomed as a deterrent to regular employment in the case of 66 percent of female-headed families, and in the case of 30 percent of families that are male-headed, as determined by interviews. Other problems, some family-related, were also identified. The number of multi-problem families was notable. Most sample families, approximately 85 percent, were migrants (that is, not native to New York City).

With this as background on the sample of welfare recipients, the study turns to relating this material to the dynamics of welfare caseloads. The most significant finding is the fact that a great majority of those accepted for welfare remain on the relief rolls for lengthy periods of time. Case history data reveal little movement back and forth between welfare and gainful employment in the private sector. A mere five percent of males and two percent of females in the sample give evidence of such movement.

The termination of persons from the welfare rolls, where such occurred, was for administrative reasons in many cases (for example, uncovering a fraudulent application), not because of one's acquiring gainful employment. Comparing findings disclosed by the sample on this point with published conclusions from other units of government prompts the authors to deduce that any averred relationship between welfare termination and the gaining of subsequent remunerative employment is pretty much unproved. The propensity to seek public assistance, rather, stems from one or another of the handicapping factors already noted (for instance, health problems); these minimize employability for long periods as a rule. The study relates well the relationship between these deterrents to employment and various family characteristics.

An especially interesting chapter (4) demonstrates that the educational level, age, sex, ethnicity, marital status, physical complaints and numbers and ages of children of welfare recipients bore a varied tie to the employment status of the recipients—whether they were employed at any time recently, were seeking a job, or had dropped out of the job search. Age categories, family size, and ethnicity were represented rather evenly among each of the three employment categories mentioned above, except for Puerto Rican women, none of whom worked currently. So was the educational level, except that older men and women were less well educated and simultaneously more likely neither to be working nor looking for work. Physical complaints or illnesses (and related problems like police records) tended to cluster largely in the "not seeking work" category, which embraced disproportionately older males (and many older females) of every ethnic background. Most women with employment potential had child-raising responsibilities and fewer reported physical problems. Most in the sample (63 percent) had effective work histories (83 percent of the men, 54 percent of the women). Only seven percent of the females in the sample and 22 percent of the males were employed at the time the sample was compiled. Hence the need for continued welfare by those in the sample, even those gainfully employed (whose income did not raise them above the poverty line, ordinarily, given their family sizes). The most current work experiences of the welfare recipients in the sample, prior to their latest entrance on the rolls, were uniformly brief, lasting but from one to two years as a rule. The recent jobs held by those in the sample, with a few exceptions, followed major trends in the New York City job market (for example, from blue collar to white collar), but sample members benefited more slowly from such developments and, as to earnings, much less munificently than the local labor force generally.

This study's importance, in sum, lies in several areas. First, it poses a reasoned and documented challenge to one assumption underlying the Social Security Act which viewed welfare as an alternative to work. Since non-work factors are presented as the main cause of being on welfare in the present study, and what employment exists for welfare recipients has proved short-lived and low-paying, this assumption is seemingly open to re-examination. Second, the study points up the case for a varied and flexible approach to welfare and work. Low-paying jobs, which the poorly trained and educated (many of those on welfare) usually qualify for, are less likely to be adjusted to minimum subsistence levels by raising the minimum wage or pushing supply-oriented labor programs (various kinds of training), in the author's judgment. Rather, the authors suggest new directions for welfare policy wherein there would be a realistic assessment of the effects on the employment potential of particularly benefited populations such as youths just out of high school, working mothers, or the unskilled. Benefit levels and work incentives, in other words, are felt likely to vary among different groups. The negative income tax, then, or the supplemental welfare payment might have more utility vis-à-vis work incentives for one group familiar to relief rolls than it would for another group. Work is not seen as the equivalent of self-support; continued use of welfare on a supplementary and selective basis is deemed wholly likely in any over-all reform of existing welfare laws and practices.

Finally, the study argues forcefully for more positive commitment by government to the promotion and maintenance of full employment, without which rising welfare rolls cannot be reversed. And it argues forcefully, by the evidence given, for the recognition of non-job-related factors as a primary clue in explaining why welfare rolls persist in being swollen. As an exercise in public program evaluation, and as an empirical analysis of the relation between work and welfare, this study is a useful model for examining aspects of welfare dysfunction and correction.

HARRY W. REYNOLDS, JR.
University of Nebraska
Omaha

## OTHER BOOKS

ABUEVA, JOSE VELOSO. *Filipino Politics: Nationalism and Emerging Ideologies.* Pp. v, 286. Manila, The Philippines: Modern Book Company, 1975. No price.

ACHEBE, CHINUA. *Morning Yet on Creation Day.* Pp. 192. New York: Doubleday, 1975. $7.95.

AGIRRE, JULEN. *Operation Ogro: The Execution of Admiral Luis Carrero Blanco.* Pp. vii, 196. New York: Quadrangle, 1975. $8.95. Paperbound.

ANN, LEE SOO. *Economic Growth and the Public Sector in Malaya and Singapore, 1948–1960.* Pp. xii, 192. New York: Oxford University Press, 1974. $20.00.

BALUTIS, ALAN P. and DARON K. BUTLER, eds. *The Political Pursestrings.* Pp. 221. New York: John Wiley & Sons, 1975. $15.00.

BARKER, THOMAS MACK. *The Military Intellectual and Battle: Raimondo Montecuccoli and the Thirty Years War.* Pp. vii, 271. Albany, N.Y.: State University of New York Press, 1975. $25.00.

BEAUMONT, ROGER A. and MARTIN EDMONDS, eds. *War in the Next Decade.* Pp. x, 217. Lexington: University of Kentucky Press, 1975. $11.00.

BECKER, ERNEST. *The Denial of Death.* Pp. ix, 315. New York: Free Press, 1975. $2.95. Paperbound.

BENEWIDK, ROBERT and TREVOR SMITH, eds.

*Direct Action and Democratic Politics.* Pp. 324. Atlantic Highlands, N.J.: Humanities Press, 1972. $16.50.

BERLANSTEIN, LEONARD R. *The Barristers of Toulouse in the Eighteenth Century (1740–1793).* Pp. ix, 210. Baltimore, Md.: Johns Hopkins University Press, 1975. $12.50.

BERNSTEIN, BASIL. *Class, Codes and Control: Theoretical Studies towards a Sociology of Language.* Pp. 282. New York: Schocken Books, 1975. $4.95. Paperbound.

BEYE, CHARLES ROWAN. *Ancient Greek Literature and Society.* Pp. 480. New York: Doubleday, 1975. $3.95. Paperbound.

BILLER, HENRY and DENNIS MEREDITH. *Father Power.* Pp. 390. New York: Doubleday, 1975. $3.50. Paperbound.

BLAU, PETER M., ed. *Approaches to the Study of Social Structure.* Pp. v, 294. New York: Free Press, 1975. $12.95.

BLOOMFIELD, LOUIS M. and GERALD F. FITZGERALD. *Crimes against Internationally Protected Persons: Prevention and Punishment.* Pp. v, 272. New York: Praeger, 1975. $18.50.

BLOUGH, ROGER M. *The Washington Embrace of Business.* Pp. 161. New York: Columbia University Press, 1975. $8.95.

BOYNTON, G. R. and CHONG LIM KIM, eds. *Legislative Systems in Developing Countries.* Pp. 286. Durham, N.C.: Duke University Press, 1975. $11.75.

BROCK, W. R. *The United States: 1789–1890.* Pp. 352. Ithaca, N.Y.: Cornell University Press, 1975. $15.00.

BROWN, R. G. S. *The Management of Welfare.* Pp. 317. Totowa, N.J.: Rowman and Littlefield, 1975. $12.50.

BROWNING, EDGAR K. *Redistribution and the Welfare System.* Pp. vi, 131. Washington, D.C.: American Enterprise Institute for Public Policy Research, 1975. $3.00. Paperbound.

BUCK, JAMES H., ed. *The Modern Japanese Military System.* Vol. V. Pp. 256. Beverly Hills, Calif.: Sage, 1975. $15.00. Paperbound, $7.50.

BUTOW, R. J. C. *The John Doe Associates: Backdoor Diplomacy for Peace, 1941.* Pp. 480. Stanford, Calif.: Stanford University Press, 1974. $16.95.

CARLSON, ROBERT O., ed. *Communications and Public Opinion: A Public Opinion Quarterly Reader.* Pp. vii, 642. New York: Praeger, 1975. $20.00. Paperbound, $7.95.

CARTER, HARRY. *A History of the Oxford University Press.* Vol. I. Pp. vi, 640. New York: Oxford University Press, 1975. $48.00.

CH'ING, YEH. *Inside Mao Tse-tung's Thought: An Analytical Blueprint of His Actions.*

Pp. v, 336. Hicksville, N.Y.: Exposition Press, 1975. $12.50.

CHOUDHURY, G. W. *India, Pakistan, Bangladesh, and the Major Powers: Politics of a Divided Subcontinent.* Pp. v, 276. New York: The Free Press, 1975. $13.95.

CHOUDHURY, G. W. *The Last Days of United Pakistan.* Pp. ix, 239. Bloomington: Indiana University Press, 1975. $10.00.

COHN, NIK. *King Death.* Pp. 143. New York: Harcourt Brace Jovanovich, 1975. $5.95.

COLMAN, WILLIAM G. *Cities, Suburbs, and States.* Pp. v, 350. New York: Free Press, 1975. $12.95.

CONRAD, JOHN B. *Crime And Its Correction: An International Survey of Attitudes and Practices.* Pp. 322. Berkeley: University of California Press, 1975. $14.50.

*The County Year Book 1975.* Pp. 232. Washington, D.C.: NACo/ICMA, 1975. $17.50.

DAVIES, DAVID. *The Last of the Tasmanians.* Pp. 284. New York: Barnes & Noble, 1974. $13.50.

DAVIES, DOROTHY KEYWORTH, ed. *Race Relations in Rhodesia.* Pp. v, 458. Totowa, N.J.: Rowman and Littlefield, 1975. $21.50.

DAVIS, HAROLD EUGENE et al. *Latin American Foreign Policies.* Pp. vii, 470. Baltimore, Md.: Johns Hopkins University Press, 1975. $18.00. Paperbound, $5.95.

DAVIS, LOUIS E. and ALBERT B. CHERNS, eds. *The Quality of Working Life: Problems, Prospects, and the State of the Art.* Vol. I. Pp. v, 450. New York: The Free Press, 1975. $12.95. Paperbound, $4.95.

DAVIS, LOUIS E., ed. *The Quality of Working Life: Cases and Commentary.* Vol. II. New York: Free Press, 1975. $12.95. Paperbound, $4.95.

DECROW, KAREN. *Sexist Justice.* Pp. 363. New York: Random House, 1974. $2.95. Paperbound.

DELFINER, HENRY. *Vienna Broadcasts to Slovakia.* Pp. 142. New York: Columbia University Press, 1974. $10.00.

DE MAUSE, LLOYD, ed. *The New Psychohistory.* Pp. 313. New York: Psychohistory Press, 1975. $12.95.

DOGAN, MATTEI, ed. *The Mandarins of Western Europe: The Political Role of Top Civil Servants.* Pp. 314. New York: Halsted Press, 1975. $17.50.

DOLAN, JAY P. *The Immigrant Church: New York's Irish and German Catholics, 1815–1865.* Baltimore, Md.: Johns Hopkins University Press, 1975. $10.00.

DREW, ELIZABETH. *Washington Journal: The Events of 1973–1974.* Pp. xii, 428. New York: Random House, 1975. $12.95.

DRUMMOND, ANTHONY DEANE. *Riot Control.* Pp. 158. New York: Crane, Russak & Co., 1975. $9.50.

DYSON, A. E. and JULIAN LOVELOCK, eds. *Education and Democracy.* Pp. v, 295. Boston, Mass.: Routledge & Kegan Paul, 1975. $17.25.

EARLE, JOHN. *Italy in the 1970s.* Pp. 208. North Pomfret, Vt.: David & Charles, 1975. $15.95.

ETCHISON, DON L. *The United States and Militarism in Central America.* Pp. vi, 150. New York: Praeger, 1975. $14.00.

ETZIONI, AMITAI. *A Comparative Analysis of Complex Organization.* Pp. vii, 584. New York: Free Press, 1975. $11.95. Paperbound, $5.95.

*Evaluating Governmental Performance: Changes and Challenges for GAO.* Pp. iii, 279. Washington, D.C.: U.S. Government Printing Office, 1975. No price.

FEIT, EDWARD. *Workers without Weapons.* Pp. 230. Hamden, Conn.: Archon Books, 1975. $12.50.

FINE, SIDNEY. *Frank Murphy: The Detroit Years.* Pp. 608. Ann Arbor: University of Michigan Press, 1975. $20.00.

FINNEY, GRAHAM S. *Drugs: Administering Catastrophe.* Pp. 135. Washington, D.C.: Drug Abuse Council, 1975. $4.00. Paperbound.

FISHER, LOUIS. *Presidential Spending Power.* Pp. vii, 345. Princeton, N.J.: Princeton University Press, 1975. $12.50. Paperbound, $3.45.

FONER, PHILIP S. *American Labor Songs of the Nineteenth Century.* Pp. xii, 356. Urbana: University of Illinois Press, 1975. $13.95.

*Foreign Relations of the United States, 1948: The Near East, South Asia, and Africa.* Vol. V. Pp. v, 532. Washington, D.C.: U.S. Government Printing Office, 1975. $8.25.

FREDERICK, KENNETH D. *Water Management and Agricultural Development.* Pp. v, 187. Baltimore, Md.: Johns Hopkins University Press, 1975. $10.00.

FULLER, PAUL E. *Laura Clay and the Woman's Rights Movement.* Pp. ix, 216. Lexington: University of Kentucky Press, 1975. $12.50.

GAIGE, FREDERICK H. *Regionalism and National Unity in Nepal.* Pp. 252. Berkeley: University of California Press, 1975. $13.75.

GALPER, JEFFRY H. *The Politics of Social Services.* Pp. ix, 236. Englewood Cliffs, N.J.: Prentice-Hall, 1975. $5.95. Paperbound.

GAMSON, WILLIAM A. *The Strategy of Social Protest.* Pp. ix, 217. Homewood, Ill.: Dorsey Press, 1975. $5.95. Paperbound.

GEYER, GEORGIE ANNE. *The Young Russians.* Pp. 295. Homewood, Ill.: ETC Publications, 1975. $10.50.

GILKES, PATRICK. *The Dying Lion: Feudalism*

and *Modernization in Ethiopia*. Pp. vii, 307. New York: St. Martin's Press, 1975. $12.95.

GRAMS, JEAN D. *Sex: Does it Make a Difference?* Pp. ix, 276. North Scituate, Mass.: Duxbury Press, 1975. No price.

GRAZIANO, ANTHONY M., ed. *Behavior Therapy with Children*. Vol. II. Pp. v, 640. Chicago, Ill.: Aldine, 1975. $19.95.

GREGERSEN, HANS M. and ARNOLDO CONTRERAS. *U.S. Investment in the Forest-Based Sector in Latin America*. Pp. vii, 113. Baltimore, Md.: Johns Hopkins University Press, 1975. $4.50. Paperbound.

GROW, LUCILLE J. and DEBORAH SHAPIRO. *Transracial Adoption Today*. Pp. 91. New York: Child Welfare League of America, 1975. $3.95. Paperbound.

HAHN, HARLAN and R. WILLIAM HOLLAND. *American Government: Minority Rights Versus Majority Rule*. Pp. vii, 203. New York: John Wiley & Sons, 1976. $6.95. Paperbound.

HAMMEED, K. A. *Enterprise: Industrial Entrepreneurship in Development*. Pp. 256. Beverly Hills, Calif.: Sage, 1975. $7.00. Paperbound.

HARDIN, CHARLES M. *Presidential Power and Accountability toward a New Constitution*. Pp. 256. Chicago, Ill.: University of Chicago Press, 1975. $3.95. Paperbound.

HARDOY, JORGE E., ed. *Urbanization in Latin America: Approaches and Issues*. Pp. 40. New York: Doubleday, 1975. $4.50. Paperbound.

HILLMAN, EUGENE. *Polygamy Reconsidered: African Plural Marriage and the Christian Churches*. Pp. v, 266. Maryknoll, N.Y.: Orbis Books, 1975. $15.00. Paperbound, $7.95.

HODSON, H. V., ed. *World Events in 1974*. Pp. v, 580. New York: St. Martin's Press, 1975. $35.00.

HOLBIK, KAREL and PHILIP L. SWAN. *Industrialization and Employment in Puerto Rico, 1950–1972*. Studies in Latin American Business, no. 16. Pp. v, 82. Austin: University of Texas Press, 1975. No price.

HOLMES, ARTHUR F., ed. *War and Christian Ethics*. Pp. 356. Grand Rapids, Mich.: Baker Book House, 1975. $7.95. Paperbound.

HORTON, PAUL B. and GERALD R. LESLIE, eds. *Readings in the Sociology of Social Problems*. 2nd ed. Pp. v, 418. Englewood Cliffs, N.J.: Prentice-Hall, 1975. $7.50. Paperbound.

HSU, IMMANUEL C. Y. *The Rise of Modern China*. 2nd ed. Pp. vii, 1002. New York: Oxford University Press, 1975. $12.95.

INTERNATIONAL MOMENTARY FUND. *Surveys of African Economies*. Vol. VI. Pp. v, 480. Washington, D.C.: International Monetary Fund, 1975. $5.00.

JACOB, HERBERT, ed. *The Potential for Reform of Criminal Justice*. Pp. 352. Beverly Hills, Calif.: Sage, 1975. $17.50. Paperbound, 7.50.

JACOBY, SUSAN. *Inside Soviet Schools*. Pp. 248. New York: Schocken, 1975. $3.95. Paperbound.

JOHNSON, JOHN M. *Doing Field Research*. Pp. ix, 225. New York: Macmillan, 1975. $9.95.

JUDSON, HORACE FREELAND. *Heroin Addiction: What Americans Can Learn from the English Experience*. Pp. xi, 200. New York: Random House, 1975. $2.95. Paperbound.

KALIN, MARTIN G. *The Utopian Flight from Unhappiness: Freud Against Marx on Social Progress*. Pp. v, 231. Totowa, N.J.: Littlefield, Adams & Co., 1975. $3.50. Paperbound.

KAPLAN, MORTON A., ed. *Isolation or Interdependence? Today's Choices for Tomorrow's World*. Pp. 254. New York: The Free Press, 1975. $10.00.

KATZENELLENBOGEN, S. E. *Railways and the Copper Mines of Katanga*. Pp. 165. New York: Oxford University Press, 1973. $12.00.

KELLEY, S. C., THOMAS N. CHIRIKOS and MICHAEL G. FINN. *Manpower Forecasting in the United States: An Evaluation of the State of the Art*. Pp. i, 257. Columbus: Ohio University Press, 1975. No price.

KENDRICK, ALEXANDER. *The Wound Within: America in the Vietnam Years, 1945–1974*. Pp. xii, 432. Boston, Mass.: Little, Brown, 1975. $4.95. Paperbound.

KENNEDY, ROBERT E., JR. *The Irish: Emigration, Marriage, and Fertility*. Pp. 254. Berkeley: University of California Press, 1975. $3.65. Paperbound.

KENT, SHERMAN. *The Election of 1827 in France*. Pp. vii, 225. Lawrence, Mass.: Harvard University Press, 1975. $12.50.

KINTON, JACK, ed. *The American Community: Creation & Revival*. Pp. i, 170. Aurora, Ill.: SSSR, 1975. $6.95. Paperbound.

KNIGHT, DAVID. *Sources for the History of Science, 1660–1914*. Pp. 223. Ithaca, N.Y.: Cornell University Press, 1975. $11.00.

KOENIGSBERG, RICHARD A. *Hitler's Ideology: A Study in Psychoanalytic Sociology*. Pp. v, 105. New York: Library of Social Science, 1975. $7.95.

KOMAROVSKY, MIRRA, ed. *Sociology and Public Policy: The Case of Presidential Commissions*. Pp. v, 183. New York: Elsevier, 1975. $10.95.

KOSSMANN, E. H. and A. F. MELLINK, eds. *Texts Concerning the Revolt of the Nether-*

*lands.* Pp. v, 295. New York: Cambridge University Press, 1975. $17.50.

KREHM, WILLIAM. *Price in a Mixed Economy: Our Record of Disaster.* Pp. ix, 255. Toronto, Ont.: Thornwood, 1975. $13.95. Paperbound, $9.95.

LENCZOWSKI, GEORGE, ed. *Political Elites in the Middle East.* Pp. 227. Washington, D.C.: American Enterprise Institute for Public Policy Research, 1975. $9.50. Paperbound, $3.50.

LEVIN, GILBERT, EDWARD B. ROBERTS and GARY B. HIRSCH. *The Persistent Poppy: A Computer-Aided Search for Heroin Policy.* Pp. vii, 229. Cambridge, Mass.: Ballinger, 1975. No price.

LEVINE, DONALD J. and MARY JO BAND, eds. *The "Inequality" Controversy.* Pp. v, 338. New York: Basic Books, 1975. $17.50. Paperbound, $6.95.

LEVY, JACQUES. *Cesar Chavez: Autiobiography of La Causa.* Pp. 546. New York: W. W. Norton, 1975. $12.95.

LINEBERRY, WILLIAM P., ed. *American Colleges: The Uncertain Future.* Pp. 218. New York: H. W. Wilson, 1975. No price.

LOVING, JEROME M., ed. *Civil War Letters of George Washington Whitman.* Pp. xii, 173. Durham, N.C.: Duke University Press, 1975. $11.75.

LU, JOSEPH K. *U.S. Government Publications Relating to the Social Sciences: A Selected Annotated Guide.* Pp. 260. Beverly Hills, Calif.: Sage, 1975. $15.00.

LUNT, JAMES. *John Burgoyne of Saratoga.* Pp. xi, 369. New York: Harcourt Brace Jovanovich, 1975. $14.95.

LUZA, RADOMIR. *Austro-German Relations in the Anschluss Era.* Pp. vii, 438. Princeton, N.J.: Princeton University Press, 1975. $20.00.

MAISEL, LOUIS and PAUL M. SACKS, eds. *The Future of Political Parties.* Pp. 280. Beverly Hills, Calif.: Sage, 1975. $17.50. Paperbound, $7.50.

MANACH, JORGE. *Frontiers in the Americas: A Global Perspective.* Pp. 108. New York: Teachers College Press, 1975. $8.50. Paperbound, $4.50.

MARCUS, HAROLD G. *The Life and Times of Menelik II: Ethiopia, 1844–1913.* Pp. viii, 298. New York: Oxford University Press, 1975. $17.00.

McFARLAND, KEITH D. *Harry H. Woodring: A Political Biography of FDR's Controversial Secretary of War.* Pp. vii, 346. Lawrence: University Press of Kansas, 1975. $12.50.

MEHNERT, KLAUS. *Moscow and the New Left.* Pp. 289. Berkeley: University of California Press, 1975. $12.50.

MEISEL, JOHN. *Working Papers on Canadian Politics.* 2nd ed. Pp. vii, 289. Quebec, Ca.: McGill-Queen's University Press, 1975. $6.00. Paperbound.

MELCHER, ARLYN J. *General Systems and Organization Theory.* Pp. 123. Kent, Ohio: Kent State University Press, 1975. $7.50.

MERKLEY, PAUL. *Reinhold Niebuhr: A Political Account.* Pp. viii, 289. Montreal, Ca.: McGill-Queen's University Press, 1975. $13.50.

MILLMAN, MARCIA and ROSABETH MOSS KANTER, eds. *Another Voice: Feminist Perspectives on Social Life and Social Science.* Pp. 400. New York: Doubleday, 1975. $3.50. Paperbound.

MOKGATLE, NABOTH. *The Autobiography of an Unknown South African.* Pp. 360. Berkeley: University of California Press, 1975. $3.95. Paperbound.

MOSHER, FREDERICK C., ed. *American Public Administration: Past, Present, Future.* Pp. 298. University: University of Alabama Press, 1975. $10.00. Paperbound, $3.50.

MUIR, RICHARD. *Modern Political Geography.* Pp. vi, 262. New York: John Wiley & Sons, 1975. $16.50.

PALUDAN, PHILLIP S. *A Covenant with Death: The Constitution, Law, and Equality in the Civil War Era.* Pp. x, 309. Urbana: University of Illinois Press, 1975. $11.50.

PENNIMAN, HOWARD R., ed. *France at the Polls: The Presidential Election of 1974.* Pp. 324. Washington, D.C.: American Enterprise Institute for Public Policy Research, 1975. $4.50. Paperbound.

PINARD, MAURICE. *The Rise of a Third Party: A Study in Crisis Politics.* Pp. v, 299. Quebec, Ca.: McGill-Queen's University Press, 1975. $6.00. Paperbound.

RAY, BENJAMIN C. *African Religions: Symbol, Ritual, and Community.* Studies in Religion Series. Pp. v, 238. Englewood Cliffs, N.J.: Prentice-Hall, 1976. No price.

REED, JOHN SHELTON. *The Enduring South: Subcultural Persistence in Mass Society.* Pp. v, 135. Chapel Hill: University of North Carolina Press, 1975. $4.95. Paperbound.

REINHOLD, MEYER, ed. *The Classick Pages.* Pp. vii, 231. New York: Interbook, 1975. $7.50. Paperbound, $3.50.

REPPETTO, THOMAS. *Residential Crime.* Pp. vi, 163. Cambridge, Mass.: Ballinger, 1974. $11.00.

RICE, OTIS K. *Frontier Kentucky.* Pp. ix, 131. Lexington: University of Kentucky Press, 1975. $3.95.

RICHARDS, GUY. *The Rescue of the Romanovs.* Pp. 215. Old Greenwich, Conn.: Devin-Adair, 1975. $8.95.

RIDLEY, F. F. *The Study of Government:*

*Political Science and Public Administration.* Pp. 240. New York: Crane, Russak & Co., 1975. $9.00. Paperbound.

RIPLEY, RANDALL B. and GRACE A. FRANKLIN, eds. *Policy-Making in the Federal Executive Branch.* Pp. vii, 209. New York: The Free Press, 1975. $11.95.

ROBERTS, BRYAN R. *Organizing Strangers: Poor Families in Guatemala City.* Pp. xi, 360. Austin: University of Texas Press, 1975. $12.50.

ROBINSON, GLEN O. *The Forest Service: A Study in Public Land Management.* Pp. v, 337. Baltimore, Md.: Johns Hopkins University Press, 1975. $16.95. Paperbound, $4.95.

ROCKART, JOHN FRALICK and MICHAEL S. SCOTT MORTON. *Computers and the Learning Process in Higher Education.* Pp. 356. New York: McGraw-Hill, 1975. $17.50.

ROSENOF, THEODORE. *Dogma, Depression, and the New Deal: The Debate of Political Leaders over Economic Recovery.* Pp. vii, 155. Port Washington, N.Y.: Kennikat Press, 1975. $12.50.

ROSS, STANLEY R., ed. *Is the Mexican Revolution Dead?* Pp. vii, 339. Philadelphia, Pa.: Temple University Press, 1975. $12.50. Paperbound, $3.95.

RUBIN, JOAN and BJORN H. JERNUDD. *Can Language be Planned?* Pp. ix, 343. Honolulu: University of Hawaii Press, 1975. $5.95. Paperbound.

SANDERS, RALPH, ed. *Science and Technology: Vital National Resources.* Pp. v, 146. Mt. Airy, Md.: Lomond Systems, Inc., 1975. $12.50.

SCHLESSINGER, ARTHUR, JR. and ROGER BRUNS, eds. *Congress Investigates: A Documented History, 1792–1974.* Vols. I to V. Pp. 4103. New York: R. R. Bowker, 1975. $75.00 per set.

SCHNEIDER, R. et al. *Applications of Meteorology to Economic and Social Development.* Technical Note No. 132. New York: UNIPUB, 1974. $15.00. Paperbound.

SHAFFER, ARTHUR H., ed. *The Politics of History: Writing the History of the American Revolution 1783–1815.* Pp. 228. Chicago, Ill.: Precedent, 1975. $12.50.

SHAPIRO, H. R. *The Bureaucratic State: Party Bureaucracy and the Decline of Democracy in America.* Pp. viii, 366. Brooklyn, N.Y.: Samizdat Press, 1975. $11.95. Paperbound, $4.95.

SIMMONS, LUIZ R. S. and ABDUL A. SAID, eds. *Drugs, Politics, and Diplomacy: The International Connection.* Pp. 312. Beverly Hills, Calif.: Sage, 1974. $17.50. Paperbound, $7.50.

SIMON, RITA JAMES, ed. *The Jury System in America: A Critical Overview.* Pp. 256. Beverly Hills, Calif.: Sage, 1975. $17.50. Paperbound, $7.50.

SMITH, E. A. *Whig Principles and Party Politics.* Pp. viii, 411. Totowa, N.J.: Rowman and Littlefield, 1975. $25.00.

SMITH, EDWARD ELLIS and DURWARD S. RIGGS, eds. *Land Use, Open Space, and the Government Process.* Pp. v, 197. New York: Praeger, 1975. No price.

SOCHEN, JUNE. *The New Woman in Greenwich Village, 1910–1920.* Pp. ix, 175. New York: Quadrangle, 1975. $3.50. Paperbound.

SOLOMON, NOAL. *When Leaders Were Bosses.* Pp. ix, 205. Hicksville, N.Y.: Exposition Press, 1975. $7.50.

STAVRIANOS, L. S. *The World to 1500: A Global History.* 2nd ed. Pp. 399. Englewood Cliffs, N.J.: Prentice-Hall, 1975. $7.95. Paperbound.

STEINBERG, CHARLES S. *The Creation of Consent: Public Relations in Practice.* Pp. 315. New York: Hastings House, 1975. $13.50. Paperbound, $6.95.

STERN, J. P. *Hitler: The Führer and the People.* Pp. 254. Berkeley: University of California Press, 1975. $3.65. Paperbound.

STOKES, GALE. *Legitimacy through Liberalism: Vladimir Jovanović and the Transformation of Serbian Politics.* Pp. vii, 279. Seattle: University of Washington Press, 1975. $11.00.

STOUMEN, LOU. *Can't Argue with Sunrise: A Paper Movie.* Pp. 185. Milbrae, Calif.: Celestial Arts, 1975. $14.95. Paperbound, $9.45.

STUB, HOLGER R. *The Sociology of Education: A Sourcebook.* 3rd ed. Pp. vii, 427. Homewood, Ill.: Dorsey Press, 1975. $7.95. Paperbound.

TAYLOR, ARTHUR J., ed. *The Standard of Living in Britain in the Industrial Revolution.* Pp. viii, 216. New York: Barnes & Noble, 1975. $18.50. Paperbound, $10.00.

TIGER, LIONEL and JOSEPH SHEPHER. *Women in the Kibbutz.* Pp. 334. New York: Harcourt Brace Jovanovich, 1975. $10.95.

TOMEH, AIDA K. *The Family and Sex Roles.* Pp. ix, 139. Toronto, Ca.: Holt, Rinehart and Winston, 1975. $2.99. Paperbound.

TOPLIN, ROBERT BRENT. *Unchallenged Violence: An American Ordeal.* Pp. v, 332. Westport, Conn.: Greenwood Press, 1975. $15.00.

TOTH, CHARLES W., ed. *The American Revolution and the West Indies.* Pp. ix, 225. Port Washington, N.Y.: Kennikat Press, 1975. $12.75.

UDRY, J. RICHARD and EARL E. HUYCK, eds. *The Demographic Evaluation of Domestic*

*Family Planning Programs.* Pp. v, 119. Cambridge, Mass.: Ballinger, 1975. No price.

VENTER, AL J. *The Zambesi Salient: Conflict in Southern Africa.* Pp. 395. Old Greenwich, Conn.: Devin-Adair, 1975. $12.50.

WATSON, HUGH SETON. *The "Sick Heart" of Modern Europe: The Problem of the Danubian Lands.* Pp. v, 76. Seattle: University of Washington Press, 1975. $4.95.

WEBER, MAX. *Roscher and Knies: The Logical Problems of Historical Economics.* Pp. v, 294. New York: Free Press, 1975. $10.95.

WEICHMANN, LOUIS J. *A True History of the Assassination of Abraham Lincoln and of the Conspiracy of 1865.* Edited by Floyd E. Risvold. Pp. xi, 492. New York: Alfred A. Knopf, 1975. $15.00.

WELCH, SUSAN and JOHN COMER, eds. *Public Opinion: Its Formation, Measurement, and Impact.* Pp. iii, 541. Palo Alto, Calif.: Mayfield, 1975. $7.50. Paperbound.

WELLBORN, STARNES R. *The Age of Trust.* Pp. 183. Jericho, N.Y.: Exposition Press, 1975. $6.00.

WEST, H. W. and O. H. M. SAWYER. *Land Administration: A Bibliography for Developing Countries.* Pp. iii, 292. New York: Cambridge University Press, 1975. No price.

WILLIAMS, EDWARD J. and FREEMAN J. WRIGHT. *Latin American Politics: A Developmental Approach.* Pp. v, 480. Palo Alto, Calif.: Mayfield, 1975. $12.95.

WILLIAMS, RAYMOND. *Television: Technology and Cultural Form.* Pp. 160. New York: Schocken Books, 1975. $7.50. Paperbound, $3.45.

WILLIS, ROY. *Man and Beast.* Pp. 142. New York: Basic Books, 1975. $7.50.

YOUNG, ORAN R., ed. *Bargaining: Formal Theories of Negotiation.* Pp. vi, 412. Urbana: University of Illinois Press, 1975. $15.00.

# New from Columbia

## TWENTIETH-CENTURY YUGOSLAVIA

### FRED SINGLETON

The most complete and up-to-date survey of modern Yugoslavia to be published in any language, this book concerns the efforts which the Yugoslavs have made since the Second World War under the leadership of the Communist Party to industrialize an economically underdeveloped country and to grapple with the problems of cultural diversity within a multinational federation.　　cloth, $15.00; paper, $5.95

## ELITE STRUCTURE AND IDEOLOGY
### A Theory With Applications to Norway

### JOHN HIGLEY, G. LOWELL FIELD, and KNUT GROHOLT

Ranging over a large number of societies, historical and contemporary, this book presents a general theory of elite structure and ideology as they relate to political stability and instability.　 There is a special emphasis on Norwegian society with information presented in the context of the general theory.　　　　　　　　$17.50
*Available in July paperback format:*

## TWENTIETH-CENTURY GERMANY

### A. J. RYDER

An exploration of the upheavals which Germany has seen in the past eight decades, from William II's Empire to the remarkable peak of prosperity Germany enjoys today. "An outstanding general history. . . . Should be . . . seriously considered as a text for undergraduate courses in German history."—*Choice*　　　　　　　$6.95, paper

## AID TO RUSSIA 1941–1946
### Strategy, Diplomacy, the Origins of the Cold War

### GEORGE C. HERRING, JR.

A reexamination of the evolution of American policies for lend-lease and aid for Russian reconstruction within the context of the formation, development, and subsequent breakdown of the wartime alliance between the United States and the Soviet Union. "A very welcome book—a concise, logical, and clearly written account."—*Annals*
*Contemporary American History Series*　　　$6.00, paper

 **COLUMBIA UNIVERSITY PRESS**

Address for orders: 136 South Broadway, Irvington, New York 10533

# INDEX

177

# EUROPEAN HISTORY SERIES

**IMPERIALISM**
The Robinson and Gallagher Controversy
*Edited by Wm. Roger Louis,*
*University of Texas at Austin*
Assesses different aspects of the controversy surrounding the theory of imperialism held by Ronald Robinson and John Gallagher. *288 pp. Paper: $6.95 (05582-5). Cloth: $12.50 (05375-X).*

**REAPPRAISALS OF FASCISM**
*Edited by Henry A. Turner, Jr.,*
*Yale University*
A compilation of ten of the most important recent re-examinations of fascism as a generic phenomenon, exploring its causes and characteristics. *256 pp. Paper: $5.95 (05579-5). Cloth: $12.50 (05372-5).*

**SEVENTEENTH-CENTURY ENGLAND**
Society in an Age of Revolution
*Edited by Paul Seaver,*
*Stanford University*
Several well-known English historians examine the basic structures of English society in an age of revolution and some of the social and political attitudes that shaped and set limits to the extent of change. *192 pp. Paper: $5.95 (05584-1). Cloth: $12.50 (05377-6).*

**STATE AND SOCIETY IN SEVENTEENTH-CENTURY FRANCE**
*Edited by Raymond F. Kierstead,*
*Catholic University*
Examines the many facets of the political and social fabric in absolutist France, focusing on the problems of elites in France's political system and on popular resistance to absolutism. *304 pp. Paper: $6.95 (05573-6). Cloth: $12.50 (05367-9).*

# topics of current and continuing the social sciences.

**THE STRENGTH IN US**
Self-Help Groups in the Modern World
*Written and edited by Alfred H. Katz,*
*University of California at Los Angeles,*
*and Eugene I. Bender,*
*California School of Professional Psychology*
*272 pp. Paper $6.95 (05585-X). Cloth: $12.50 (05378-4).*

**UGANDAN ASIANS IN BRITAIN**
Forced Migration and Social Absorption
*by William G. Kuepper, G. Lynne Lackey,*
*and E. Nelson Swinerton,*
*University of Wisconsin at Green Bay*
*122 pp. Cloth: $10.00 (05380-6).*

**MAN AND ENVIRONMENT**
(A New York Times Book)
*Edited by Amos A. Hawley,*
*University of North Carolina*
*256 pp. Paper: $5.95 (05574-4).*

**NEW VIEWPOINTS**
A Division of
Franklin Watts
730 Fifth Avenue
New York, N.Y. 10019

*Kindly mention* THE ANNALS *when writing to advertisers*

# The American Academy of Political and Social Science

3937 Chestnut Street                                    Philadelphia, Pennsylvania 19104

---

Origin and Purpose. The Academy was organized December 14, 1889, to promote the progress of political and social science, especially through publications and meetings. The Academy does not take sides in controverted questions, but seeks to gather and present reliable information to assist the public in forming an intelligent and accurate judgment.

Meetings. The Academy holds an annual meeting in the spring extending over two days.

Publications. THE ANNALS is the bimonthly publication of The Academy. Each issue contains articles on some prominent social or political problem, written at the invitation of the editors. Also, monographs are published from time to time, numbers of which are distributed to pertinent professional organizations. These volumes constitute important reference works on the topics with which they deal, and they are extensively cited by authorities throughout the United States and abroad. The papers presented at the meetings of The Academy are included in THE ANNALS.

Membership. Each member of The Academy receives THE ANNALS and may attend the meetings of The Academy. Annual dues for individuals are $15.00 (for clothbound copies $20.00 per year). A life membership is $500. All payments are to be made in United States dollars.

Libraries and other institutions may receive THE ANNALS paperbound at a cost of $15.00 per year, or clothbound at $20.00 per year. Add $1.50 to above rates for membership outside U.S.A.

Single copies of THE ANNALS may be obtained by nonmembers of The Academy for $4.00 ($5.00 clothbound) and by members for $3.50 ($4.50 clothbound). A discount of 5 percent is allowed on orders for 10 to 24 copies of any one issue, and of 10 percent on orders for 25 or more copies. These discounts apply only when orders are placed directly with The Academy and not through agencies. The price to all bookstores and to all dealers is $4.00 per copy less 20 percent, with no quantity discount. Monographs may be purchased for $4.00, with proportionate discounts. Orders for 5 books or less must be prepaid (add $.75 for postage and handling). Orders for 6 books or more must be invoiced.

All correspondence concerning The Academy or THE ANNALS should be addressed to the Academy offices, 3937 Chestnut Street. Philadelphia, Pa. 19104.